고득점으로 가는 최적의 토플 *i*BT 종합서
NEW EDITION
HOOKED ON TOEFL SPEAKING

LinguaForum

NEW EDITION
HOOKED ON TOEFL SPEAKING

지은이	링구아포럼 리서치센터
선임연구원	Daniel K. Paxitzis
감수	William Winchester, Brantley Smith
디자인	링구아포럼 디자인팀
표지사진	Cpubrp (Microphone on stand)
편집인	장기용
발행인	이길호
발행처	링구아포럼

1판6쇄	2011. 8. 30				
교재문의	02) 3480-6627	대표전화	1577-6167		
등록번호	제2000-000335호	등록일자	2000. 5. 17	ISBN 978-89-5563-533-1 (98740)	가격 17,000원

Copyright © 2009-2011 by LinguaForum
No unauthorized photocopying.
All rights reserved. No part of this book may be reproduced or transmitted in any form or by any means, electronic or mechanical, including photocopying, recording, or any other information storage and retrieval system without the written permission of the publisher.

이 책은 링구아포럼이 독창적으로 개발하였습니다. 이 책의 내용, 사진 등 일부 혹은 전체 내용을 어떠한 방법으로도 무단 복사, 복제, 전재하는 것은 저작권법에 의해 금지되어 있습니다.

Printed in the Republic of Korea

R/N(CRnehoTFSG): 09240950KB/11110950KB/12180950KB/04091050KB/03301150KB/08301150KB

고득점으로 가는 최적의 토플 *i*BT 종합서

NEW EDITION
HOOKED ON TOEFL SPEAKING

LinguaForum

Foreword　　　　　　　　　　　　　　　　　　　　　　　　　/ 머리말 /

토플을 단순히 시험으로만 생각하는 사람이 의외로 많다. 그래서 토플을 대하는 요령이나 방법을 배우려 하는 사람을 어렵지 않게 찾아볼 수 있다. 하지만 토플은 시험이기 전에 영어라는 언어이다. 무엇보다도 TOEFL iBT Speaking은 언어에 대한 이해 없이 단순한 암기나 요령으로는 좋은 결과를 얻기 어렵다. TOEFL iBT는 본인의 생각을 조리 있게 표현할 수 있는 능력(TASK 1 & 2), 읽고 들은 내용을 종합해서 말할 수 있는 능력(TASK 3 & 4), 그리고 대학 생활이나 교수의 강의 내용을 정리하고 paraphrase 할 수 있는 능력(TASK 5 & 6)을 요구한다. TASK 1 & 2는 기본적인 영어 실력만 갖춰져 있다면 고득점을 획득할 수 있다. 하지만 TASK 3 – 6까지의 문제들을 풀기 위해서는 단순히 말하기 능력만 필요한 것이 아니라 지문을 빠른 시간 내에 읽고 정리할 수 있는 능력과 듣기 능력을 필요로 한다.

토플을 준비하는 학생들이 가장 먼저 생각해야 할 것은 어휘 능력이다. 토플을 공부함과 동시에 좋은 토플 어휘 책을 구입해서 꾸준히 암기해야 한다. 또한 매일 50분 이상은 듣기 연습을 해야 한다. 대학 생활을 바탕으로 한 영화나 미국 대학 (하버드, 예일, MIT, NYU, etc)에서 제공하는 무료 수업을 청강하는 것도 좋은 방법이다. 대부분의 토플 스피킹 문제가 대학 생활에 관련된 문제이기에 직접적인 관련이 있는 내용을 듣는 것이 더 현명할 수 있겠다. 대학 강의를 들을 때는 여러 강의를 많이 듣는 것 보다 들었던 강의를 반복해서 들으면서 강의를 이해하는 감각을 높이는 것이 중요하다. 반복해서 청취하다 보면 들리는 내용이 조금씩 많아 진다. 그 때부터는 Dictation 연습을 통해 강의 내용을 정리하는 연습을 하자.

이와 함께, New Edition Hooked On TOEFL iBT Speaking책에서 제공하는 학습 방법을 체계적으로 익히기 바란다. 갑자기 어떤 어려운 주제나 학습분야에 관해서 토론을 해야 한다면 스피킹이 어렵게 느껴질 수도 있겠지만 New Edition Hooked On TOEFL iBT Speaking에서 제공하는 가장 기본적인 표현법을 응용해서 패턴 드릴을 연습하다 보면 나도 모르는 사이에 자연스럽게 영어로 생각을 표현하고 편안하게 말 할 수 있는 실력을 갖출 수 있을 것이다.

New Edition Hooked On TOEFL iBT Speaking은 "Study smarter, not harder." 라는 표어를 실천하기 원하는 학생들을 위해서 제작된 교재라 할 수 있겠다. 이 책은 무작정 광범위한 내용을 공부하는 것이 아니라 꼭 필요한 내용을 체계적으로 학습자가 응용해서 사용할 수 있는 방법을 제시한다. 이 책의 안내를 따라 꼼꼼히, 그리고 충실하게 문제를 풀어나가다 보면 어느덧 주어진 문제에 자신 있게 영어로 답하는 자신의 모습을 발견하게 될 것이다.

　　　　　　　　　　　　　　　　　　　　　　　　　　　　　　LinguaForum Research Center
　　　　　　　　　　　　　　　　　　　　　　　　　　　　　　TOEFL iBT Speaking 연구팀

Structure
/이 책의 구성과 특징/

Part I — Task Types
Overview를 통해 모든 문제의 특징과 문제 해결 방법을 단계적으로 설명하였다. Pre-Speaking 단계에서 기본적인 답변을 준비하는 연습을 거친 후 말하기를 준비한다. 무엇보다 말하기를 준비하는 요령을 익히기 위해 각 Task에서 필요한 모든 기본문장의 응용 및 반복학습을 통해 자연스럽게 익힐 수 있게 구성하였다.

Part II — Practice Test
앞에서 배운 내용을 바탕으로 다양한 실전 문제들을 다뤄볼 수 있도록 Practice Test을 한층 강화 하였다. 영역별 출제 빈도가 높은 주제와 실전 길이의 지문을 통해 효과적으로 실전 감각을 기를 수 있도록 Task마다 각각 8개의 실전 연습문제를 제공하였다.

Part III — Actual Test
Part I과 Part II에서 학습한 내용을 바탕으로 실제 시험을 치른다는 마음가짐으로 연습할 수 있도록 실전과 같은 환경을 제공하였다.

Appendix
TOEFL iBT Speaking에 도움이 되는 발음법, 강세, Note-taking 방법, 그리고 대학 생활 관련 어휘 등을 수록하였다.

Answer Key & Explanations
어휘, 지문 번역과 함께 ETS에서 요구하는 기준에 맞는 Sample Answer를 제시하였다.

HOOKED ON TOEFL SPEAKING L·I·N·G·U·A·F·O·R·U·M·H·

Contents

PART I **Task Types**

A. Independent Speaking Tasks

1	Personal Preference	12
2	Paired Choice	26

B. Integrated Speaking Tasks

3	Fit and Explain	42
4	General / Specific	60
5	Problem / Solution	78
6	Summary	96

PART II Practice Test

Task 1	116
Task 2	132
Task 3	148
Task 4	164
Task 5	180
Task 6	196

PART III Actual Test

Actual Test 1	215
Actual Test 2	223

*링구아포럼 웹사이트 (http://test.linguaforum.com)에서 교재 인증 절차를 거쳐 실제 시험과 같은 환경에서 연습할 수 있습니다.

Appendix	232
Orientation	250

Answer Key & Explanations

HOOKED ON TOEFL SPEAKING

Task Types

A. Independent Speaking Tasks
1. Personal Preference
2. Paired Choice

B. Integrated Speaking Tasks
3. Fit and Explain
4. General / Specific
5. Problem / Solution
6. Summary

L·I·N·G·U·A·F·O·R·U·M·H·O·O·K·E·D·O·N·T·O·E·F·L·S·P·E·A·K·I·N·G

PART I

Independent Speaking Tasks

Basic information

In the speaking section, the first and second tasks are Independent Speaking questions. When answering these questions, no materials or information related to the questions will be given. This means you should learn to speak from your personal knowledge and experience.

Task 1
Personal Preference

Preparation : 15 seconds
Answer : 45 seconds

Task 2
Paired Choice

Preparation : 15 seconds
Answer : 45 seconds

Task Solving Process

There is a certain sequence you need to go through in order to organize and deliver your response in a logical manner. As you respond in a sequence, you will learn to handle various topics and present relevant and coherent answers for given topics.

Step 1
Learn what the questions ask you to do

Outline

Step 2
Organize your ideas in a logical sequence

Topic > Reason > Detail

Things to consider when you speak

Confidence, Grammar, Pronunciation, & Time

TASK 01 Personal Preference

Overview

Task 1 consists of a question related to your personal life, choices, or interests. You will have 15 seconds to prepare your answer and 45 seconds to speak the answer. When preparing for your answer, try to come up with 1 topic, 2 reasons, and 2 details as quickly as you can. You should then speak in a calm but firm voice.

Question Types

- What is your favorite part of the day and why?
- Choose a famous person that you admire as a hero.
- Describe the most enjoyable activity that you did last year.
- Who is the person you go to when you need advice, and why do you rely on that person?
- Where would you like to have your dream vacation?
- Describe a valuable lesson you had in your life.
- Choose a type of house you would like to live in.

Strategies

- Understand what the prompt asks you to do.
- Make a detailed outline, but don't spend much time outlining.
- Relax and speak as clearly as you can.
- Do not hesitate or mumble.
- Be aware that there is no right or wrong answer.
- Remember your time is limited!

1. Personal Preference

Sample Question

Q Describe an important decision you made in your life and explain why it was important to you. Include details and examples in your response.

Topic	Studying in America	
Reason 1		**Reason 2**
Learning English		New experiences
Details		**Details**
• Attending ESL classes • Making English speaking friends		• Trying tasty foreign foods • Experiencing a new life style

🎙 Sample Response

Topic	One of the most important decisions I made was to study in America.
Reason 1	First, studying in America allowed me to learn English.
Details	I attended ESL classes and made a lot of friends who were native English speakers.
Reason 2	Second, studying in America helped me experience many new things.
Details	I tried delicious foreign foods and experienced a new lifestyle while studying in America.
Conclusion	The opportunity to learn English and to have many experiences was the main reason why I believe studying in America was the most important decision I made in my life.

Pre-Speaking

STEP 1 • **Basic Outlining**

>> Read the questions and fill in the blanks with key ideas.

1 What is your favorite part of the day and why? Please include specific details and examples in your explanation.

Topic	Dawn
Reason 1 Relaxing	**Reason 2** Do the things I like
Details • Only me awake • Atmosphere, sit back & relax	**Details** • Write & Read

2 Choose a famous person that you admire as a hero and explain why you admire him or her. Please include examples and details in your explanation.

Topic	
Reason 1	**Reason 2**
Details	**Details**

3 Describe your favorite hangout and explain why it is your favorite. Include details and examples in your response.

Topic	
Reason 1	**Reason 2**
Details	**Details**

4 Describe the most enjoyable activity that you did last year and explain why you found it enjoyable. Use examples and details in your response.

Topic	
Reason 1	**Reason 2**
Details	**Details**

5 Choose one thing you would do if you could travel back in time and explain why. Please include specific examples and details in your explanation.

6 Choose an activity you'd like to do when you're on a date and explain why you like it. Please include details and examples in your response.

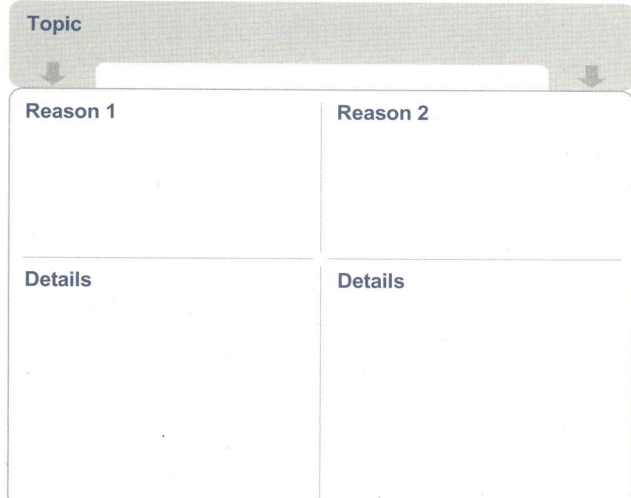

7 Describe the most valuable lesson you had in your life and explain why you find it valuable. Include details and examples to support your explanation.

8 Describe an important quality of a good teacher. Explain why it is important to you. Include details and examples in your response.

STEP 2 • Speaking

Topic / Reason / Detail

Expressions for Topic Sentences

- I think ...
- It seems to me ...
- I believe ...
- I would say ...
- In my opinion,
- As far as I'm concerned,
- In my case,
- Without a doubt,

I think ...	**I think** the luckiest day of my life was the day I was awarded a full scholarship.
It seems to me ...	**It seems to me** that electricity is the most useful invention in the world.
I believe ...	**I believe** the most memorable experience of my life is the trip I took to Africa.
I would say ...	**I would say** the best way to spend a week's vacation is lounging on a beach.

Tip Task 1 does not require you to make complicated sentences. Rather, it is designed to evaluate your ability to make simple but grammatically well-structured sentences. So, your main concern is to make clear, concise and sensible sentences quickly. As soon as you read the question, you should come up with a topic sentence right away.

In my opinion,	**In my opinion,** Chemistry is the most exciting subject among all my high school subjects.
As far as I'm concerned,	**As far as I'm concerned,** the finest vacation spot would be the Alps in Switzerland.
In my case,	**In my case,** Indian food is my favorite cuisine.
Without a doubt,	**Without a doubt,** my mother is the person I go to when I need advice.

Tip These conversation expressions help you speak more smoothly. Use these expressions to give an impression that you're properly trained in English. Again, your main concern here is to make a topic sentence as quickly as you can. Memorize these expressions and get ready to use them at any moment when speaking your opinions.

>> Read the questions and make topic sentences.

1 What is your favorite part of the day and why? Please include specific details and examples in your explanation.

   Topic I think that my favorite part of the day is dawn, when it starts to get bright.

2 Choose a famous person that you admire as a hero and explain why you admire him or her. Please include examples and details in your explanation.

   Topic

3 Describe your favorite hangout and explain why it is your favorite. Include details and examples in your response.

   Topic

4 Describe the most enjoyable activity that you did last year and explain why you found it enjoyable. Use examples and details in your response.

   Topic

5 Choose one thing you would do if you could travel back in time and explain why. Please include specific examples and details in your explanation.

   Topic

6 Choose an activity you'd like to do when you're on a date and explain why you like it. Please include details and examples in your response.

   Topic

7 Describe one of the most valuable lessons you had in your life and explain why you find it valuable. Include specific details and examples to support your explanation.

   Topic

8 Describe an important quality of a good teacher and explain why it is important to you. Include details and examples in your response.

   Topic

STEP 2 • Speaking

Topic / **Reason** / Detail

Expressions for Reason Sentences

- What I like about ...
  Another reason is that ...

- One of the reasons ...
  The other reason is that ...

- One reason why ...
  I like it also because ...

- First,
  Second,

What I like about ... Anther reason is that ...	Reason 1	**What I like about** this day is that my work was recognized by an award.
	Reason 2	**Another reason is that** I pleased my parents.
One of the reasons ... The other reason is that ...	Reason 1	**One of the reasons** why I choose electricity is that it enabled indoor lighting so that we can work and play even late at night.
	Reason 2	**The other reason is that** I can use a lot of electronic devices.
One reason why ... I like this also because ...	Reason 1	**One reason why** I like this trip is that I was able to enjoy the beautiful scenery.
	Reason 2	**I like this** trip **also because** I was able to see a lot of wild animals I've never seen before.
First, Second,	Reason 1	**First,** when I lounge on a beach, I am able to get rid of my stress.
	Reason 2	**Second,** I can meet lots of people that come all over the world.

Tip It's not only important to make a topic sentence, but also crucial to provide sound reasons for the topic sentence. Even if you speak fluent English, you will not receive a high score if your answer is not well-supported. Try to memorize these expressions to make reason sentences to support your topic.

» Read the questions and make reason sentences.

1 What is your favorite part of the day and why? Please include specific details and examples in your explanation.

- **Topic:** Dawn
  - **Reason 1:** What I like about dawn is that it's so relaxing and everything seems so peaceful.
  - **Reason 2:** Another reason is that I can concentrate on doing the things I like.

2 Choose a famous person that you admire as a hero and explain why you admire him or her. Please include examples and details in your explanation.

- **Topic:** _____
  - **Reason 1:** _____
  - **Reason 2:** _____

3 Describe your favorite hangout and explain why it is your favorite. Include details and examples in your response.

- **Topic:** _____
  - **Reason 1:** _____
  - **Reason 2:** _____

4 Describe the most enjoyable activity that you did last year and explain why you found it enjoyable. Use examples and details in your response.

- **Topic:** _____
  - **Reason 1:** _____
  - **Reason 2:** _____

5 Choose one thing you would do if you could travel back in time and explain why. Please include specific examples and details in your explanation.

- Topic
  - Reason 1
  - Reason 2

6 Choose an activity you'd like to do when you're on a date and explain why you like it. Please include details and examples in your response.

- Topic
  - Reason 1
  - Reason 2

7 Describe one of the most valuable lessons you had in your life and explain why you find it valuable. Include specific details and examples to support your explanation.

- Topic
  - Reason 1
  - Reason 2

8 Describe an important quality of a good teacher and explain why you find it important. Include details and examples in your response.

- Topic
  - Reason 1
  - Reason 2

STEP 2 • Speaking

Topic / Reason / **Detail**

Expressions for Detail Sentences

- It means that ...   (= I mean ...)
- For example,   (= For instance,)
- To give a specific example,   (= To illustrate,)
- What I am saying is that ...   (= In other words,)

It means that ... **I mean ...**	**Details** **It means that** I can achieve anything if I strive to do my best. With this in mind, I studied very hard day and night.
	Details **I mean** my parents were so pleased that they told this news to everyone in my town. I am truly happy that I could please my parents and make them proud.
For example, **For instance,**	**Details** **For example,** he is always humble despite his pre-eminence. He doesn't exaggerate his ability or get overexcited even when performing at his best. He just persistently focuses on doing his best.
	Details **For instance,** he never settles down, and continues to strive for excellence. This honest effort enabled him to become one of the finest soccer players in the world. For this reason, he is my role model and hero.
To give a specific example ... **To illustrate ...**	**Details** **To give a specific example,** I went to Africa last summer, and one of the best parts of this trip was enjoying the beautiful scenery of Africa. I've never seen such beautiful, scenic views of natural landscapes. It was worth spending all my savings.
	Details **To illustrate,** I saw giraffes, wallaroos, and hedgehogs for the first time in my life.
What I am saying is that ... **In other words,**	**Details** **What I am saying is that** I often get exhausted and become extremely tired after a long day's work every day. I would be more than pleased if I could spend a week's vacation on a beach to get rid of all my stress.
	Details **In other words,** I could meet Mexicans, Chinese people, Americans, Canadians, and other people of different nationalities as I get rest on a beautiful beach.

» Read the questions and make detail sentences.

1 What is your favorite part of the day and why? Please include specific details and examples in your explanation.

- **Topic**: Dawn
  - **Reason 1**: Relaxing
    - **Details**: It means that I am the only one awake at dawn. I can just enjoy the peaceful atmosphere and sit back and relax.
  - **Reason 2**: Do the things I like
    - **Details**: For instance, I can solve math questions easily at dawn. I love it that I can fully concentrate on what I like to do.

2 Choose a famous person that you admire as a hero and explain why you admire him or her. Please include examples and details in your explanation.

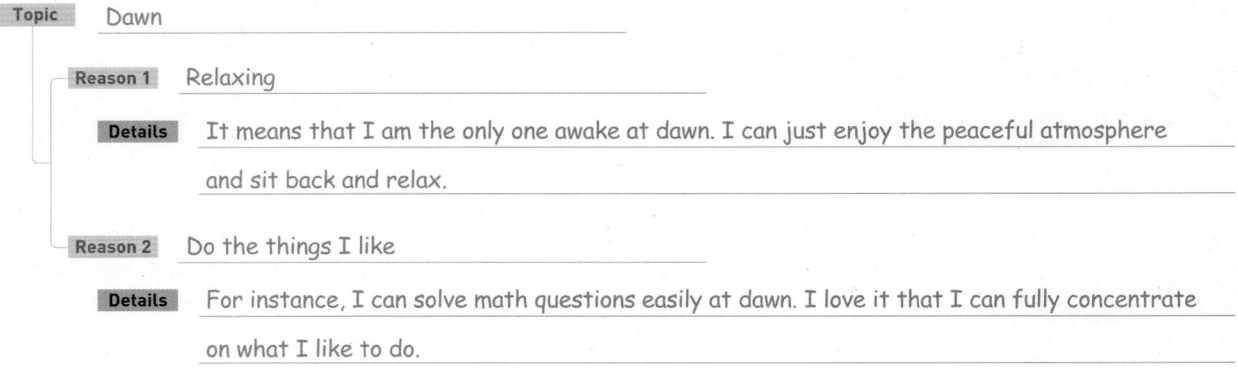

3 Describe your favorite hangout and explain why it is your favorite. Include details and examples in your response.

4 Describe the most enjoyable activity that you did last year and explain why you found it enjoyable. Use examples and details in your response.

- Topic: _____
    - Reason 1: _____
        - Details: _____
        _____
    - Reason 2: _____
        - Details: _____
        _____

5 Choose one thing you would do if you could travel back in time and explain why. Please include specific examples and details in your explanation.

- Topic: _____
    - Reason 1: _____
        - Details: _____
        _____
    - Reason 2: _____
        - Details: _____
        _____

6 Choose an activity you'd like to do when you're on a date and explain why you like it. Please include details and examples in your response.

- Topic: _____
    - Reason 1: _____
        - Details: _____
        _____
    - Reason 2: _____
        - Details: _____
        _____

7 Describe one of the most valuable lessons you had in your life and explain why you find it valuable. Include specific details and examples to support your explanation.

- **Topic** _____
  - **Reason 1** _____
    - **Details** _____
      _____
  - **Reason 2** _____
    - **Details** _____
      _____

8 Describe an important quality of a good teacher and explain why it is important to you. Include details and examples in your response.

- **Topic** _____
  - **Reason 1** _____
    - **Details** _____
      _____
  - **Reason 2** _____
    - **Details** _____
      _____

Practice Questions

>> Fill in the notes and speak your answers.

1 Describe your favorite type of weather and explain why you like it. Use specific details and examples in your response. MP3 2

2 Describe a friend who is special to you and explain why you find him or her special. Use specific details and examples in your response. MP3 3

3 Describe your favorite month of the year and explain why you like it. Include details and examples in your response. MP3 4

TASK 02 Paired Choice

Overview

Task 2 also consists of one question which asks you to choose one of two perspectives on a given issue or one of two alternative ways of doing something. You can select one point of view and support it with reasons and detail sentences.

Question Types

- Some people prefer to watch movies at home. Others prefer to go to the theater. Which do you prefer and why?
- Some people enjoy going to the mall with friends. Others choose to go by themselves. Which of the two ways of shopping do you prefer and why?
- Should children be allowed to go to school without adult supervision? State your opinion and explain why.

Strategies

- Understand what the prompt asks you to do!
- Choose one point of view as quickly as possible!
- Speak clearly and try not to mumble!
- Be confident when you speak!
- Be aware that there is no right or wrong answer.
- Remember your time is limited!

2. Paired Choice

Sample Question

Q Some people think that cities should spend a lot of money on parks and museums. Others think that cities should spend that money on services for poor citizens. Which opinion do you agree with and why?

Topic	Spend money on parks and museums	
Reason 1 Enriches the city		**Reason 2** Fairer to taxpayers
Details • Everyone can use • Educational and cultural values • Free admission		**Details** • Their money being used fairly

Sample Response

Topic	As far as I'm concerned, cities should spend their tax revenue on civic projects rather than on the poor.
Reason 1	One reason why I think these things are a better investment is that they add cultural and aesthetic value to the city.
Details	For example, parks beautify the city and can be enjoyed by everyone. Museums and galleries have educational and cultural value, and sometimes offer free admission, so they can be enjoyed by everyone.
Reason 2	Also, taxpayers work hard to earn their money, so they should derive a direct benefit from the city.
Details	I mean it should definitely be confirmed that their money is not just being taken from them.

Pre-Speaking

STEP 1 • Basic Outlining

>> Read the questions and fill in the blanks with key ideas.

1 Some people prefer to read news in print while others prefer online news. Which way of getting news do you prefer and why?

Topic	Online News	
Reason 1	Fits my lifestyle	**Reason 2** Cost-effective
Details • No need to subscribe - turn on computer watch news online at any time I want.		**Details** • No payment - Don't pay a penny to read online news.

2 Some people enjoy going to the mall with friends. Other people choose to go by themselves. Which of the two ways of shopping do you prefer and why?

Topic		
Reason 1		**Reason 2**
Details		**Details**

3 Some people are against the idea of having plastic surgery and others find nothing wrong with it. Which opinion do you agree with and why?

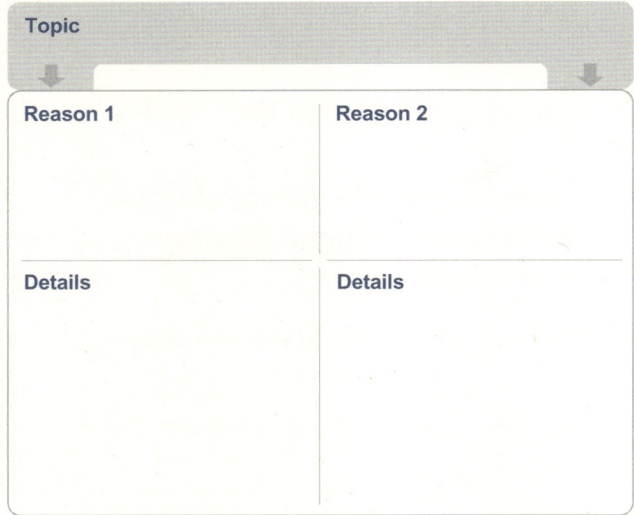

4 Should children be allowed to go to school without adult supervision? State your opinion and explain why.

5 Some students prefer a study group when preparing for exams, while others prefer to have a private tutor. Which way of studying do you prefer and why?

Topic	
Reason 1	Reason 2
Details	Details

6 When doing research, some people use online materials and others use actual books. Which method of finding information do you prefer and why?

Topic	
Reason 1	Reason 2
Details	Details

7 Some people believe that children should learn to follow strict rules and others the exact opposite. Which opinion do you prefer and why?

Topic	
Reason 1	Reason 2
Details	Details

8 Some students get part-time jobs and others choose to work for their parents. Which way of working do you prefer and why?

Topic	
Reason 1	Reason 2
Details	Details

STEP 2 • **Speaking** .... **Topic** / Reason / Detail

Expressions for Topic Sentences

- I prefer (A) to (B)
- I think (A) is better than (B)
- I'd rather (A) than (B)
- I would say that (A) is more ~ than (B)

- Personally,
- In my opinion,
- The way I see it,
- As I see it,

I prefer (A) to (B)	**I prefer** spending **to** saving money.
I think (A) is better than (B)	**I think** watching movies at home **is better than** going to the theater.
I'd rather (A) than (B)	**I'd rather** write a letter **than** make a phone call.
I would say that (A) is more ~ than (B)	**I would say that** studying in the morning **is more** effective **than** studying in the evening.

Tip As soon as you understand the prompt, you should pick one of the two perspectives and make a clear, affirmative topic sentence. It doesn't matter whether you choose A or B, but it matters how fast you can make your choice and get ready to handle the topic.

Personally,	**Personally,** I believe that online communication puts more strain on relationships rather than making them stronger.
In my opinion,	**In my opinion,** professions shouldn't be exclusive to any gender.
The way I see it ...	**The way I see it,** cities should spend their tax revenue on civic projects rather than on the poor.
As I see it ...	**As I see it,** seeing a doctor is better than self-medicating.

Tip These are some additional expressions with which you can make topic sentences. It's always better to learn various phrases to express your opinions more effectively.

≫ Read the questions and make topic sentences.

1 Some people prefer to read news in print while others prefer online news. Which way of getting news do you prefer and why?

Topic   I prefer reading online news to reading news in print.

2 Some people enjoy going to the mall with friends. Other people choose to go by themselves. Which of the two ways of shopping do you prefer and why?

Topic

3 Some people are against the idea of having plastic surgery and others find nothing wrong with it. Which opinion do you agree with and why?

Topic

4 Should children be allowed to go to school without adult supervision? State your opinion and explain why.

Topic

5 Some students prefer a study group when preparing for exams, while others prefer to have a private tutor. Which way of studying do you prefer and why?

Topic

6 When doing research, some people use online materials and others use actual books. Which method of finding information do you prefer and why?

Topic

7 Some people believe that children should learn to follow strict rules and others the exact opposite. Which opinion do you prefer and why?

Topic

8 Some students get part-time jobs and others choose to work for their parents. Which way of working do you prefer and why?

Topic

STEP 2 • Speaking

Topic / **Reason** / Detail

Expressions for Reason Sentences

- That's because …
  Furthermore,

- One of the reasons why I prefer …
  Another reason is that …

- One reason why …
  I like it also because …

- First,
  Second,

That's because … Furthermore,	Reason 1	**That's because** it's more comfortable to be with my friend.
	Reason 2	**Furthermore,** I can have an enjoyable time with my friend.
One of the reasons I prefer … Another reason is that …	Reason 1	**One of the reasons I prefer** watching movies at home is because it's convenient.
	Reason 2	**Another reason is that** it's less expensive to watch movies at home.
One reason is that … The other reason is that …	Reason 1	**One reason is that** I can express my thoughts more profoundly if I have enough time to think what to say as I write.
	Reason 2	**The other reason is that** it's less expensive to write a letter.
First, Second,	Reason 1	**First,** I can intensively concentrate on studying in the morning since my brain operates very actively at morning time.
	Reason 2	**Second,** you will be prepared for the day early in the morning.

Tip These are the most common phrases to make reason sentences. Learn to use these expressions thoroughly so that you can support your topic sentences more effectively.

≫ Read the questions and make reason sentences.

1 Some people prefer to read news in print while others prefer online news. Which way of getting news do you prefer and why?

- **Topic**: Online news
  - **Reason 1**: That's because it fits my lifestyle.
  - **Reason 2**: Furthermore, it's cost-effective.

2 Some people enjoy going to the mall with friends. Other people choose to go by themselves. Which of the two ways of shopping do you prefer and why?

- **Topic**: _____
  - **Reason 1**: _____
  - **Reason 2**: _____

3 Some people are against the idea of having plastic surgery and others find nothing wrong with it. Which opinion do you agree with and why?

- **Topic**: _____
  - **Reason 1**: _____
  - **Reason 2**: _____

4 Should children be allowed to go to school without adult supervision? State your opinion and explain why.

- **Topic**: _____
  - **Reason 1**: _____
  - **Reason 2**: _____

5 Some students prefer a study group when preparing for exams, while others prefer to have a private tutor. Which way of studying do you prefer and why?

- Topic
  - Reason 1
  - Reason 2

6 When doing research, some people use online materials and others use actual books. Which method of finding information do you prefer and why?

- Topic
  - Reason 1
  - Reason 2

7 Some people believe that children should learn to follow strict rules and others the exact opposite. Which opinion do you prefer and why?

- Topic
  - Reason 1
  - Reason 2

8 Some students get part-time jobs and others choose to work for their parents. Which way of working do you prefer and why?

- Topic
  - Reason 1
  - Reason 2

STEP 2 • Speaking

Topic / Reason / **Detail**

Expressions for Detail Sentences

- It means that ...
  What I mean is that ...
- I mean ...
  Also,
- In fact ...
  In contrast to ...
- That is to say ...
  In other words,

It means that ... **What I mean is that ...**	Details	**It means that** I can freely act and do whatever I want at my friend's house.
	Details	**What I mean is that** we can enjoy our time together since my friend and I enjoy playing sports and computer games that most people in our age group enjoy.
I mean ... **Also,**	Details	**I mean** I don't need to spend much time to get to the movie theater to watch movies. All I need to do is to rent a movie at a video store nearby my house.
	Details	This **also** helps me save money as I enjoy watching movies comfortably at home.
In fact, **In contrast to ...**	Details	**In fact,** it takes a long time when I try to handle delicate and complicated issues of my personal relationships in writing.
	Details	**In contrast to** making an expensive phone call, writing a letter doesn't cost too much money, especially when it comes to contacting a person who lives abroad.
That is to say, **In other words,**	Details	I am refreshed in the morning; **that is to say**, I'm very much ready to study even difficult subjects in the morning.
	Details	**In other words,** I won't be late for school or work if I can manage to wake up early to begin my day.

PART I Task Types

≫ Read the questions and make detail sentences.

1 Some people prefer to read news in print while others prefer online news. Which way of getting news do you prefer and why?

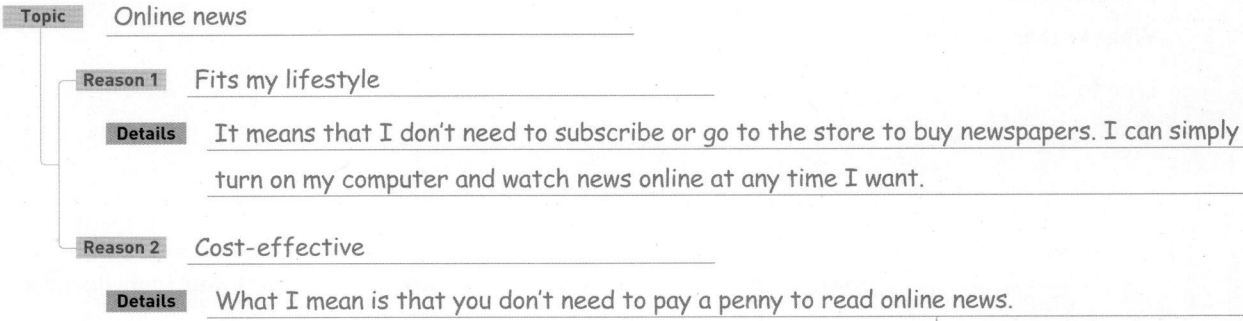

Topic: Online news
Reason 1: Fits my lifestyle
Details: It means that I don't need to subscribe or go to the store to buy newspapers. I can simply turn on my computer and watch news online at any time I want.
Reason 2: Cost-effective
Details: What I mean is that you don't need to pay a penny to read online news.

2 Some people enjoy going to the mall with friends. Other people choose to go by themselves. Which of the two ways of shopping do you prefer and why?

Topic:
Reason 1:
Details:
Reason 2:
Details:

3 Some people are against the idea of having plastic surgery and others find nothing wrong with it. Which opinion do you agree with and why?

Topic:
Reason 1:
Details:
Reason 2:
Details:

4 Should children be allowed to go to school without adult supervision? State your opinion and explain why.

- Topic: _____
  - Reason 1: _____
    - Details: _____
  - Reason 2: _____
    - Details: _____

5 Some students prefer a study group when preparing for exams, while others prefer to have a private tutor. Which way of studying do you prefer and why?

- Topic: _____
  - Reason 1: _____
    - Details: _____
  - Reason 2: _____
    - Details: _____

6 When doing research, some people use online materials and others use actual books. Which method of finding information do you prefer and why?

- Topic: _____
  - Reason 1: _____
    - Details: _____
  - Reason 2: _____
    - Details: _____

7 Some people believe that children should learn to follow strict rules and others the exact opposite. Which opinion do you prefer and why?

- Topic: _____
  - Reason 1: _____
    - Details: _____
  - Reason 2: _____
    - Detail 2: _____

8 Some students get part-time jobs and others choose to work for their parents. Which way of working do you prefer and why?

- Topic: _____
  - Reason 1: _____
    - Details: _____
  - Reason 2: _____
    - Details: _____

Practice Questions

≫ Fill in the notes and speak your answers.

1 Some people prefer to eat foods which they are familiar with. Others prefer to experiment and try exotic or unusual foods. Which do you prefer and why? **MP3 5**

2 Some people think that women should not have certain jobs, such as being a police officer. Others think that women should be able to have any jobs they want. Which opinion do you agree with and why? **MP3 6**

3 Some people like to spend their vacation with their friends. Others like to spend it with their family. Which way do you prefer and why? **MP3 7**

Integrated Speaking Tasks

Basic information

In TOEFL speaking, the third, fourth, fifth, and sixth tasks are Integrated Speaking questions. For tasks 3 and 4, you will read a short passage and listen to a conversation between a man and a woman. For tasks 5 and 6, you will listen to a lecture or a discussion. You're allowed to take notes if you want. Unlike Independent Speaking Tasks, you are not speaking from your experience or knowledge. Here, you should learn to speak about the readings and the listening material for tasks 3 and 4 and he listening material for tasks 5 and 6.

TASK 3
Fit & Explain

TASK 4
General / Specific

Preparation : 30 seconds
Answer : 60 seconds

TASK 5
Problem & Solution

TASK 6
Summary

Preparation : 20 seconds
Answer : 60 seconds

Problem Solving Process

There is a certain sequence you need to go through in order to organize and deliver your response in a logical manner. As you respond in a sequence, you will learn to handle various topics and present relevant and coherent answers for given topics.

Step 1
Learn what the questions ask you to do

Task 3 & 4	Task 5 & 6
Synthesize (Reading & Listening)	Paraphrase (Listening)

Step 2
Organize your ideas in a logical sequence

Task 3
Opinion > Reason > Detail

Task 5
Problem > Solution > Reason

Task 4
Definition > Citation > Explanation

Task 6
Topic > Classification > Detail

Things to consider when you speak

Confidence, Grammar, Pronunciation, & Time

TASK 03 Fit and Explain

Overview

Task 3 is about synthesizing both reading and listening passages. You will read a reading passage related to college life. The passage might be an announcement, a notice, an E-mail, or even a memo left on a bulletin board. You have 45 seconds to read the passage. As soon as the reading time expires, you will listen to a conversation between a male and a female student discussing the announcement for 60 to 80 seconds.

Question Types

- What is the woman's opinion of the policy? What reasons does she give for holding that opinion?
- The woman expresses her opinion of the university's policy on its mentoring program. State her opinion and explain the reasons she gives for holding that opinion.
- The woman expresses her opinion of the change regarding the hiring policy for the computer labs. State her opinion and explain the reasons she gives for holding that opinion.

Strategies

- Summarize the reading passage in a couple of sentences.
- Take good notes on the conversation.
  (1) Find the standpoint of a male or a female student.
  (2) Find the reasons why the student is holding that opinion.
  (3) Find the details with which the student supports his or her reasons.
- Remember that your time is limited!

3. Fit and Explain

Sample Question

Reading Read the announcement about the university's policy to limit admission to audit courses.

Announcement from the University President

Please be informed that starting next semester, admission to audit courses shall be limited to a maximum of three students per class [— Policy]. This is in line with the university's effort to address the shortage of space availability and effective management of [— Reason] classes. As the student population continues to increase each academic year, the [— Detail —] university is in full support of ensuring that all students be given quality education to [— Detail —] help them reach their academic goals. For further details, please contact the Academic Affairs department.

Reading Checkpoints
- ✓ Policy
- ✓ Reason
- ✓ Details

Listening Now listen to two students as they discuss the announcement.

W: Jesse, you seem really happy today ... Did anything happen that I should know about?

M: Finally, the school's come up with a good plan for us ... [— Opinion]

W: Oh, did you mean the cap on audit courses? Why, aren't you a fan of audit students?

M: It's not that at all. I'm just glad that students who actually need to attend those [— Reason 1 —] classes and pass the course will be prioritized. I mean, audit students don't have [— Detail —] the same things at stake, like passing the course exams or submitting major papers and requirements. Like me, I won't have to worry about not getting into a class because someone wants to just sit in class ... know what I mean?

W: Well, audit students also want to learn ...

M: I understand where they're coming from ... it's just that putting a limit on the number of students does give everyone a chance at a better learning [— Reason 2 —] environment. I mean, the professor won't have to sacrifice his lecture time trying [— Detail —] to figure out how to be heard clearly by everyone ...

Listening Checkpoints
- ✓ Opinion
- ✓ Reason 1
- ✓ Details
- ✓ Reason 2
- ✓ Details

Reading Note

Policy

Limiting admission to audit courses
- to max. 3 students / class

Reason 1

To secure space
- stu. population increase
- quality education

Listening Note

Opinion

Agree

Reason 1

Giving priority to those who need to attend the class – reasonable

Reason 2

A better learning environment
- everyone can hear prof's voice.

Question The man expresses his opinion of the announcement from the university president. State his opinion and explain the reasons he gives for holding that opinion.

Sample Response

Opinion	The man agrees with the plan to limit participation of audit students in classes.
Reason 1	He provides two reasons for holding his opinions. First, he says that those who need to take the classes for their course requirements can be prioritized more than the audit students, which is quite a fair move.
Details	In other words, he says it will limit unfair situations where there are many students in a class who are not required to submit things but have spots.
Reason 2	Second, he also agrees with the announcement that this change will bring more space to classrooms.
Details	Especially, it will give students the chance to have a better learning environment, and for professors to have a class size that is more manageable, so everyone in class can hear the professor without any trouble.

Pre-Speaking

STEP 1 • Reading & Listening

» Read the passage and listen to the conversation and fill out the reading and listening notes with key ideas.

1

Reading   The university library is planning to reduce the number of days allowed for borrowed books to 7 days. Read the announcement about the new policy from the library staff.

New Borrowing Policy for Library Books

In line with the university's goal of pursuing a more competitive and progressive learning environment, and due to the challenges concerning the preservation of valuable contents in libraries, the 30-day limit on the number of days allowed for borrowed books shall be reduced to 7 days, including weekends. A fine of one dollar ($1.00) for every day a book is past due shall be applied. This new policy shall take effect next semester and affect all campus staff and students enrolled in the various colleges of the university with the exception of faculty members. All parties will be held to strict compliance.

Listening   Now listen to two students as they discuss the announcement. MP3 8

Reading Note

Policy

Borrowing period for library books
• Reducing the period from 30 days to 7
• Fine of $1 a day

Reason 1

Better learning environment

Reason 2

To preserve valuable contents in library

Listening Note

Opinion

It is just stupid - Disagree

Reason 1

A week is too short
• cannot read & remember info that fast
• has many classes

Reason 2

Expenses
The fine ($1) is heavy when added up
• making photocopies costs money.

2

Reading   The university is planning to purchase sculptures for the campus. Read the student's letter to the university newspaper about the plan.

Letter to the Editor – University Press

I am writing with regard to the planned purchase of sculptures for the campus by the university. It is my firm belief that such a move is a waste of school finances. I do not wish to have my tuition and housing fees, which were both increased by 15% last year, to be used for anything other than the further development of my education. Furthermore, the campus quad is used by many students for athletic and recreational activities. My friends and I play soccer on the quad, and we won't be able to do this if the quad is cluttered with sculptures. I think most students would agree that having good recreational facilities is more important than beautifying the campus.

Josh Smith/ Senior

Listening   Now listen to two students as they discuss the student's letter. MP3 9

Reading Note

Policy

Letter (Agree or Disagree)

Reason 1

Reason 2

Listening Note

Opinion

Reason 1

Reason 2

3

Reading The university is planning to suspend grants for foreign study programs. Read the announcement about the plan from the university president.

University Scrapping its Varsity Teams

Talks about the university's plan to scrap its varsity teams have now been confirmed. In an interview, Sports Director Dr. McGuire indicated that the school will temporarily suspend operations of its varsity teams for a minimum of two years. He said that the university can no longer shoulder the required budget to develop teams for inter-school competitions. Dr. McGuire, however, implied that varsity teams may be organized again after the two-year deferral, if financial prospects get better by that time. It remains to be seen what impact this announcement will have on students, professors, and alumni of this sports-crazed university.

Listening Now listen to two students discussing the article. [MP3 10]

Reading Note

Policy

Reason 1

Listening Note

Opinion

Reason 1

Reason 2

4

Reading The university is planning to enforce a car ban for first year students. Read the announcement about the plan made by the university.

Car Ban for Freshmen Students

Starting next semester, the university will enforce a vehicle ban for all incoming freshmen to lessen air pollution and relieve traffic congestion on the campus. As the student population continues to steadily rise each year, the volume of automobiles on campus and human traffic will also increase. Only vehicles with special permits are exempt from said ban. Existing students are required to procure new vehicle permits before the end of the current semester. Free shuttle service will be provided for students affected by the ban. Location and drop-off schedules will be announced at a later date.

Listening Now listen to two students as they discuss the announcement.

Reading Note

Policy

Reason 1

Listening Note

Opinion

Reason 1

Reason 2

STEP 2 • Speaking

Opinion / Reason / Detail

Expressions for Opinion Sentences

- The man / woman agrees with ...
- The man / woman approves of ...
- The man / woman supports ...
- The man / woman shares the view that ...
- The man / woman disagrees with ...
- The man / woman is against ...
- The man / woman is opposed to ...
- The man / woman has a different opinion from ...

The man agrees with ...	**The man agrees with** increasing the number of school buses.
The woman approves of ...	**The woman approves of** banning cars on campus.
The man supports ...	**The man supports** the plan to limit participation of audit students in classes.
The woman shares the view that ...	**The woman shares the view that** it is a good idea to purchase more sculptures.

The man disagrees with ...	**The man disagrees with** the university's policy to increase tuition.
The woman is against ...	**The woman is against** making first-year students live in the dorm.
The man is opposed to ...	**The man is opposed to** suspending grants for foreign study programs.
The woman has a different opinion from ...	**The woman has a different opinion from** the student who wrote the letter.

Tip Here, you're not listening to a random talk. The topics you have in Task 3 will include announcements, statements, or letters made by the University president, student affairs center, school library, computer departments, university officials, foreign studies department, dormitory staff, or concerned students. After reading a passage related to campus life, get ready to jot down a brief summary of a student's opinion about the given topic.

Read the passage and listen to part of a conversation. As you read underline the policy and as you listen fill in the blanks and make opinion sentences.

1

New Borrowing Policy for Library Books

In line with the university's goal of pursuing a more competitive and progressive learning environment, and due to the challenges concerning the preservation of valuable contents in libraries, the 30-day limit on the number of days allowed for borrowed books shall be reduced to 7 days, including weekends. A fine of one dollar ($1.00) for every day a book is past due shall be applied. This new policy shall take effect next semester and affect all campus staff and students enrolled in the various colleges of the university with the exception of faculty members. All parties will be held to strict compliance.

MP3 12

W: "Have you heard about the new policy on the library books? _I am all for it._"

➡ Opinion

The woman agrees with the university's policy to limit the number of days allowed for borrowed books from 30 days to 7, including weekends.

2

Letter to the Editor – University Press

I am writing with regard to the planned purchase of sculptures for the campus by the university. It is my firm belief that such a move is a waste of school finances. I do not wish to have my tuition and housing fees, which were both increased by 15% last year, to be used for anything other than the further development of my education. Furthermore, the campus quad is used by many students for athletic and recreational activities. My friends and I play soccer on the quad, and we won't be able to do this if the quad is cluttered with sculptures. I think most students would agree that having good recreational facilities is more important than beautifying the campus.

Josh Smith/ Senior

MP3 13

W: "Really? I think it's a great idea. Whoever wrote that is _____, if you ask me."

➡ Opinion

3

University Scrapping its Varsity Teams

Talks about the university's plan to scrap its varsity teams have now been confirmed. In an interview, Sports Director Dr. McGuire indicated that the school will temporarily suspend operations of its varsity teams for a minimum of two years. He said that the university can no longer shoulder the required budget to develop teams for inter-school competitions. Dr. McGuire, however, implied that varsity teams may be organized again after the two-year deferral, if financial prospects get better by that time. It remains to be seen what impact this announcement will have on students, professors, and alumni of this sports-crazed university.

MP3 14

W: "_____ For more than twenty years they've never been able to join the championship at the National College League ... I think the university's plan to scrap its varsity teams is _____ "

➡ **Opinion**

_____
_____
_____

4

Car Ban for Freshmen Students

Starting next semester, the university will enforce a vehicle ban for all incoming freshmen to lessen air pollution and relieve traffic congestion on the campus. As the student population continues to steadily rise each year, the volume of automobiles on campus and human traffic will also increase. Only vehicles with special permits are exempt from said ban. Existing students are required to procure new vehicle permits before the end of the current semester. Free shuttle service will be provided for students affected by the ban. Location and drop-off schedules will be announced at a later date.

MP3 15

M: "Well, _____ If they want to help save the environment, they should ask everyone to drive a bit less.

➡ **Opinion**

_____
_____
_____

STEP 2 • Speaking   Opinion / **Reason** / Detail

Expressions for Reason Sentences

- There are two reasons why … The first reason is that …
  The second reason is that …
- She gives two reasons for holding her opinion. First, she points out that …
  Second, she mentions that …
- His reasons for holding that opinion are twofold. First, he explains that …
  Second, he also says that …
- The professor provides two reasons for holding his opinion. First,
  Second,

There are two reasons why … The first reason is that … The second reason is that …	**There are two reasons why** she opposes the new policy on smoking, which prohibits smoking on all university premises. **The first reason is that** she thinks banning smoking in all of the buildings is way too harsh on smokers. **The second reason is that** there are problems with the process of enforcing the policy.
She gives two reasons for holding her opinion. First, she points out that … Second, she mentions that …	**She gives two reasons for holding her opinion. First, she points out that** students with disabilities will have difficulty commuting to school every day. **Second, She mentions that** commuting will cost them much more money than other students.
His reasons for holding that opinion are twofold. First, he explains that … Second, he also says that …	**His reasons for holding that opinion are twofold. First, he explans that** it will lessen the chance of getting unwanted email. **Second, he also says that** large email distributions might overpower or cause problems with the university's internet server.
The professor provides two reasons for holding his opinion. First, Second,	**The professor prorides two reasons for holding his opinion. First,** one week is not enough time for her to read the materials she needs. **Second,** she is worried about the expenses she will have in case of delay.

> **Tip** When listening to the conversation, you need to find out who the main person in the conversation is as quickly as you can and listen carefully to his or her claim about the given issue. You sould then expect to write down two reasons the student provides for his or her claim.

>> As you listen to part of a conversation, fill in the blanks and make detail sentences.

1 New Borrowing Policy for Library Books

MP3 16

W: "How do they expect me to read a book in a week? _That's too little time for me_. I don't read and retain info that fast."

W: "Well, how about my expenses? Money doesn't exactly _grow on trees_ in my household. One dollar doesn't seem like a lot, but if you add 'em up, that's a lot of money."

➡ **Reason**

She gives two reasons for holding that opinion. First, one week is not enough time for her to read the materials she needs. Second, she thinks the fine is heavy when added up.

2 Letter to the Editor – University Press

MP3 17

W: "Well, for starters, the school budget won't be used to buy the sculptures. It'll be coming from _____."

W: "No ... I think what's really _____ is the fact that the sculptures will be located on the quad and he plays soccer there."

➡ **Reason**

3 University Scrapping its Varsity Teams

> **MP3 18**
>
> W: "Just two years ago they were _____ at the National College League ... we were all over the news ..."
>
> W: "It's also unfair for the students, you know ... because _____ ... Hmmm ... I think this will send the wrong signal to the whole academic community-that our school is way below par ..."

➡ **Reason**

_____
_____
_____

4 Car Ban for Freshmen Students

> **MP3 19**
>
> M: "I mean, telling freshmen that they can't bring a car to school in their first year won't help them settle in school."
>
> M: "Even if they offer free rides, _____. What if the service schedule doesn't fit with the students' schedules? You're going to have a lot of late students."

➡ **Reason**

_____
_____
_____

STEP 2 • Speaking

Opinion / Reason / **Detail**

Expressions for Detail Sentences

- For example / For instance ...
- In other words / What he means is that ...
- Especially / Particularly / In particular ...
- That's because / because / as / since ...
- But / Unlike ...
- While / Whereas ...
- However / On the other hand ...
- Although / In contrast ...

For example / For instance ...	**For example,** expanding the operation of shuttle buses will set the problem to rest.
In other words / What he means is that ...	**In other words,** he doesn't believe that raising tuition will lead to better education.
Especially / Particularly / In particular ...	Students with disabilities will have difficulty commuting to school every day, **especially** during the rush hour.
That's because / because / as / since ...	**That's because** it takes more time and effort for them to get to school. Moreover, commuting will cost them much more money than other students **because** they would have to take a cab instead of using public transportation.

But / Unlike ...	**But** the man believes that building a parking lot is not the best solution to the problem.
While / Whereas ...	**While** the student who wrote the letter agrees with the plan to limit participation of audit students in classes, the woman wants to allow audit students without any restrictions.
However / On the other hand ...	The woman, **however,** points out that this is not true.
Although / In contrast ...	**In contrast,** he says that the number of cars increased even though the parking fees were increased last year.

>> As you listen to part of a conversation, fill in the blanks and make detail sentences.

1 New Borrowing Policy for Library Books

> MP3 20
>
> W: "I don't read and retain info that fast. You know what I mean? Plus, it's not ___as if___ ___I only have one class___ to think about."

➡ **Detail**

That's because she can't read and retain information that fast. And she also has many other classes to worry about.

2 Letter to the Editor – University Press

> MP3 21
>
> W: "Well, for starters, the school budget _____ to buy the sculptures. It'll be coming from an anonymous donor. So, he _____ part of his fees being used for this move by the school to make the grounds look more appealing."

➡ **Detail**

3 University Scrapping its Varsity Teams

> **MP3 22**
>
> **W:** "This is totally unfair! Just two years ago _____ our overall championship at the National College League ... _____ ...
> I think it's really sick to scrap the teams after what they have done for the school ..."

➡ **Detail**

_____
_____
_____

4 Car Ban for Freshmen Students

> **MP3 23**
>
> **M:** "You're going to have a lot of late students. And some of them might live far from school. They can't just _____ that easily ..."

➡ **Detail**

_____
_____
_____

Practice Questions

1

Reading The university is planning to adopt a new policy on academic probation. Read the announcement about the new policy made by the university.

Reading Time : 45 seconds

New Policy on Academic Probation

In an effort to improve the academic excellence of the university, and to foster student discipline on campus, students who have a grade point average (GPA) below 2.0, or are on academic probation, will not be allowed to participate in extra-curricular activities. Effective next term, students on academic probation will not be allowed to participate in athletic activities or participate in any foreign exchange program until their GPA rises to meet university standards. Students who fail to improve their academic standing after the probationary period will be required to take a voluntary leave of absence for one term to review their academic goals.

Listening Now listen to two students as they discuss the announcement. MP3 24

Question The man expresses his opinion of the university's policy on academic probation. State his opinion and explain the reasons he gives for holding that opinion.

Reading Note

Listening Note

2

Reading The university is planning to cut its budget for the drama club. Read a student's letter to the university newspaper about the plan.

Reading Time : 45 seconds

Letter to the Editor

I would like to voice my outrage at the university's decision to slash the budget of the drama club. The drama club has been a central element of cultural and artistic life on campus for many years. Its productions are well received by both the student body and the art community. Given the drama club's importance on campus, the university should be increasing its budget rather than reducing it. Furthermore, the university has obviously not thought about how this will impact the reputation of our school. What will applicants think when they learn that the university doesn't even have a decently funded drama club?

A Concerned Thespian

Listening Now listen to two students as they discuss the student's letter. [MP3 25]

Question The man expresses his opinion of the student's letter. State his opinion and explain the reasons he gives for holding that opinion.

Reading Note

Listening Note

TASK 04 General / Specific

Overview

In Task 4, you will read an article, a textbook, or a journal taken from various academic subjects including social studies, humanities, natural science, et cetera. You have 45 seconds to read the passage. As soon as the reading time expires, you will listen to a lecture on an academic subject for 60 to 90 seconds.

Question Types

- The professor describes the concept of deception in animals by giving examples. Explain how these examples demonstrate animal deception.
- The professor explains the principle of mountain-building through folding by giving examples. Explain how the examples illustrate the concept of mountain-building through folding.
- Using the examples given by the professor, explain why deviant behavior is a relative concept.

Strategies

- Take good notes on the reading and the lecture.
- Summarize the key points of reading and listening passages.
- Find the relationship of the reading passage with the listening passage as quickly as you can.
- (1) Present a topic sentence which represents the given information in both the reading and listening passages. (2) Provide specific details to support your topic sentence.
- Your answer should not include your personal opinions.

4. General / Specific

Sample Question

Reading Now read the passage about the zone of proximal development.

Zone of Proximal Development — Topic

The zone of proximal development is an educational concept first developed by the Russian psychologist Lev Vygotsky. According to Vygotsky's theory, there is always <u>a distance between the actual developmental level as determined by independent</u> — Main Idea <u>problem solving and the level of potential development as determined through solving under adult guidance, or in collaboration with more capable peers</u>. If that gap is too great, the learner will not be able to learn the new material and will become frustrated. — Detail — If the gap is too small, the learner will find the task too easy and will lose interest. — Detail

Reading Checkpoints
- ✓ Topic
- ✓ Main Idea
- ✓ Details

Listening Now listen to part of a lecture on this topic in an education class.

OK, when you put students into pairs for group assignments, you need to think about how you pair students up very carefully. Uh, it's not just matching up the students' personalities so that you avoid arguments... you need to, uh, consider their ability levels as well. Ideally, you want to place students of slightly different levels together. — Example 1 — This way the more capable students can help guide those who are less capable. This works out well for both students. — Detail — The less capable student receives the support of the better student, and therefore finds the assignment within his range of ability... uh, and the better student is challenged because he has to help teach the less capable student. — Detail — But you need to be careful in doing this ... uh, don't place the best student in the class with the worst student in the class. — Example 2 — Their ability levels are too different. The worst student just isn't ready to function at the level of the best student ... uh, even with help, it's just not within his range of ability yet. — Detail — Such a pairing will only lead to frustration and discouragement. — Detail

Listening Checkpoints
- ✓ Example 1
- ✓ Details
- ✓ Example 2
- ✓ Details

PART I Task Types

Reading Note

Topic
Zone of proximal development

Main Idea
Gap between a learner's level of current development & potential development

Details
- Too great → gets frustrated & gives up
- Too small → loses interest

Listening Note

Example 1
1) Pairing students of similar ability levels
   - Less capable stu. → supported
   - Better stu. → challenged

Example 2
2) Pairing the best with the worst
   - The worst → not ready, beyond his ability
     → frustrated & discouraged.

Question The professor discusses appropriate pairings of students for group work. Explain how these pairings relate to Vygotsky's zone of proximal development.

Sample Response

The professor says that teachers must be careful in the way that they pair students for group work. He argues that the ability levels of the students should be different but not too different because, if the difference in abilities is too great, it will lead to frustration. This directly relates to the idea of a zone of proximal development. If the best student in the class is paired with the worst student in the class, the gap between their knowledge levels will be too great. The poor student isn't able to perform at the good student's level because the gap between his knowledge and the good student's knowledge is too great.

Pre-Speaking

STEP 1 • Reading & Listening

» Read the passage and listen to the conversation and fill out the reading and listening notes with key ideas.

1

Reading   Now read the passage about the concept of animal deception.

Animal Deception

Survival is a natural progression for various species. Animals, in particular, adapt and show certain traits and characteristics in order to protect themselves from other predatory creatures moving in the same habitat. As a defense mechanism, deception is a fundamental adaptive ability for certain species used to elude other animals they deem to be threats to their lives. Some animals may pretend to belong to another species, resembling its physical appearance, while others may pretend to be injured to deceive predators.

Listening   Now listen to part of a lecture on this topic in a biology class. The professor is discussiong animal deception. MP3 26

Reading Note

Topic
Animal Deception

Main Idea
Animals adopt certain features to protect themselves from predators.

Details
1) Pretend to be another species
2) Pretend to be injured

Listening Note

Example 1
1) Mimicry (copy another animal)
   Ex) copy the sound of a larger animal

Example 2
2) Pretending to be injured to protect their young
   Ex) Some bird species
      - Female pretends to have a broken wing

2

Reading Now read the passage about mountain formation.

Folded Mountains

The earth's crust is its outermost layer. The crust is made up of sections of rocks called plates. When subjected to heat and pressure, the plates move against each other and the crust is deformed. This pressure and the resultant upward movement of sections of the earth's crust can tilt, bend or wrinkle them, creating wavelike formations of ridges and valleys. This process of deformation of the earth's surface, which only occurs when certain types of rock are present in the earth's crust, is called folding.

Listening Now listen to part of a lecture in a geology class. The professor is discussing the folding process. MP3 27

Reading Note

Topic

Main Idea

Details

Listening Note

Example 1

Example 2

3

Reading Now read the passage about deviant behavior.

Deviant Behavior

A society creates laws and corresponding sanctions based on what it considers to be desirable and ideal behavior, and expects its members to conform to such norms. Any recognized violation of the social norm is called deviant behavior, and it varies from relatively trivial things to actions deemed social problems. Deviant behavior is relative, as norms vary from one culture to the other. What is considered appropriate in one culture may not be acceptable in another society.

Listening Now listen to part of a lecture in a sociology class. The professor is discussing the relativity of deviant behavior. MP3 28

Reading Note

Topic

Main Idea

Details

Listening Note

Example 1

Example 2

4

Reading   Now read the passage about cognitive biases.

Cognitive Biases

People generally perceive others using their own predispositions and biases. These are called social biases, or, in a psychological term, cognitive biases, and they affect our daily social interactions. One of them is the halo effect, where one's good assessment of one quality of a person serves to influence and affect the judgment of other qualities. A person who has "quality X" is also seen as having "quality Y," even if the two qualities are not related. Attractive people or those who have admirable skills are often judged as having more competence than someone of average appearance or abilities.

Listening   Now listen to part of a talk in a psychology class. The professor is discussing the halo effect.

MP3 29

Reading Note

Topic

Main Idea

Details

Listening Note

Example 1

Example 2

STEP 2 • Speaking

Definition / Citation / Explanation

Expressions for Definition Sentences

- (A) is (B)
- (A) refers to (B)
- (A) is defined as (B)
- (A) is a term that describes (B)
- (A) implies that …
- (A) occurs when …
- (A) is seen where …
- (A) illustrates that …

(A) is (B)	Creative destruction **is** a process in which newly created products take the place of existing ones.
(A) refers to (B)	Symbiosis **refers to** a close relationship between two organisms living together.
(A) is defined as (B)	The reading **defines** a keystone species **as** one whose presence is essential to the proper functioning of its ecosystem.
(A) is a term that describes (B)	Risk compensation **is a term that describes** the corresponding adjustment of a person's behavior in response to anticipated risk.

(A) implies that …	The professor **implies that** teachers must be careful in the way that they pair students for group work.
(A) occurs when …	The reading says that folding **occurs when** two of the earth's plates meet and push against each other.
(A) is seen where …	The halo effect **is** often **seen where** the interviewer might be attracted to the interviewee's appearance and believe he has other qualities.
(A) illustrates that …	The professor **illustrates that** our ecosystem's survival depends on the diversity of the living organisms that comprise it.

Tip Unlike Task 3, you will find Task 4 intricate and somewhat difficult to answer. For this reason you need to take good notes on all the key information provided in the reading passage and the lecture. One thing you should keep in mind is that you need to understand the topic of the reading passage and expect to listen to the example from the lecture. This way, you will know what to expect from both the reading passage and the lecture.

>> Underline the main idea as you read the passage and make definition sentences.

1

Animal Deception

Survival is a natural progression for various species. Animals, in particular, adapt and show certain traits and characteristics in order to protect themselves from other predatory creatures moving in the same habitat. As a defense mechanism, deception is a fundamental adaptive ability for certain species used to elude other animals they deem to be threats to their lives. Some animals may pretend to belong to another species, resembling its physical appearance, while others may pretend to be injured to deceive predators.

➡ **Definition**

Deceit is a term that describes a means for animals to protect themselves from predators.

2

Folded Mountains

The earth's crust is its outermost layer. The crust is made up of sections of rocks called plates. When subjected to heat and pressure, the plates move against each other and the crust is deformed. This pressure and the resultant upward movement of sections of the earth's crust can tilt, bend or wrinkle them, creating wavelike formations of ridges and valleys. This process of deformation of the earth's surface, which only occurs when certain types of rock are present in the earth's crust, is called folding.

➡ **Definition**

_____
_____
_____

3

Deviant Behavior

A society creates laws and corresponding sanctions based on what it considers to be desirable and ideal behavior, and expects its members to conform to such norms. Any recognized violation of the social norm is called deviant behavior, and it varies from relatively trivial things to actions deemed social problems. Deviant behavior is relative, as norms vary from one culture to the other. What is considered appropriate in one culture may not be acceptable in another society.

➡ **Definition**

_____
_____
_____

4

Cognitive Biases

People generally perceive others using their own predispositions and biases. These are called social biases, or, in a psychological term, cognitive biases, and they affect our daily social interactions. One of them is the halo effect, where one's good assessment of one quality of a person serves to influence and affect the judgment of other qualities. A person who has "quality X" is also seen as having "quality Y," even if the two qualities are not related. Attractive people or those who have admirable skills are often judged as having more competence than someone of average appearance or abilities.

➡ **Definition**

_____
_____
_____

STEP 2 • Speaking

Definition / **Citation** / Explanation

Expressions for Citation Sentences

- The reading says that ...
- The professor says that ...
- The reading describes ...
- The lecture describes ...
- What the professor points out is that ...
- According to the professor ...
- According to the lecture ...
- As discussed by the professor ...

The reading says that ...	**The reading says that** some animals may pretend to be other, physically similar animals.
The professor says that ...	**The professor explains that** the old office machines were replaced by more efficient modern ones.
The reading describes ...	**The reading describes** a kind of art that requires the spontaneous participation of the audience.
The lecture describes ...	**The lecture describes** the relationship between humans and these bacteria.

What the professor points out is that ...	**What the professor points out is that** a non-disturbing environment is needed for flow to occur.
According to the professor ...	**According to the professor**, creative destruction renders old products obsolete.
According to the lecture ...	**According to the lecture**, humans and gut flora get mutual benefits through their relationship.
As discussed by the professor ...	**As discussed by the professor**, some animals are able to deceive potential predators through mimicry.

Tip You first discuss the reading passage and then listening next. You might want to spend the preparation time preparing detailed notes. If you write well-organized notes, you will have more confidence when you speak. Good note-taking is a must for Tsak 4.

≫ As you listen to part of a lecture, fill in the blanks and make citation sentences.

1 Animal Deception

MP3 30

... Some animals are able to ___deceive a potential predator through mimicry___. This means they are able to copy, or mimic, the behavior, movements, or sounds of another animal. ...

➡ **Citation**

The lecture explains how some animals deceive their predators through mimicry.

2 Folded Mountains

MP3 31

... Now, in order for folding to occur, rocks must have the _____. Imagine that a rock is like a piece of plastic. When you heat plastic, it bends and deforms easily, but when it cools, it takes a rigid form again. ...

➡ **Citation**

3 Deviant Behavior

MP3 32

... For example, divorce, while considered a legal and _____ in most cultures, is still frowned upon in other _____ ... say, a Catholic society? So, if you are a Catholic, seeking a divorce may be seen as deviant, but in _____, divorce is accepted, or at least not as frowned upon as it is in the Catholic church. ...

➡ **Citation**

_____
_____
_____

4 Cognitive Biases

MP3 33

... The halo effect often occurs at job interviews, where the interviewer may be influenced by _____. If the interviewee is physically attractive, the interviewer may ignore his/her other weaknesses. ...

➡ **Citation**

_____
_____
_____

STEP 2 • Speaking

Definition / Citation / **Explanation**

Expressions for Explanation Sentences

- The professor gives an example of ...
- The professor discusses ... to demonstrate ...
- The first/second example of ...
- Another example ... is ...
- The professor illustrates the concept of ...
- The professor relates the story of ... to ...
- The first/second example shows how ...
- This is seen in the way ...

The professor gives an example of ...	**The professor gives an example of** risk compensation which refers to the tendency of individuals to take as much risk as they can afford, compensating for the protection they have.
The professor discusses ... to demonstrate ...	**The professor discusses** the memories of her childhood **to demonstrate** lateral thinking.
The first / second example of ...	**The first example of** animal deception discussed by the professor is mimicry.
Another example ... is ...	**Another example** that shows creative destruction **is** the development of the automobile.

The professor illustrates the concept of ...	**The professor illustrates the concept of** parasitic relationship by giving an example.
The professor relates the story of ... to ...	**The professor relates the story of** his friend **to** the concept of flow.
The first / second example shows how ...	**The first example shows how** the halo effect is applied in business.
This is seen in the way ...	**This is seen in the way** animals deceive predators by copying the behavior of another animal.

> **Tip** After citing what the professor said, you need to explain what that citation means or give further information about the issue discussed by the professor. Above are eight different sentences to help with citations. Of course, there would be many other expressions. But the focus is not to learn many expressions, but to learn effective ways to explain the lecture. For this reason, you need to focus on learning a few good expressions.

≫ As you listen to part of a lecture, fill in the blanks and make explanation sentences.

1 Animal Deception

> **MP3 34**
>
> ... For example, some animals are able _to replicate the sound of a larger_, _more threatening animal_. When a predator comes by, they are able to scare it away _by mimicking_ the sound of this larger animal. ...

⇨ **Explanation**

The professor gives an example of some animals replicating the sound of larger and more threatening animals.

2 Folded Mountains

> **MP3 35**
>
> ... Some rocks are the same way, and thus _____.
> Others which don't have this property of plasticity, just shatter when they are subjected to heat and pressure, and the mountains they form are _____ ...

⇨ **Explanation**

_____
_____
_____

3 Deviant Behavior

> **MP3 36**
>
> ... Take the teens of the 1960s for example. They had, uh, to say the least, _____ _____ than those of their parents' generation. So the actions of teens, uh, wearing unusual clothing, experimenting with drugs, or whatever ... it seemed _____ but perfectly acceptable to the teens themselves. ...

➡ **Explanation**

_____
_____
_____

4 Cognitive Biases

> **MP3 37**
>
> ... This is because the interviewer presumes that the other qualities of that person are as good as his/her looks, although there is no proof that _____. ...

➡ **Explanation**

_____
_____
_____

Practice Questions

1

Reading Now read a passage about the fragility of apex predators.

Reading Time : 45 seconds

The Fragility of Apex Predators

Apex predators are animals which are at the top of the food chain, meaning that they have no natural predators themselves. This has made apex predators synonymous with strength in the minds of many people. In truth, however, the life cycles of apex predators are remarkably fragile and subject to disruption. The reason for this is that apex predators are ultimately affected by anything that impacts their prey species. Thus apex predators are subject to far greater environmental stress than other animal species.

Listening Now listen to part of a lecture on this topic in a biology class. MP3 38

Question The professor discusses the population decline of the American bald eagle. Explain how this population decline demonstrates the fragility of apex predators.

Reading Note	Listening Note

2

Reading   Now read a passage about punishment and reinforcement.

Reading Time : 45 seconds

Punishment and Reinforcement

Punishment and reinforcement are the two methods by which we may attempt to modify behavior. Punishment is used to discourage a behavior that is undesirable. When an undesirable behavior is engaged in, it is punished by adding an unpleasant stimulus or by removing a pleasant one. Reinforcement works to encourage a desired behavior by rewarding that behavior. Rewards may involve either the addition of a pleasant stimulus or the removal of a negative one. In general, reinforcement is a more effective form of behavior modification because it directly encourages a desired behavior, whereas punishment does not always lead to the adoption of the desired behavior.

Listening   Now listen to part of a lecture on this topic in a psychology class.   MP3 39

Question   The professor discusses methods of toilet training a child. Explain how these methods demonstrate concepts of punishment and reinforcement.

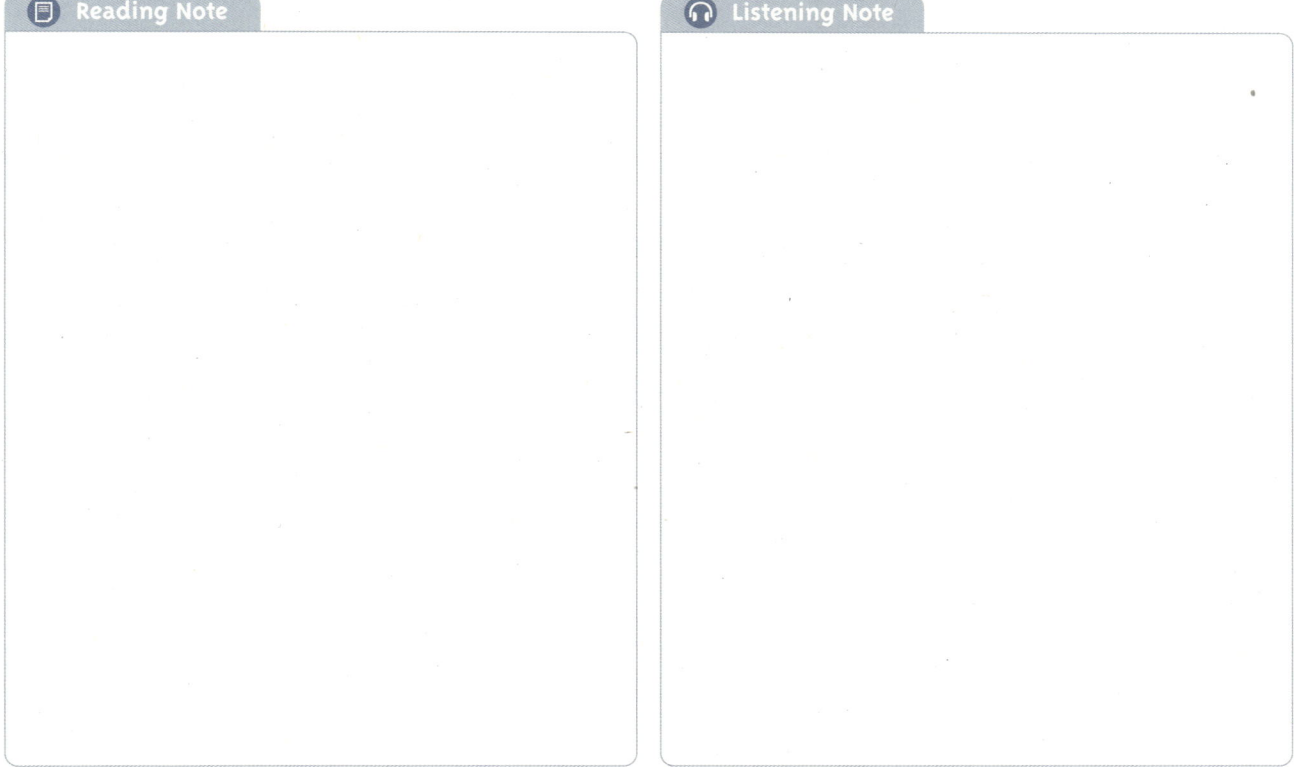

TASK 05 Problem / Solution

Overview

Task 5 consists of a conversation between two speakers which normally lasts from 60 to 90 seconds. One of the two speakers will explain his or her problem directly or indirectly related to campus life. Your task is to summarize the problem and present two possible solutions mentioned in the conversation. Then, choose one solution that you think is better and explain why.

Question Types

- The students discuss two possible solutions to the man's problem. Describe the problem. Then state which of the two solutions you prefer and explain why.
- The female student offered two solutions to the male student's problem. Describe the problem. Then state which of the two solutions you prefer and explain why.
- The male and female students discuss two possible solutions to the woman's problem. Describe the problem. Then state which of the two solutions you prefer and explain why.

Strategies

- Understand the overall theme of the conversation.
- Take good notes simply by writing key points.
- Think about the following questions: (1) What is the problem or the main issue? (2) What are the solutions to the problem or the issue? (3) Which solution do you personally prefer and why?
- Support your opinion with sound reasons and/or examples.
- Try to be confident when you speak and do not hesitate or mumble.
- Remember that your time is limited.

5. Problem / Solution

Sample Question

Listening Listen to a conversation between two students.

W: How come I don't see you at the gym on Saturdays anymore? Seems you've been busy with something else lately ...

M: Oh, nothing interesting, trust me. I haven't been showing up at the gym because <u>I'm trying to look for a meaningful job.</u> [Problem] My dad wants me to take over one of his stores some day. But he doesn't think I'm ready. He says I should start getting serious about my future and that I should be finding a job. He says it'll help me build character ... you know how parents are ...

W: Uh-huh. Well, <u>I'm doing temp work for this management firm near the university. Just clerical stuff</u> [Solution 1] ... I know they're always hiring part-time students for their personnel department. Why don't you try it out and apply? If you get in, you can see how the company manages its staff. Wouldn't that be great? And you'd get some spending money to boot!

M: Yeah, that looks promising ... an actual paying job ... although I'm not sure if that's the right job for me ...

W: Hmmm. Okay then, <u>why not just ask your dad if you can work at one of his stores?</u> [Solution 2] Even though he doesn't exactly trust you with the business yet, <u>maybe he could just hire you for stacking boxes or something ... or doing inventory work ... even greeting customers in the store</u> [Reason 1] ... anything. He might not pay you, but <u>it will certainly better prepare you for managing the store yourself someday.</u> [Reason 2]

M: Well, let me go over everything first. Then maybe I'll see you at the gym again.

Listening Checkpoints

✓ Problem
✓ Solution 1
✓ Solution 2
✓ Reason 1
✓ Reason 2

🎧 Listening Note

Problem

Looking for a job - according to his father's wish

Solutions

1) Get a job in the personnel dept. at a management company.
   - can learn how to manage staff
   - can earn spending money

2) Work at his father's store
   - may not pay him
   - will better prepare him for managing the store in the future

Reasons
① Will get valuable experience
   - will be exposed to the business
② Preparing for the future
   - the experience will be helpful when he manages his father's store

Question The students discuss two possible solutions to the man's problem. Describe the problem. Then state which of the two solutions you prefer and explain why.

🎤 Sample Response

The man is looking for a job to prepare him for the future. His father wants him to get a job that is meaningful. The woman tells him that he could apply where she works, since there's an opening. She also suggests that he just work at one of his dad's stores. Between the two, I think he should work for his dad. Even if he doesn't get paid, the experience will help prepare him to take over his father's stores one day. He won't need as much training when he manages one of the stores because he will have already been exposed to the business.

Pre-Speaking

STEP 1 • **Listening**

≫ Fill in the note with key ideas as you listen to a conversation.

1

Listening Now listen to a conversation between two students. MP3 40

Listening Note

Problem
Can't take a required course needed to graduate
• Not offered this semester

Solutions

1) Take the course for grad students
   • More difficult than her level

2) Take the course at an affiliate college
   • Far away
   • The same level

Reasons
① Save time & money
   • can take the course at her univ.
② Might look impressive on her resume
   • b/c she took a harder course.

2

Listening Now listen to a conversation between two students. MP3 41

Listening Note

Problem

Solutions

3

Listening Now listen to a conversation between two students. `MP3 42`

Listening Note

Problem

Solutions

4

Listening Now listen to a conversation between two students. `MP3 43`

🎧 **Listening Note**

Problem

Solutions

STEP 2 • Speaking

Problem / Solution / Reason

Expressions for Problem Sentences

- The man's problem is that ...
- The man has a problem with ...
- The man is in trouble because ...
- The man is having a hard time ~ ing ...
- The problem they discuss is that ...
- The man has difficulty with ...
- The man is facing a dilemma.
- The man wants to ~, but he isn't able to ~

The man's problem is that ...	**The man's problem is that** he doesn't get along with his roommate.
The man has a problem with ...	**The man has a problem with** his recent purchase of an expensive laptop.
The man is in trouble because ...	**The man is in trouble because** he won't be able to use the library's computers to do research for his papers.
The man is having a hard time ~ ing ...	**The man is having a hard time** pay**ing** his tuition.

The problem they discuss is that ...	**The problem they discuss is that** the pay from the internship is not enough for her to pay tuition.
The man has difficulty with ...	**The man has difficulty with** sleeping at night because the air-conditioner is not working.
The man is facing a dilemma.	**The man is facing a dilemma.** His school is renovating the free parking lot for students, so he has to find another parking space for his car.
The man wants to ~, but he isn't able to~	**The man wants to** get a job on campus, **but he isn't able to** find a job on campus.

Tip Write down key points and paraphrase the speakers' conversation. You should then clearly state the problem, present the first and second solutions, and make your suggestion supported by descriptive reasons and details.

➤ As you listen to part of a conversation, fill in the blanks and make problem sentences.

1

MP3 44

W: I can't seem to _get a break with my schedule_. I'm about to graduate, and this is what I get ...
M: Oh, you're having problems getting into _your required courses_, huh?
W: You got it. I need to take this course to graduate ... and now they tell me the course isn't offered this semester. My graduation is on the line here, and I have no idea _how I'll be able to get through this_.

➡ **Problem**

The woman is in trouble because she hasn't gotten into a class that she needs to graduate.

2

MP3 45

M: Hey, Alice, what's up with all those forms?
W: Oh these? _____; that's all. I got offers from two grad schools. I'm trying to figure out which one's the best for me ...

➡ **Problem**

_____
_____
_____

86 HOOKED ON TOEFL SPEAKING

3 　MP3 46

W: Whoa! Hold it ... those boxes look heavy. Let me help. _____?
M: Oh, thanks. _____ over to my cousin's place ... just two blocks away from here. My lease won't expire 'til after next month, but my landlord wants me out by next week. I forgot that I forfeited my last month's stay the last time I renewed my lease ... I just don't know how I'll manage to get all my stuff out on time ...
W: Why? What do you mean?
M: I mean I don't have the time this week because I have to be out of town ... part of my internship with Prof. Miller. I missed the last two sessions. _____.

➡ **Problem**

_____
_____
_____

4 　MP3 47

M: Hey, do you know _____ this coming summer?
W: No, I don't think so ... Why, what's up? Aren't you attending the same class?
M: Yeah, I am. Thing is ... _____ in class lately. Ever since I sprained my hand, my writing's been slower. And if I push too hard, it gets really painful.

➡ **Problem**

_____
_____
_____

STEP 2 • Speaking

Problem / **Solution** / Reason

Expressions for Solution Sentences

- The man suggests two solutions. One is … The other is …
- There are two solutions presented. The first is …The second is …
- The man suggests that she either … or …
- The man advises that she should … or …
- The man advises that she could …
- The man says that she would …
- The man tells her to …
- The man recommends that she …

The man suggests two solutions. One is … The other is …	**The man suggests two solutions. One is** that she could ask her employer to change her working shift to the morning or the evening. **The other is** that she could take other similar courses available in the morning.
There are two solutions presented. The first is … The second is …	**There are two solutions presented. The first is** to change his major to something else. **The second is** to take some time off and wait for his old zeal for art to come back.
The man suggests that she either … or …	**The man suggests that she either** ask a fellow volunteer who has a car for help **or** use public transportation.
The man advises that she should … or …	**The man advises that she should** take the course for graduate students **or** take the course at an affiliate college.

The man advises that she could …	**The man advises that she could** get a job in the personnel department at a management company.
The man says that she would …	**The man says that she would** ask her friends for help.
The man tells her to …	**The man tells her to** work at his father's store.
The man recommends that she …	**The man recommends that she** study at home with borrowed books.

Tip Choose a solution that you can easily support with your background knowledge. Focus on answering the prompt in a logical manner with sensible reasons and details.

» As you listen to part of a conversation, fill in the blanks and make solution sentences.

1 MP3 48

M: It's not really the end of the world, you know. If you really have to, you could take the course taken by the graduate students. _It's probably harder than your typical course_, but you'll be able to graduate if you pass it.

W: Well, there is that … and it is going to be harder than my usual level …

M: _Or you can try cross-registering to our affiliate collage_ for the same course. It's a long distance from our school, but you'll have the exact course you need in order to graduate.

➡ **Solution**

The man suggests two solutions. The first option is to take a harder graduate course to satisfy the graduation requirement. The other option is to take the class she needs at a different college campus.

2 MP3 49

W: Here's the thing. _____, but it's three hours away from home and where I'm working right now ... the other one's only given me _____, but it's just a stone's throw away from my apartment ... And you know I can't afford the tuition or lose my part-time job ...

M: Don't you think it's better to accept the partial scholarship, since as you said, it's near your apartment and all? You don't have to travel all that far just to get to school, and you can use your extra time for your part-time job.

W: _____ ... still, I'm not sure about the school expenses ...

M: Well ... then take the full scholarship. That way, you won't have to worry about paying for your tuition. _____. And if it's the job you're worried about, you could start looking for jobs within the school area ... that way, you won't have to worry about not having one.

➡ **Solution**

3   MP3 50

W: Oh, I see ... that's a tough one ... hmmm, well, why don't you ask some of your close friends to do the moving for you while you're away? See if one of them has a truck you could use to make it easier ...

M: Well, yeah, I could probably ask them ... but I was also thinking of _____ _____ to do the job. They'll know what to do with my stuff ... what do you think?

W: That's actually up to you ... _____ and then decide, hopefully by tomorrow morning ... see what works for you?

→ Solution

_____
_____
_____

4   MP3 51

W: Hmmm. Well, maybe _____ for the day and photocopy them or something ... _____ trying to keep up with the lectures on the board ... you could ask your seatmate or someone close to you taking the same class for the day's lecture notes.

M: That seems simple enough ... though, I'm not too sure about it.

W: Well, maybe _____. You could try and sit at the front or near the professor so that the audio will be clear enough to listen to afterwards. Later, you can have _____. You can borrow my recorder, if you want.

→ Solution

_____
_____
_____

STEP 2 • Speaking

Problem / Solution / **Reason**

Expressions for Reason Sentences

- I think he should ... because otherwise ...
- Between the two solutions, I prefer ... to ... because ...
- I think that (A) is better than (B). This is because ...
- I believe the best way is to ... One reason is ... The other is ...
- I think the first solution is better because ...
- I suggest he follow the woman's first suggestion because ...
- I believe the first solution is better. That is because ...
- I consider (A) to be the most reasonable solution because ...

I think he should ... because otherwise	**I think he should** keep his job **because otherwise** he can't have work experiences that university courses can't offer.
Between the two solutions, I prefer ... to ... because ...	**Between the two solutions, I prefer** getting another roommate **to** living alone **because** he would never get lonely.
I think that (A) is better than (B). This is because ...	**I think that** asking her boss to change her shift **is better than** adjusting her course schedule. **This is because** it's more important for a student to study than to work.
I believe the best way is to ... One reason is ...The other is ...	**I believe the best way is to** take some time off. **One reason** is that he can have time to think about the matter. **The other is** that it will help him make a good decision.

I think the first solution is better because ...	**I think the first solution is better because** asking for money may jeopardize the internship.
I suggest he follow the woman's first suggestion because ...	**I suggest he follow the woman's first suggestion because** he won't have to worry about other people disturbing him.
I believe the first suggestion is better. That is because ...	**I believe the first suggestion is better. That is because** her problem will be fixed permanently.
I consider (A) to be the most reasonable solution because ...	**I consider** taking the course for graduate students **to be the most reasonable solution because** it will save her time and money.

Tip Don't spend too much time describing what the problem is. Simply state the problem and get to the point. Briefly explain what are the solutions mentioned in the conversation and choose a solution you prefer, as quickly as you can. Time management is an important skill when it comes to handling integrated speaking tasks. You should learn to distinguish important issues from less important details and paraphrase them in your own style.

>> As you listen to part of a conversation, fill in the blanks and make solution sentences.

1 MP3 52

M: It's not really the end of the world, you know. If you really have to, you could _take the course taken by the graduate students_. It's probably harder than your typical course, but you'll be able to graduate if you pass it.

W: Well, there is that ... and it is going to be harder than my usual level ...

M: Or you can try cross-registering to our affiliate college for the same course. It's a long distance from our school, but you'll have _the exact course you need in order to graduate_.

➡ **Reason**

I think the woman should take the graduate level course because otherwise she will end up spending too much time and doing too much work as she attempts to take her class at a different campus.

2 MP3 53

W: Here's the thing. One's offering me a full scholarship, but it's three hours away from home and where I'm working right now ... the other one's only given me a partial scholarship, but it's just a stone's throw away from my apartment ... _____ ...

M: Don't you think it's better to accept the partial scholarship, since as you said, it's near your apartment and all? You don't have to travel all that far just to get to school, _____.

W: That seems logical ... still, I'm not sure about the school expenses ...

M: Well ... then take the full scholarship. That way, you won't have to worry about _____. Not a lot of people get offers like yours. And if it's the job you're worried about, you could start looking for jobs within the school area ... that way, you won't have to worry about not having one.

➡ **Reason**

3
MP3 54

W: Oh, I see ... that's a tough one ... hmmm, well, why don't you ask some of your close friends to do the moving for you while you're away? See if one of them has a truck you could use to make it easier ...

M: Well, yeah, I could probably ask them ... but I was also thinking of just paying a couple of professional movers to do the job. _____ ... what do you think?

W: That's actually up to you ... _____, hopefully by tomorrow morning ... see what works for you?

➡ **Reason**

_____
_____
_____

4
MP3 55

W: Hmmm. Well, maybe you could just borrow someone else's notes for the day and photocopy them or something ...
_____
_____ ... you could ask your seatmate or someone close to you taking the same class for the day's lecture notes.

M: That seems simple enough ... though, I'm not too sure about it.

W: Well, maybe you could just bring a tape recorder to class. _____
_____ so that the audio will be clear enough to listen to afterwards. Later, you can have someone transcribe the tape for you. You can borrow my recorder, if you want.

➡ **Reason**

_____
_____
_____

Practice Questions

1

Listening Listen to a conversation between two students. MP3 56

Question The students discuss two possible solutions to the man's problem. Describe the problem. Then state which of the two solutions you prefer and explain why.

Listening Note

2

Listening Listen to a conversation between two students. MP3 57

Question The students discuss two possible solutions to the woman's problem. Describe the problem. Then state which of the two solutions you prefer and explain why.

Listening Note

PART I Task Types 95

TASK 06 Summary

Overview

Task 6 contains a lecture which normally lasts 60 to 90 seconds. This lecture is mainly about an academic subject. You need to summarize the contents of the lecture and provide specific examples and details that are worth mentioning.

Question Types

- Using points and examples from the talk, explain how the two methods of lowering temperature and reducing humidity prevent food deterioration.
- Using points and examples from the lecture, explain how fragmentation and ambiguity affect the illusion of space in cubist paintings.
- Using specific examples and points from the talk, explain how the two illustrations presented by the professor demonstrate the social effects of the early use of fire.

Strategies

- Understand the overall information of the listening passage.
- Learn to develop effective note-taking skills.
- You won't have time to talk about everything mentioned in the lecture. Thus, it's essential for you to improvise a well-organized summary as you listen to the lecture.
- Remember that you are not just summarizing the lecture, but also providing the information about the lecture's main topic along with specific details.

6. Summary

Sample Question

Listening Now listen to part of a talk in an anthropology class.

When early pre-human creatures started using fire about three to five hundred thousand years ago, there began a series of developments that would culminate in the rise of modern humans. Uh, the discovery of fire is the greatest of all prehistoric and cultural advancements. Most of us already know the advantages that fire provided our ancestors. Of course, with fire, they could warm themselves in cold weather, keep out animals and insects, harden their weapons, and soften food through cooking. But what most of us are not aware of are the social consequences brought about by the early use of fire. *— Topic*

One of these social effects was a better group relationship among these creatures. *— Example 1 —* Imagine yourself as one of them, and as your group or tribe rests at night, a fire is set inside your cave. Of course you will tend to go near the fire, and as others go near the fire also, we now have a whole group of creatures facing each other. In time, this *— Main Idea 1 —* nightly activity would become a sort of regular **leisure period**, and as each creature *— Details —* tried to closely **communicate with the other group members**, their language would have been sharpened, resulting in **better understanding and communication**.

Hmm ... With fire also came an early form of social hierarchy within these primitive *— Example 2 —* groups. Fire brought about the emergence of fire specialists—you know, those who *— Main Idea 2 —* knew the secret of making fires and guarding this important tool. These fire specialists were looked up to in their group, and they must have **used this knowledge** *— Details —* to claim **admiration among the creatures**. Mastering the use of fire, they began to be regarded as **the most valuable members of their group**.

Listening Checkpoints

✓ Topic
✓ Example 1
✓ Main Idea 1
✓ Details
✓ Example 2
✓ Main Idea 2
✓ Details

🎧 Listening Note

Topic
Social effects of the early use of fire.

Example 1
A better group relationship

Example 2
Establishment of social hierarchy

Main Idea 1
People gathered around the fire, facing each other.

Main Idea 2
Emergence of fire specialists

Details
→ Became a regular leisure period
→ Language development
→ Better communication

Details
→ Had special knowledge
→ Admired by other group members
→ Their skill gave them value and status

Question   Using points and examples from the talk, explain how the two illustrations presented by the professor demonstrate the social effects of the early use of fire.

🎤 Sample Response

The professor illustrates the social effects of the early use of fire by giving two examples. In the first example, a better group relationship resulted as people gathered around the fire, facing each other. This time became a regular leisure period and encouraged better communication through language development. In the second example, a social hierarchy was established by the emergence of fire specialists. These experts had special knowledge and were admired by other group members. Their skill gave them value and status in their social group.

Pre-Speaking

STEP 1 • **Listening**

» Fill out the note with key ideas as you listen to the lecture.

1

Listening   Now listen to part of a lecture in an economics class. MP3 58

🎧 Listening Note

Topic
Related products - dependent on one another

Example 1
Substitute prod.

Example 2
Complementary prod.

Main Idea 1
Price increase of one prod. Increases sale of similar, cheaper prod.

Main Idea 2
Some items serve a purpose in relation to other prod.

Details
Butter is too expensive → switch to margarine
price of butter drops → switch back

Details
CDs can only used with a CD player
→ CDs will only sell if many people also buy CD players
→ Prices of either item may be dropped to encourage sales of the other.

2

Listening Now listen to part of a lecture in a psychology class. MP3 59

Listening Note

Topic

| Example 1 | Example 2 |

| Main Idea 1 | Main Idea 2 |

| Details | Details |

3

Listening Now listen to part of a lecture on agriculture. [MP3 60]

Listening Note

Topic

Example 1

Example 2

Main Idea 1

Main Idea 2

Details

Details

4

Listening Now listen to part of a talk in a social psychology class. [MP3 61]

Listening Note

Topic

| Example 1 | Example 2 |

| Main Idea 1 | Main Idea 2 |

| Details | Details |

STEP 2 • Speaking

Topic | Classification | Detail

Expressions for Topic Sentences

- The lecture is mainly about ...
- The topic of the lecture is ...
- The professor discusses ...
- The professor talks about ...
- According to the professor, (A) is ...
- According to the lecture, (A) + (B) are two ways to ...
- According to the professor, (A) is defined as ...
- According to the professor, (A) refers to ...

The lecture is mainly about ...	**The lecture is mainly about** the use of perspective in Renaissance paintings.
The topic of the lecture is ...	**The topic of the lecture is** cognitive dissonance and the different ways it can be resolved.
The professor discusses ...	**The professor discusses** the effects of the Industrial Revolution.
The professor talks about ...	**The professor talks about** the social effects of the early use of fire by giving two examples.

According to the professor, (A) is ...	**According to the professor,** slash-and-burn farming **is** something that damages the environment in two basic ways.
According to the lecture, (A) + (B) are two ways to ...	**According to the lecture,** lowering temperature **and** reducing humidity **are two ways to** prevent food from spoiling.
According to the professor, (A) is defined as ...	**According to the professor,** latent learning **is defined as** learning without apparent need or reward.
According to the professor, (A) refers to ...	**According to the professor,** selective attention **refers to** the ability to focus on one stimulus at a time.

Tip If you don't have solid listening skills, task 6 will be more than overwhelming. First, having good listening skills is a must. You definitely need to spend a lot of time listening to English lectures or conversations. Second, you need to learn dictation skills. Even if you have good listening skills, you won't be able to remember all the contents of the lecture. It's vitally important for you to acquire effective dictation skills, especially to handle Task 6.

» As you listen to part of a lecture, fill in the blanks and make topic sentences.

1 MP3 62

Unlike normal goods that can stand alone, related products <u>are dependent on or affect one another</u>, in terms of function. As pricing depends on the need for one or both products, they can either balance one another ... or replace one another.

➡ **Topic**

The professor talks about related products in his lecture.

2 MP3 63

Our cognition, _____, affects our behavior and everyday decisions. There is cognitive dissonance whenever a situation arises wherein there is an apparent conflict between our beliefs and our actions.

➡ **Topic**

3

MP3 64

Slash-and-burn farming is a type of farming that is _____,
especially in rainforests. In slash-and-burn farming, all the large trees are cut down and then intentionally set on fire. The resulting fire burns away _____
_____, leaving a clear field that may then be planted with crops. But as you'll see in a few minutes, slash-and-burn farming is heavily destructive to the environment.

➡ **Topic**

_____
_____
_____

4

MP3 65

When people aspire to climb the social ladder, _____
_____ in their lives than they had before. The acquisition of luxury goods and other high dollar items serves as a visual symbol, not only to others, but also to oneself, of one's rising status in society. _____
through material possessions fees into the culture of consumerism.

➡ **Topic**

_____
_____
_____

STEP 2 • Speaking

Topic / **Classification** / Detail

Expressions for Classification Sentences

- The professor gives two types of ... One is ... The other is ...
- There are two factors of ... One is ... The other is ...
- The professor explains two definitions of ... One is ... the other is ...
- The professor demonstrates the concept of ...
- The professor illustrates this by talking about ...
- The professor discusses ... as an example of ...
- The professor gives another example of ...
- The professor describes ... by giving two examples.

The professor gives two types of ... One is ... The other is ...	**The professor gives two types of** artistic imitation. **One** example **is** exaggerated drawings in newspapers. **The other is** impersonation, wherein good imitators try to look and to act like their subjects.
There are two factors of ... One is ... The other is ...	**There are two factors of** Cubism that achieve the illusion of space in paintings. **One is** fragmentation. **The other is** ambiguity.
The professor explains two methods of ... One is ... The other is ...	**The professor explains two methods of** protecting food from deteriorating. **One is** to lower the temperature. **The other is** to reduce the humidity.
The professor demonstrates the concept of ...	**The professor demonstrates the concept of** cognitive dissonance by giving two examples.

The professor illustrates this by talking about ...	**The professor illustrates this by talking about** specific examples of latent learning.
The professor discusses ... as an example of ...	**The professor discusses** brain death **as an example of** death.
The professor gives another example of ...	**The professor gives another example of** organisms that can build up a resistance to toxins.
The professor describes ... by giving two examples.	**The professor describes** the culture of consumerism and its effects **by giving two examples**.

> **Tip** Task 6 is difficult since it is about handling academic topics taken from social science, natural science, history, psychology, arts, biology, et cetera. For this reason, it will be helpful if you read various college-level books. It's unwise to expect a high score on TOEFL unless you have both a good command of English and general knowledge of academic subjects. Your priority, therefore, should be achieving English proficiency and acquiring knowledge about various academic subjects.

As you listen to part of a lecture, fill in the blanks and make classification sentences.

1

MP3 66

If a product undergoes a price increase, like the price of butter, for example ... people, as a natural tendency, may opt to buy an alternative product that basically serves the same use as butter and is much cheaper. They may start buying margarine instead, and if this happens, it will be the latter product that will be more in demand. As demand for butter decreases, its price will drop, and _people may switch back to buying butter_. Products that are involved in this kind of cyclical relationship are what we call substitute products.

One the other hand, _there are complementary products_, where a product out in the market serves a particular purpose in relation to another product. For example a CD is only useful to the consumer if he or she goes out and buys a CD player. Uh… therefore, CDs can't perform well in the market unless CD players also sell well. So, to arrange this, retailers may reduce the price of the player in order to encourage higher sales of CDs. The relationship is reciprocal ... if CDs were priced too highly, _then consumers would not have much motivation to buy CD players_.

➡ **Classification**

The professor describes related products by giving two examples. First he talks about butter and margarine, which is an alternative to butter, to help us understand how the price of butter is related to another product. The other example is that of CD players and CDs, which are complimentary products.

2

MP3 67

Let's say you have a family that is planning a vacation, but the only money available to take the vacation is money that they have set aside for their son's education. Um, in this situation, _____ _____ because the family's wish to take a vacation conflicts with their belief in providing a good education for their son. This _____. Most likely the family will decide that their son's education is more important and decide not to take the vacation.

Uh, in another situation, let's say you have a man who is starving but has no money. He can steal food to feed himself, but he has always been taught that stealing is wrong. Again, _____ _____. This time, however, the man resolves this by altering his beliefs. He reasons that it isn't really wrong to steal food to feed himself. By altering his previously held beliefs, he is able to resolve the dissonance.

➡ **Classification**

3

OK, first of all, uh, slash-and-burn farming destroys large areas of forest. Not only does a farmer have to cut down a section of forest to create a field for farming, _____ _____. Slash-and-burn farming quickly exhausts the nutrients in the soil, and so farmers constantly have to move to a new field. Obviously that means they have to cut down more trees. Thus, slash-and-burn farming presents _____, which is helping to cause global warming. Another way that slash-and-burn farming destroys the environment is that, uh, well, as I said ... it destroys all the large trees. _____ _____. The crops that farmers plant in place of those large trees have very shallow root structures and don't do nearly as good a job at holding the soil together. It becomes loose and easily blown or washed away. So slash-and-burn farming also contributes to soil erosion.

⇒ **Classification**

_____
_____
_____
_____

4

In a culture of consumerism, class is not only your own needs that determine your purchases; _____. If your lifestyle doesn't meet the expectations of society, you will likely view your life as inadequate. Like, say you earn decent money, have a car and a house… this would seem to be enough, right? But then you look around you, and it seems that everyone has a nicer car or a bigger house. _____, you will be driven to purchase a nicer car or a bigger house, simply to gain the same social stature as those around you. Uh, in addition to creating a culture of excess, uh, consumerism also worsens the effects of poverty. Not everyone has the money for the big car or the big house ... but everyone in society feels _____. Thus the poor are often pressured to buy items they really can't afford. Think about the young teenager in a poor family who just has to have a $150 pair of tennis shoes. Given his family's financial situation, this isn't a logical purchase, but _____ to buy them anyway.

⇒ **Classification**

_____
_____
_____
_____

STEP 2 • Speaking

Topic / Classification / **Detail**

Expressions for Detail Sentences

- (A) enabled (B)
- (A) paved the way for (B)
- (A) caused (B)
- (A) resulted in (B)
- (A) led to (B)
- (A) had a great influence on (B)
- According to someone, (A) is the most important factor in …
- (A) occurred mainly because of …

(A) enabled (B)	The development of technology **enabled** distance learning and teaching.
(A) paved the way for (B)	A series of events **paved the way for** the collapse of the Soviet Union.
(A) caused (B)	The innovation of the assembly line invented by Henry Ford **caused** a great improvement in efficiency, since it enabled the workers to do a single task when making a product.
(A) resulted in (B)	The steam engine **resulted in** the development of industries based on not human but mechanical energy, and this gave rise to large scale production.

(A) led to (B)	The invention of electricity **led to** the rapid growth of the American economy in the 20th century.
(A) had a great influence on (B)	Changes in the natural environment **had a great influence on** the biodiversity of aquatic wildlife
According to someone, (A) is the most important factor in …	**According to** Freud, experience at one's early stage of life **is the most important factor in** determining one's personality.
(A) occurred mainly because of …	Food deterioration **occurred mainly because of** the high level of temperature and moisture.

Tip When taking the TOEFL Speaking test, you are the only one speaking. For this reason you might feel nervous and timid. Try to visualize a person sitting right in front of you. This way, you can speak with a lively voice and possibly some gestures. Remember you are talking to a machine but the test graders are humans. They will expect you to speak as normally as you can.

» As you listen to part of a lecture, fill in the blanks and make detail sentences.

1 MP3 70

If a product undergoes a price increase, like the price of butter, for example… people, as a natural tendency, may opt to buy _an alternative product that basically serves the same use_ as butter and is much cheaper. They may start buying margarine instead, and if this happens, it will be the latter product that will be more in demand. As demand for butter decreases, its price will drop, and people may switch back to buying butter. _Products that are involved in this kind of cyclical relationship_ are what we call substitute products.

➡ **Detail**

The high price of butter caused people to purchase margarine, which is comparatively cheaper than butter. And this would lower the price of butter as the demand for butter decreases. As soon as the price of butter drops, people may switch back to buying butter, according to the professor; thus, this is what we call a substitute product.

2 MP3 71

Um, in this situation, _____ _____ conflicts with their belief in providing a good education for their son. This conflict must be resolved in some way. Most likely the family will decide that their son's education is more important and decide not to take the vacation.

➡ **Detail**

3 [MP3 72]

Not only does a farmer have to cut down _____,
but that field also will only be productive for maybe three or four years. Slash-and-burn farming quickly _____, and so farmers constantly have to move to a new field.

➡ **Detail**

_____
_____
_____
_____

4 [MP3 73]

You see, class, _____, it's not only your own needs that determine your purchases; societal expectations play a large role as well. It doesn't matter if what you have is enough to sustain you; if _____, you will see it as inadequate. Like, say you earn decent money, have a car and a house ... this would seem to be enough, right? But then you look around you, and it seems that everyone has a nicer car ... or a bigger house. Since _____
_____, you will be driven to purchase a bigger car or a bigger house, simply to gain the same social stature as those around you ... even though you may not really need the bigger car or the bigger house.

➡ **Detail**

_____
_____
_____
_____

Practice Questions

1

Listening Now listen to part of a lecture in a creative writing class. MP3 74

Question Using points and examples from the talk, explain two literary techniques discussed by the professor.

🎧 Listening Note

2

Listening Now listen to part of a lecture in a biology class. MP3 75

Question Using points and examples from the lecture, explain how angler fish represent an adaptation to an extreme environment.

🎧 Listening Note

HOOKED ON TOEFL SPEAKING

Practice Test

- TASK 1 Personal Preference
- TASK 2 Paired Choice
- TASK 3 Fit and Explain
- TASK 4 General / Specific
- TASK 5 Problem / Solution
- TASK 6 Summary

L·I·N·G·U·A·F·O·R·U·M·H·O·O·K·E·D·O·N·T·O·E·F·L·S·P·E·A·K·I·N·G

PART II

Task 01 — Personal Preference

MP3 76

TOEFL SPEAKING — Sample Question

What is the dream job you would like to have and why? Use specific examples and details in your explanation.

Preparation time : 15 seconds
Response time   : 45 seconds

Topic	Travel Photographer
Reason 1 Travel around the world	**Reason 2** Become more informed about the world.
Details • Meet various people • New experiences	**Details** • Observe different cultures • Show people what is happening in the world

Personal Preference

- **Speaking Expressions**

  Topic
  - In my case
  - I think ...
  - I believe ...
  - In my opinion,
  - It seems to me ...
  - As far as I'm concerned,
  - I would say ...
  - Without a doubt,

  Reason
  - What I like about ...
  - Another reason is that ...
  - One of the reasons I think ...
  - The other reason is that ...
  - One reason why ...
  - I like this also because ...
  - First,
  - Second,

  Detail
  - It means that ...
    = I mean ...
  - For example
    = For instance,
  - To give a specific example,
    = To illustrate,
  - What I am saying is that ...
    = In other words,

- **Idiomatic Expressions**

  Itchy feet: Have strong desire to travel very badly or try something new.

  Ex) His **itchy feet** caused him travel all over Europe to get a different perspective on life.

Sample Response

- Topic

  I definitely have itchy feet. For this reason, I think my dream job is to become a travel photographer.

- Reason 1

  One reason why I want to become a travel photographer is because I think it would be exciting to travel around the world.

  - Details

    For instance, I would be able to meet a variety of people from different walks of life. Every assignment would be an adventurous new experience.

- Reason 2

  The other reason is that I want to learn about the world.

  - Details

    I mean traveling and observing many different cultures would be very educational.

Conclusion

For the reasons presented above, I want to become a travel photographer.

* It's not necessary to make a concluding sentence if you don't have enough time.

Evaluation		1	2	3	4
Topic Development	Could you complete your response?				
	Is your response coherent and unified?				
	Do you find a sequence in your response?				
Language Use	How is the use of vocabulary?				
	Is the grammatical structure good?				
	How is the use of idiomatic expressions?				
Delivery	Is your response fluent and smooth?				
	Is your pronunciation clear?				
	How is the use of stress and intonation?				

Task 1

2 MP3 77

TOEFL SPEAKING

Choose a type of house (e.g., a single family home, an apartment, a farmhouse, or a trailer) you would like to live in and explain why. Please include specific examples and details in your explanation.

Preparation time : 15 seconds
Response time   : 45 seconds

Topic

Reason 1	Reason 2
Details	Details

Personal Preference

Speaking Expressions

Topic
- In my case
- I think ...
- I believe ...
- In my opinion,
- It seems to me ...
- As far as I'm concerned,
- I would say ...
- Without a doubt,

Reason
- What I like about ...
- Another reason is that ...
- One of the reasons I think ...
- The other reason is that ...
- One reason why ...
- I like this also because ...
- First,
- Second,

Detail
- It means that ...
  = I mean ...
- For example
  = For instance,
- To give a specific example,
  = To illustrate,
- What I am saying is that ...
  = In other words,

Idiomatic Expressions

There is no place like home: Regardless of its size or beauty, everyone's home is the best place to reside and get rest.

Ex) I sometimes stay at my parents' house even though I have my own place, because **there is no place like home**.

🎤 My Response

- Topic

- Reason 1

  - Details

- Reason 2

  - Details

Evaluation		1	2	3	4
Topic Development	Could you complete your response?				
	Is your response coherent and unified?				
	Do you find a sequence in your response?				
Language Use	How is the use of vocabulary?				
	Is the grammatical structure good?				
	How is the use of idiomatic expressions?				
Delivery	Is your response fluent and smooth?				
	Is your pronunciation clear?				
	How is the use of stress and intonation?				

Task 1

3

TOEFL SPEAKING

Describe your favorite subject in school and explain why you like it the most. Provide specific examples and details in your explanation.

Preparation time : 15 seconds
Response time   : 45 seconds

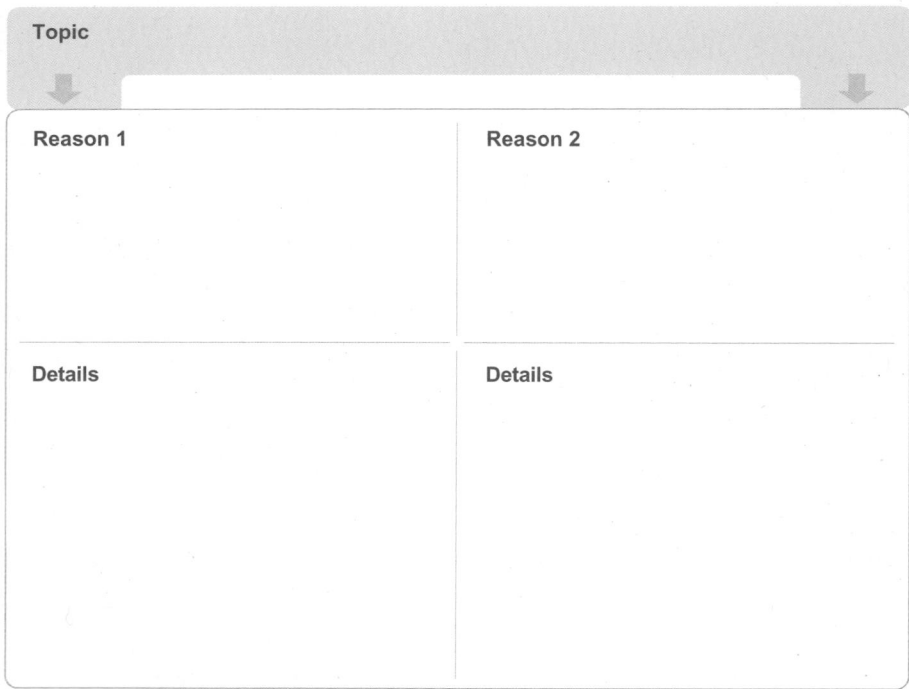

Personal Preference

Speaking Expressions

Topic
- In my case
- I think ...
- I believe ...
- In my opinion,
- It seems to me ...
- As far as I'm concerned,
- I would say ...
- Without a doubt,

Reason
- What I like about ...
- Another reason is that ...
- One of the reasons I think ...
- The other reason is that ...
- One reason why ...
- I like this also because ...
- First,
- Second,

Detail
- It means that ...
  = I mean ...
- For example
  = For instance,
- To give a specific example,
  = To illustrate,
- What I am saying is that ...
  = In other words,

🎤 My Response

- Topic

- Reason 1

  – Details

- Reason 2

  – Details

Idiomatic Expressions

A breath of fresh air:
Something that is new and different and makes everything more exciting.

Ex) The unexpected arrival of the twins was **a breath of fresh air** to the boring party.

Evaluation		1	2	3	4
Topic Development	Could you complete your response?				
	Is your response coherent and unified?				
	Do you find a sequence in your response?				
Language Use	How is the use of vocabulary?				
	Is the grammatical structure good?				
	How is the use of idiomatic expressions?				
Delivery	Is your response fluent and smooth?				
	Is your pronunciation clear?				
	How is the use of stress and intonation?				

Task 1

4

TOEFL SPEAKING

Where would you like to have your dream vacation and why? Include details and examples in your response.

Preparation time	: 15 seconds
Response time	: 45 seconds

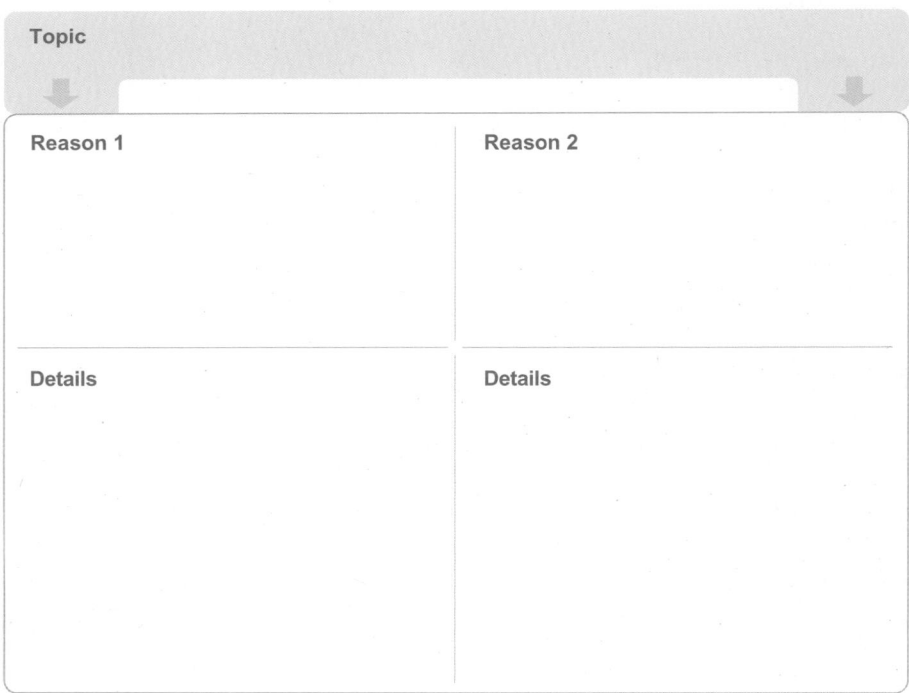

Personal Preference

Speaking Expressions

Topic
- In my case
- I think ...
- I believe ...
- In my opinion,
- It seems to me ...
- As far as I'm concerned,
- I would say ...
- Without a doubt,

Reason
- What I like about ...
- Another reason is that ...
- One of the reasons I think ...
- The other reason is that ...
- One reason why ...
- I like this also because ...
- First,
- Second,

Detail
- It means that ...
  = I mean ...
- For example
  = For instance,
- To give a specific example,
  = To illustrate,
- What I am saying is that ...
  = In other words,

Idiomatic Expressions

A shoulder to cry on: Someone who gives you sympathy when you are upset.

Ex) Even if they just want **a shoulder to cry on**, students should not hesitate to approach their guidance counselors.

🎤 My Response

- Topic

- Reason 1

  – Details

- Reason 2

  – Details

Evaluation		1	2	3	4
Topic Development	Could you complete your response?				
	Is your response coherent and unified?				
	Do you find a sequence in your response?				
Language Use	How is the use of vocabulary?				
	Is the grammatical structure good?				
	How is the use of idiomatic expressions?				
Delivery	Is your response fluent and smooth?				
	Is your pronunciation clear?				
	How is the use of stress and intonation?				

Task 1

5 MP3 80

TOEFL SPEAKING

Describe the type of music you usually listen to and explain why you like listening to it. Include details and examples to support your explanation.

Preparation time : 15 seconds
Response time   : 45 seconds

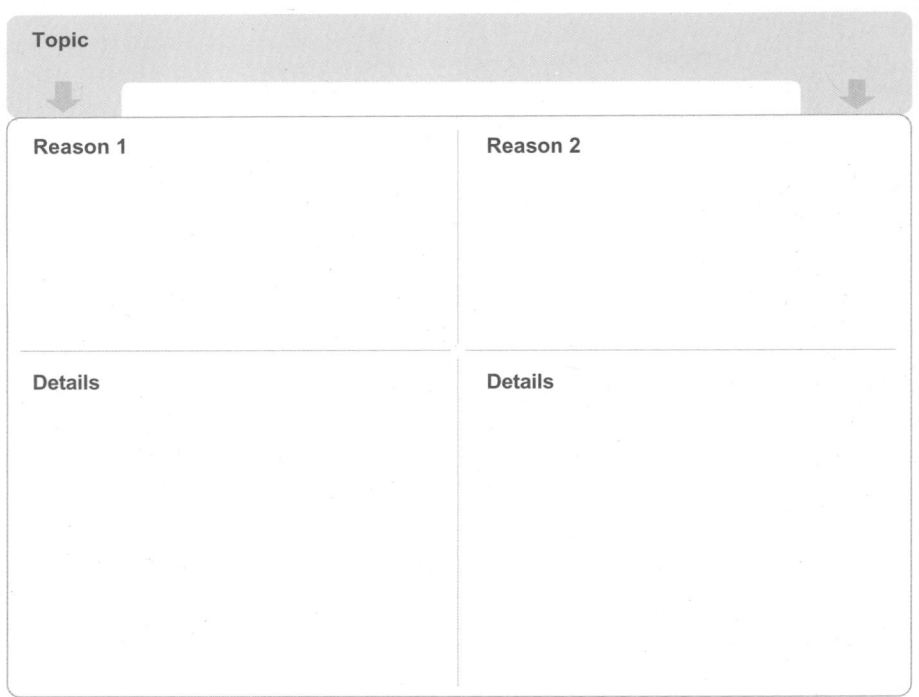

Topic

Reason 1	Reason 2
Details	Details

Personal Preference

- **Speaking Expressions**

Topic
- In my case
- I think ...
- I believe ...
- In my opinion,
- It seems to me ...
- As far as I'm concerned,
- I would say ...
- Without a doubt,

Reason
- What I like about ...
- Another reason is that ...
- One of the reasons I think ...
- The other reason is that ...
- One reason why ...
- I like this also because ...
- First,
- Second,

Detail
- It means that ...
  = I mean ...
- For example
  = For instance,
- To give a specific example,
  = To illustrate,
- What I am saying is that ...
  = In other words,

- **My Response**

- Topic

- Reason 1

  – Details

- Reason 2

  – Details

- **Idiomatic Expressions**

Cost an arm and a leg:
Extremely expensive.

Ex) I bought a new car. It **cost** me **an arm and a leg**.

	Evaluation	1	2	3	4
Topic Development	Could you complete your response?				
	Is your response coherent and unified?				
	Do you find a sequence in your response?				
Language Use	How is the use of vocabulary?				
	Is the grammatical structure good?				
	How is the use of idiomatic expressions?				
Delivery	Is your response fluent and smooth?				
	Is your pronunciation clear?				
	How is the use of stress and intonation?				

Task 1

6 MP3 81

TOEFL SPEAKING

Describe an animal that you have or would like to have as a pet. Explain why you like that kind of animal as a pet. Include specific examples and details in your explanation.

Preparation time : 15 seconds
Response time   : 45 seconds

Topic	
Reason 1	Reason 2
Details	Details

Personal Preference

🎤 My Response

- Topic

- Reason 1

  - Details

- Reason 2

  - Details

• Speaking Expressions

Topic

- In my case
- I think ...
- I believe ...
- In my opinion,
- It seems to me ...
- As far as I'm concerned,
- I would say ...
- Without a doubt,

Reason

- What I like about ...
- Another reason is that ...
- One of the reasons I think ...
- The other reason is that ...
- One reason why ...
- I like this also because ...
- First,
- Second,

Detail

- It means that ...
  = I mean ...
- For example
  = For instance,
- To give a specific example,
  = To illustrate,
- What I am saying is that ...
  = In other words,

• Idiomatic Expressions

Feel blue: Feel depressed or gloomy.

Ex) I **feel blue** because my boyfriend joined the army. I can't call or write him for three months because he started his basic training yesterday.

Evaluation		1	2	3	4
Topic Development	Could you complete your response?				
	Is your response coherent and unified?				
	Do you find a sequence in your response?				
Language Use	How is the use of vocabulary?				
	Is the grammatical structure good?				
	How is the use of idiomatic expressions?				
Delivery	Is your response fluent and smooth?				
	Is your pronunciation clear?				
	How is the use of stress and intonation?				

Task 1

7 MP3 82

TOEFL SPEAKING

Describe your favorite holiday of the year. Include details and examples in your response.

Preparation time	: 15 seconds
Response time	: 45 seconds

Personal Preference

Speaking Expressions

Topic
- In my case
- I think ...
- I believe ...
- In my opinion,
- It seems to me ...
- As far as I'm concerned,
- I would say ...
- Without a doubt,

Reason
- What I like about ...
- Another reason is that ...
- One of the reasons I think ...
- The other reason is that ...
- One reason why ...
- I like this also because ...
- First,
- Second,

Detail
- It means that ...
  = I mean ...
- For example
  = For instance,
- To give a specific example,
  = To illustrate,
- What I am saying is that ...
  = In other words,

🎤 My Response

- Topic

- Reason 1

  - Details

- Reason 2

  - Details

Idiomatic Expressions

Keep late hours: To stay up until late at night.

Ex) My sister **keeps late hours** because she is studying for the bar exam.

	Evaluation	1	2	3	4
Topic Development	Could you complete your response?				
	Is your response coherent and unified?				
	Do you find a sequence in your response?				
Language Use	How is the use of vocabulary?				
	Is the grammatical structure good?				
	How is the use of idiomatic expressions?				
Delivery	Is your response fluent and smooth?				
	Is your pronunciation clear?				
	How is the use of stress and intonation?				

Task 1

8 MP3 83

TOEFL SPEAKING

What is your favorite cuisine (e.g. Italian, Chinese, Indian, Mexican) and why? Include specific details and examples in your response.

Preparation time	: 15 seconds
Response time	: 45 seconds

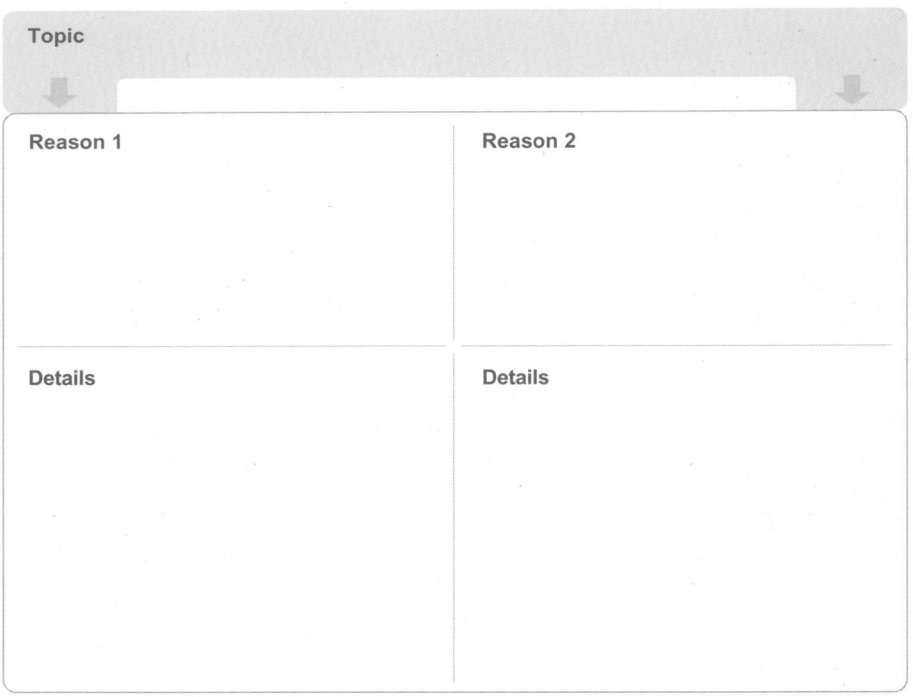

Personal Preference

Speaking Expressions

Topic
- In my case
- I think ...
- I believe ...
- In my opinion,
- It seems to me ...
- As far as I'm concerned,
- I would say ...
- Without a doubt,

Reason
- What I like about ...
- Another reason is that ...
- One of the reasons I think ...
- The other reason is that ...
- One reason why ...
- I like this also because ...
- First,
- Second,

Detail
- It means that ...
  = I mean ...
- For example
  = For instance,
- To give a specific example,
  = To illustrate,
- What I am saying is that ...
  = In other words,

🎤 My Response

- Topic

- Reason 1

  - Details

- Reason 2

  - Details

Idiomatic Expressions

Burn the midnight oil: Study or work until late at night.

Ex) I think I am not ready for the mid-term test. I definitely need to **burn the midnight oil** tonight.

Evaluation		1	2	3	4
Topic Development	Could you complete your response?				
	Is your response coherent and unified?				
	Do you find a sequence in your response?				
Language Use	How is the use of vocabulary?				
	Is the grammatical structure good?				
	How is the use of idiomatic expressions?				
Delivery	Is your response fluent and smooth?				
	Is your pronunciation clear?				
	How is the use of stress and intonation?				

Task 02 — Paired Choice

MP3 84

TOEFL SPEAKING — Sample Question

Some people buy new products right after they are produced. Others wait for a while and delay their purchase until they listen to those who have already used the products. Which way do you prefer and why?

Preparation time : 15 seconds
Response time : 45 seconds

Topic	Wait for a while	
Reason 1		**Reason 2**
New products have a high failure rate.		Other companies will make similar products that are less expensive.
Details		**Details**
All the bugs haven't been discovered or fixed. Usually end up with disappointment.		If you wait, you can pay less and get more.

Paired Choice

Speaking Expressions

Topic
- I prefer A to B
- I think A is better than B
- I'd rather A than B
- I would say that A is more ~ than B
- In my opinion,
- Personally,
- The way I see it ...
- As I see it ...

Reason
- That's because ...
- Furthermore,
- One reason is that ...
- The other reason is that ...
- One of the reasons why I prefer ...
- Another reason is that ...
- First,
- Second,

Detail
- It means that ...
- What I mean is that ...
- I mean ...
- Also,
- In fact,
- In contrast to...
- That is to say ...
- In other words,

Idiomatic Expressions

It never hurts to~: Worth trying

Ex) Why don't you go to the lady over there and ask about the information? **It never hurts to** ask.

🎤 Sample Response

- **Topic**

  I think it never hurts to wait until a product has been on the market for a while. Waiting is definitely better than rushing right out to buy one for a couple of reasons.

- **Reason 1**

  One reason is that new products have a high failure rate.

  - Details

  It means that if you buy something right away, it's possible that all the bugs haven't been discovered or fixed. You're just setting yourself up for disappointment.

- **Reason 2**

  The other reason is that a few months after the release of a new product, other companies will design similar ones that are less expensive and have more features.

  - Details

  In fact, if you're patient, you can pay less and get more.

Evaluation		1	2	3	4
Topic Development	Could you complete your response?				
	Is your response coherent and unified?				
	Do you find a sequence in your response?				
Language Use	How is the use of vocabulary?				
	Is the grammatical structure good?				
	How is the use of idiomatic expressions?				
Delivery	Is your response fluent and smooth?				
	Is your pronunciation clear?				
	How is the use of stress and intonation?				

Task 2

2 MP3 85

TOEFL SPEAKING

Some people prefer to take medication and go to see a doctor when they are ill. Others just rest and wait until they get better. Which way do you prefer and why?

Preparation time : 15 seconds
Response time   : 45 seconds

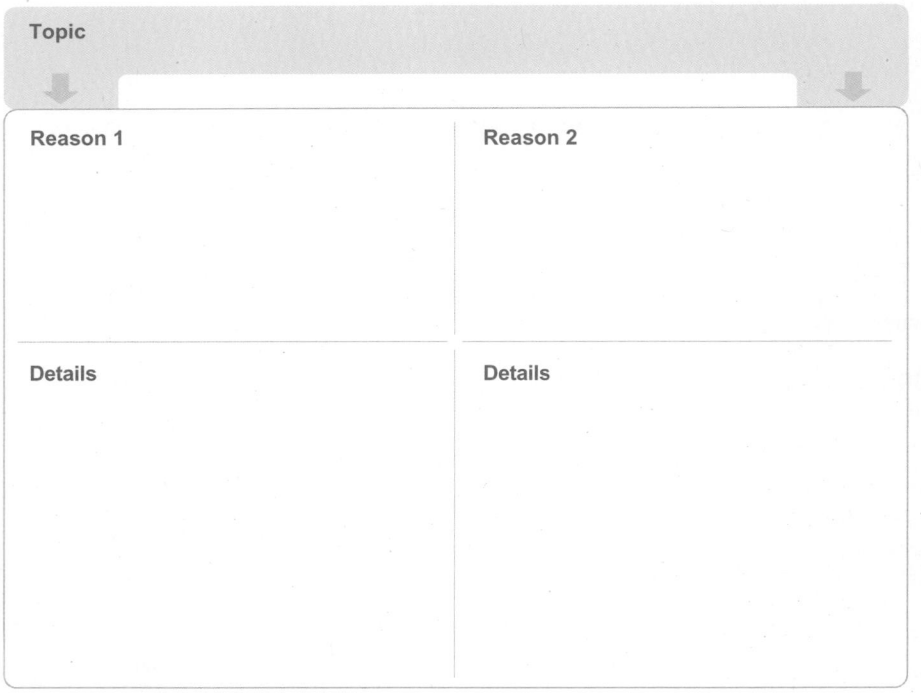

Topic

Reason 1

Details

Reason 2

Details

Paired Choice

Speaking Expressions

Topic
- I prefer A to B
- I think A is better than B
- I'd rather A than B
- I would say that A is more ~ than B
- In my opinion,
- Personally,
- The way I see it ...
- As I see it ...

Reason
- That's because ...
- Furthermore,
- One reason is that ...
- The other reason is that ...
- One of the reasons why I prefer ...
- Another reason is that ...
- First,
- Second,

Detail
- It means that ...
- What I mean is that ...
- I mean ...
- Also,
- In fact,
- In contrast to...
- That is to say ...
- In other words,

Idiomatic Expressions

Beauty is only skin deep: Character is more important than appearance.

Ex) She couldn't mask her bad attitude with her gorgeous looks because **beauty is only skin deep**.

🎤 My Response

- Topic

- Reason 1

  - Details

- Reason 2

  - Details

Evaluation		1	2	3	4
Topic Development	Could you complete your response?				
	Is your response coherent and unified?				
	Do you find a sequence in your response?				
Language Use	How is the use of vocabulary?				
	Is the grammatical structure good?				
	How is the use of idiomatic expressions?				
Delivery	Is your response fluent and smooth?				
	Is your pronunciation clear?				
	How is the use of stress and intonation?				

Task 2

3 MP3 86

TOEFL SPEAKING

Some people want to live in a city and others in a small town. Which do you prefer and why?

| Preparation time : 15 seconds |
| Response time   : 45 seconds |

Paired Choice

Speaking Expressions

Topic
- I prefer A to B
- I think A is better than B
- I'd rather A than B
- I would say that A is more ~ than B
- In my opinion,
- Personally,
- The way I see it ...
- As I see it ...

Reason
- That's because ...
- Furthermore,
- One reason is that ...
- The other reason is that ...
- One of the reasons why I prefer ...
- Another reason is that ...
- First,
- Second,

Detail
- It means that ...
- What I mean is that ...
- I mean ...
- Also,
- In fact,
- In contrast to...
- That is to say ...
- In other words,

Idiomatic Expressions

Tip of the iceberg: The surface area of something, but not the rest of it, which is hidden.

Ex) His failing grades became just the **tip of the iceberg** after he was notified about the bigger problem of getting expelled.

🎤 My Response

- Topic

- Reason 1

  - Details

- Reason 2

  - Details

Evaluation		1	2	3	4
Topic Development	Could you complete your response?				
	Is your response coherent and unified?				
	Do you find a sequence in your response?				
Language Use	How is the use of vocabulary?				
	Is the grammatical structure good?				
	How is the use of idiomatic expressions?				
Delivery	Is your response fluent and smooth?				
	Is your pronunciation clear?				
	How is the use of stress and intonation?				

Task 2

4

TOEFL SPEAKING

Some students think that smoking should be banned on campus, while others believe smokers should be given the right to smoke. Which opinion do you agree with and why?

| Preparation time : 15 seconds |
| Response time   : 45 seconds |

Paired Choice

Speaking Expressions

Topic
- I prefer A to B
- I think A is better than B
- I'd rather A than B
- I would say that A is more ~ than B
- In my opinion,
- Personally,
- The way I see it ...
- As I see it ...

Reason
- That's because ...
- Furthermore,
- One reason is that ...
- The other reason is that ...
- One of the reasons why I prefer ...
- Another reason is that ...
- First,
- Second,

Detail
- It means that ...
- What I mean is that ...
- I mean ...
- Also,
- In fact,
- In contrast to...
- That is to say ...
- In other words,

My Response

- Topic

- Reason 1

  - Details

- Reason 2

  - Details

Idiomatic Expressions

Pain in the neck:
A bother or an annoyance.

Ex) Robert was such a **pain in the neck** that he annoyed anyone he worked with at the office.

Evaluation		1	2	3	4
Topic Development	Could you complete your response?				
	Is your response coherent and unified?				
	Do you find a sequence in your response?				
Language Use	How is the use of vocabulary?				
	Is the grammatical structure good?				
	How is the use of idiomatic expressions?				
Delivery	Is your response fluent and smooth?				
	Is your pronunciation clear?				
	How is the use of stress and intonation?				

PART II Practice Test

Task 2

5

TOEFL SPEAKING

Some people want to have intelligent friends and others honest friends. Which type of friends do you prefer and why?

Preparation time : 15 seconds
Response time : 45 seconds

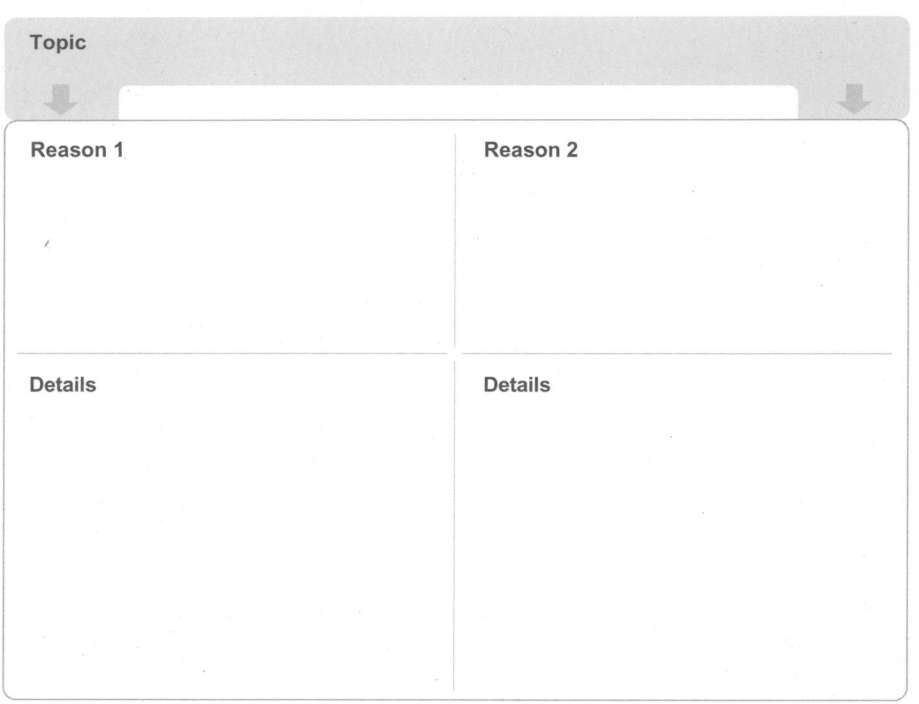

Topic

Reason 1

Reason 2

Details

Details

Paired Choice

Speaking Expressions

Topic
- I prefer A to B
- I think A is better than B
- I'd rather A than B
- I would say that A is more ~ than B
- In my opinion,
- Personally,
- The way I see it ...
- As I see it ...

Reason
- That's because ...
- Furthermore,
- One reason is that ...
- The other reason is that ...
- One of the reasons why I prefer ...
- Another reason is that ...
- First,
- Second,

Detail
- It means that ...
- What I mean is that ...
- I mean ...
- Also,
- In fact,
- In contrast to...
- That is to say ...
- In other words,

Idiomatic Expressions

Easy as pie: Very easy

Ex) The problem is, my brother makes everything sound as **easy as pie**.

🎤 My Response

- Topic

- Reason 1

  - Details

- Reason 2

  - Details

Evaluation		1	2	3	4
Topic Development	Could you complete your response?				
	Is your response coherent and unified?				
	Do you find a sequence in your response?				
Language Use	How is the use of vocabulary?				
	Is the grammatical structure good?				
	How is the use of idiomatic expressions?				
Delivery	Is your response fluent and smooth?				
	Is your pronunciation clear?				
	How is the use of stress and intonation?				

Task 2

6

TOEFL SPEAKING

Some people prefer to watch movies at home. Others prefer to go to the theater. Which do you prefer and why?

| Preparation time : 15 seconds |
| Response time   : 45 seconds |

Topic	
Reason 1	**Reason 2**
Details	**Details**

Paired Choice

Speaking Expressions

Topic
- I prefer A to B
- I think A is better than B
- I'd rather A than B
- I would say that A is more ~ than B
- In my opinion,
- Personally,
- The way I see it ...
- As I see it ...

Reason
- That's because ...
- Furthermore,
- One reason is that ...
- The other reason is that ...
- One of the reasons why I prefer ...
- Another reason is that ...
- First,
- Second,

Detail
- It means that ...
- What I mean is that ...
- I mean ...
- Also,
- In fact,
- In contrast to...
- That is to say ...
- In other words,

Idiomatic Expressions

Have nothing against: Having no objections.

Ex) **I have nothing against** freedom of speech, but I get angry at those who destroy a person's reputation through false accusations.

🎤 My Response

- Topic

- Reason 1

    - Details

- Reason 2

    - Details

Evaluation		1	2	3	4
Topic Development	Could you complete your response?				
	Is your response coherent and unified?				
	Do you find a sequence in your response?				
Language Use	How is the use of vocabulary?				
	Is the grammatical structure good?				
	How is the use of idiomatic expressions?				
Delivery	Is your response fluent and smooth?				
	Is your pronunciation clear?				
	How is the use of stress and intonation?				

Task 2

7

TOEFL SPEAKING

Some people say that online communication has made people closer, while others think the opposite. Which opinion do you agree with and why?

| Preparation time : 15 seconds |
| Response time   : 45 seconds |

Topic	
Reason 1	Reason 2
Details	Details

Paired Choice

Speaking Expressions

Topic
- I prefer A to B
- I think A is better than B
- I'd rather A than B
- I would say that A is more ~ than B
- In my opinion,
- Personally,
- The way I see it ...
- As I see it ...

Reason
- That's because ...
- Furthermore,
- One reason is that ...
- The other reason is that ...
- One of the reasons why I prefer ...
- Another reason is that ...
- First,
- Second,

Detail
- It means that ...
- What I mean is that ...
- I mean ...
- Also,
- In fact,
- In contrast to...
- That is to say ...
- In other words,

Idiomatic Expressions

In a flash: Very quickly

Ex) As far as I know, the car accident occurred **in a flash**.

🎤 My Response

- Topic

- Reason 1

  - Details

- Reason 2

  - Details

	Evaluation	1	2	3	4
Topic Development	Could you complete your response?				
	Is your response coherent and unified?				
	Do you find a sequence in your response?				
Language Use	How is the use of vocabulary?				
	Is the grammatical structure good?				
	How is the use of idiomatic expressions?				
Delivery	Is your response fluent and smooth?				
	Is your pronunciation clear?				
	How is the use of stress and intonation?				

Task 2

8 MP3 91

TOEFL SPEAKING

Some people prefer to buy their own CDs. Other people prefer to borrow CDs from their friends. Which do you prefer and why?

| Preparation time : 15 seconds |
| Response time   : 45 seconds |

Topic	
Reason 1	**Reason 2**
Details	**Details**

Paired Choice

Speaking Expressions

Topic
- I prefer A to B
- I think A is better than B
- I'd rather A than B
- I would say that A is more ~ than B
- In my opinion,
- Personally,
- The way I see it ...
- As I see it ...

Reason
- That's because ...
- Furthermore,
- One reason is that ...
- The other reason is that ...
- One of the reasons why I prefer ...
- Another reason is that ...
- First,
- Second,

Detail
- It means that ...
- What I mean is that ...
- I mean ...
- Also,
- In fact,
- In contrast to...
- That is to say ...
- In other words,

🎤 My Response

- Topic

- Reason 1

  - Details

- Reason 2

  - Details

Idiomatic Expressions

Kill two birds with one stone: Handling two problems with a single action.

Ex) I clean the house and exercise at the same time. It's definitely **killing two birds with one stone**.

Evaluation		1	2	3	4
Topic Development	Could you complete your response?				
	Is your response coherent and unified?				
	Do you find a sequence in your response?				
Language Use	How is the use of vocabulary?				
	Is the grammatical structure good?				
	How is the use of idiomatic expressions?				
Delivery	Is your response fluent and smooth?				
	Is your pronunciation clear?				
	How is the use of stress and intonation?				

Task 03 — Fit and Explain

TOEFL SPEAKING Sample Question

Reading Time : 45 seconds

New Hiring Policy in Computer Laboratories

Due to the shortage of employment opportunities for students, and the small demographic of computer majors in the university, it has been decided that employment in the computer laboratories shall now be open not only to computer majors, but to any and all college students seeking possible employment with the school. This change shall be put into effect starting next Monday. Revised application forms are now available at the student affairs office and at the computer labs.

Listening Now listen to two students as they discuss the announcement.

Question The woman expresses her opinion of the change regarding hiring policy for the computer labs. State her opinion and explain the reasons she gives for holding that opinion.

Preparation time : 30 seconds
Response time : 60 seconds

Reading Note

Policy
Employment in the computer laboratories is opened to all college students.

Reason 1
The shortage of employment opportunities for students

Reason 2
The small demographic of computer majors in the university

Listening Note

Opinion
Disagree!

Reason 1
Students who want to work can find jobs in the local stores.

Reason 2
Non-computer majors won't be much help to the students using the computer labs.

Fit and Explain

Speaking Expressions

Opinion
- The man agrees with ...
- The man disagrees with ...
- The man approves of ...
- The man is against ...
- The man supports ...
- The man is opposed to ...
- He shares the view that ...
- He has a different opinion from ...

Reason
- The woman says that ...
- She also mentions that ...
- The first reason is that ...
- The second reason is that ...
- He points out that ...
- He comments on ...
- First,
- Second,

Detail
- For example,
- So,
- In other words,
- What he means is that ...
- Instead,
- Especially,
- That's because ...
- Since ...

Sample Response

- **Opinion**

The woman disagrees with the university's plan to allow all students to apply for jobs in the computer lab.

- **Reason 1**

Although the announcement says this plan is due to the shortage of employment opportunities for students, the woman says that there are plenty of other places that students who aren't computer majors can find jobs.

- Details

So, the university does not have to open the computer lab positions to students from all majors.

- **Reason 2**

She also mentions that it is a bad idea because students who aren't computer majors, nine times out of ten, won't know enough about computers to actually be of any help in the computer lab.

- Details

In other words, they won't be able to do anything in case some problems occur with the computers.

Idiomatic Expressions

Nine times out of ten: Almost, always, or very often.

Ex) I really don't understand calculus. **Nine times out of ten**, I have no idea what my professor is talking about.

Evaluation		1	2	3	4
Topic Development	Could you complete your response?				
	Is your response coherent and unified?				
	Do you find a sequence in your response?				
Language Use	How is the use of vocabulary?				
	Is the grammatical structure good?				
	How is the use of idiomatic expressions?				
Delivery	Is your response fluent and smooth?				
	Is your pronunciation clear?				
	How is the use of stress and intonation?				

Task 3

2 MP3 93

TOEFL SPEAKING

Reading Time : 45 seconds

Letter to the Editor – University Journal

This is to reiterate an earlier appeal to our concerned university officials for the beautification of the school by putting up trees and plants around the university. This is because the school appears quite barren. Most of its areas are covered by cement or asphalt, making the university environment hotter than usual. Said proposal will result in many benefits–among them added study places for students, and a greener university environment, which would promote better appreciation of our university.

A Concerned Student

Listening Now listen to two students discussing the letter to the editor.

Question The woman expresses her opinion of the letter in the university paper. State her opinion and explain the reasons she gives for holding that opinion.

Preparation time : 30 seconds
Response time   : 60 seconds

Reading Note

Policy

Letter (Agree or Disagree)

Reason 1

Reason 2

Listening Note

Opinion

Reason 1

Reason 2

Fit and Explain

- **Speaking Expressions**

  Opinion
  - The man agrees with ...
  - The man disagrees with ...
  - The man approves of ...
  - The man is against ...
  - The man supports ...
  - The man is opposed to ...
  - He shares the view that ...
  - He has a different opinion from ...

  Reason
  - The woman says that ...
  - She also mentions that ...
  - The first reason is that ...
  - The second reason is that ...
  - He points out that ...
  - He comments on ...
  - First,
  - Second,

  Detail
  - For example,
  - So,
  - In other words,
  - What he means is that ...
  - Instead,
  - Especially,
  - That's because ...
  - Since ...

🎤 **My Response**

- Opinion

- Reason 1

  - Details

- Reason 2

  - Details

- **Idiomatic Expressions**

  Pave the way for~:
  A preparation which will make it possible for something to happen in the future.

  Ex) The introduction of direct debit cards **paved the way for** an era of convenience in banking.

	Evaluation	1	2	3	4
Topic Development	Could you complete your response?				
	Is your response coherent and unified?				
	Do you find a sequence in your response?				
Language Use	How is the use of vocabulary?				
	Is the grammatical structure good?				
	How is the use of idiomatic expressions?				
Delivery	Is your response fluent and smooth?				
	Is your pronunciation clear?				
	How is the use of stress and intonation?				

Task 3

3

TOEFL SPEAKING

Reading Time : 45 seconds

Announcement from the Director of Campus Affairs

In our ongoing attempts to improve the quality of on-campus life, we are pleased to announce that Wednesday night will be designated World Cuisine Night in all student cafeterias. Each Wednesday night, students will get to sample cuisine from a different part of the world. The goal is to expose students to authentic cuisine from each region, and the university has consulted chefs from leading ethnic restaurants to obtain recipes. We hope you will enjoy this change and the chance to experience other cultures through their cuisine.

Listening Now listen to two students as they discuss the announcement.

Question The woman expresses her opinion of the announcement. State her opinion and explain the reasons she gives for holding that opinion.

Preparation time : 30 seconds
Response time   : 60 seconds

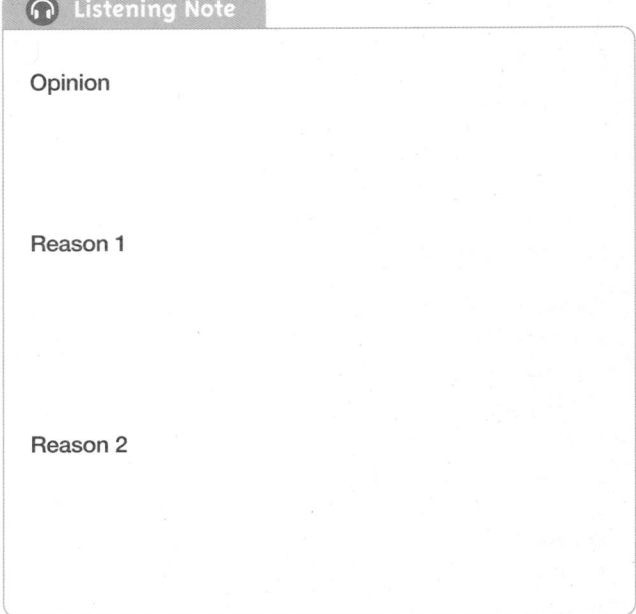

Fit and Explain

Speaking Expressions

Opinion
- The man agrees with ...
- The man disagrees with ...
- The man approves of ...
- The man is against ...
- The man supports ...
- The man is opposed to ...
- He shares the view that ...
- He has a different opinion from ...

Reason
- The woman says that ...
- She also mentions that ...
- The first reason is that ...
- The second reason is that ...
- He points out that ...
- He comments on ...
- First,
- Second,

Detail
- For example,
- So,
- In other words,
- What he means is that ...
- Instead,
- Especially,
- That's because ...
- Since ...

🎤 My Response

- Opinion

- Reason 1

  – Details

- Reason 2

  – Details

Idiomatic Expressions

(A) is at odds with (B):
(A) is in opposition to (B).

Ex) Alex had a lot of trouble adjusting to university life. He found that he **was** often **at odds with** his friends.

Evaluation		1	2	3	4
Topic Development	Could you complete your response?				
	Is your response coherent and unified?				
	Do you find a sequence in your response?				
Language Use	How is the use of vocabulary?				
	Is the grammatical structure good?				
	How is the use of idiomatic expressions?				
Delivery	Is your response fluent and smooth?				
	Is your pronunciation clear?				
	How is the use of stress and intonation?				

Task 3

4

TOEFL SPEAKING

Reading Time : 45 seconds

Announcement from the Music Department

Due to the need for greater classroom space, the instrument storage rooms on the first floor of the Performing Arts building will be converted to classrooms during the winter break. The music department understands that this will pose some hardship to music majors, as they will no longer be able to store their instruments at school. However, the classroom space is needed to accommodate the rising numbers of freshmen enrolling in the program. The department will reserve one room on the third floor for the storage of extremely large instruments such as cellos and tubas.

Listening Now listen to two students discussing the announcement.

Question The man expresses his opinion of the university's plan to do away with instrument storage rooms. State his opinion and explain the reasons he gives for holding that opinion.

| Preparation time : 30 seconds |
| Response time   : 60 seconds |

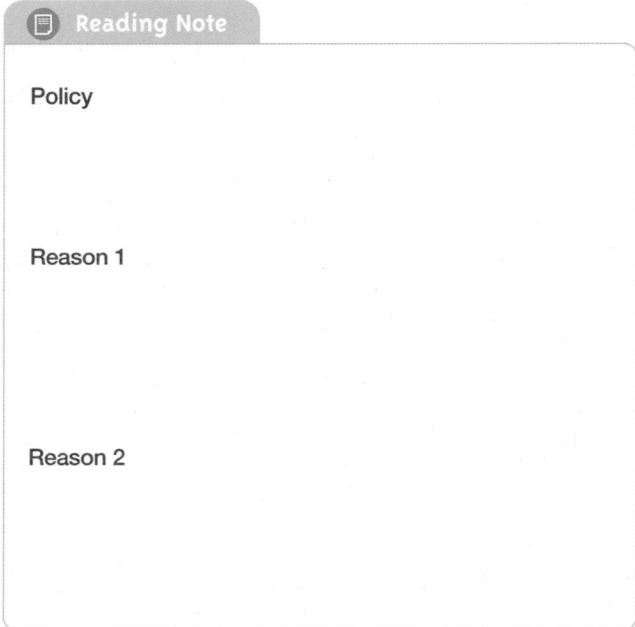

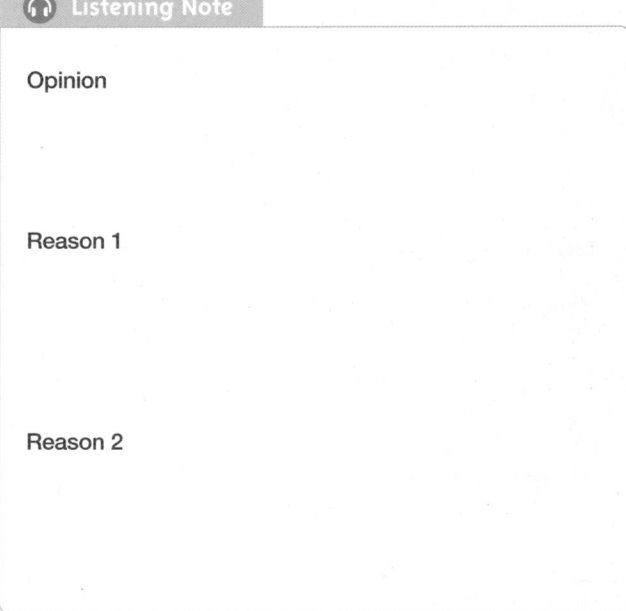

Fit and Explain

- **Speaking Expressions**

  Opinion
  - The man agrees with ...
  - The man disagrees with ...
  - The man approves of ...
  - The man is against ...
  - The man supports ...
  - The man is opposed to ...
  - He shares the view that ...
  - He has a different opinion from ...

  Reason
  - The woman says that ...
  - She also mentions that ...
  - The first reason is that ...
  - The second reason is that ...
  - He points out that ...
  - He comments on ...
  - First,
  - Second,

  Detail
  - For example,
  - So,
  - In other words,
  - What he means is that ...
  - Instead,
  - Especially,
  - That's because ...
  - Since ...

- 🎤 **My Response**

  - Opinion

  - Reason 1

    – Details

  - Reason 2

    – Details

- **Idiomatic Expressions**

  (A) gives (B) a hard time:
  (A) troubles (B) or sometimes gives mental or physical stress to (B).

  Ex) The customer in front of me was arguing with the store manager and generally **giving** her a **hard time**.

Evaluation		1	2	3	4
Topic Development	Could you complete your response?				
	Is your response coherent and unified?				
	Do you find a sequence in your response?				
Language Use	How is the use of vocabulary?				
	Is the grammatical structure good?				
	How is the use of idiomatic expressions?				
Delivery	Is your response fluent and smooth?				
	Is your pronunciation clear?				
	How is the use of stress and intonation?				

Task 3

5

TOEFL SPEAKING

Reading Time : 45 seconds

Announcement from the Universitiy President

In order to curb growing financial expenses, grants for foreign study programs offered by the university shall be suspended for the next two semesters. Rest assured that the university's commitment to first-class education is still a top priority. This action is just part of the school's goal to identify unnecessary costs in the academic budget. Students who intended to participate in said programs are advised to contact their respective colleges for complete details.

Listening Now listen to two students as they discuss the announcement.

Question The man expresses his opinion of the announcement regarding foreign study programs. State his opinion and explain the reasons he gives for holding that opinion.

| Preparation time : 30 seconds |
| Response time   : 60 seconds |

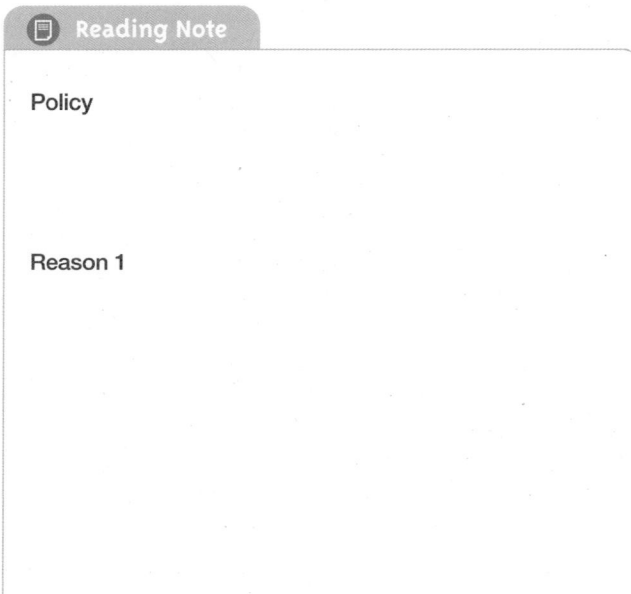

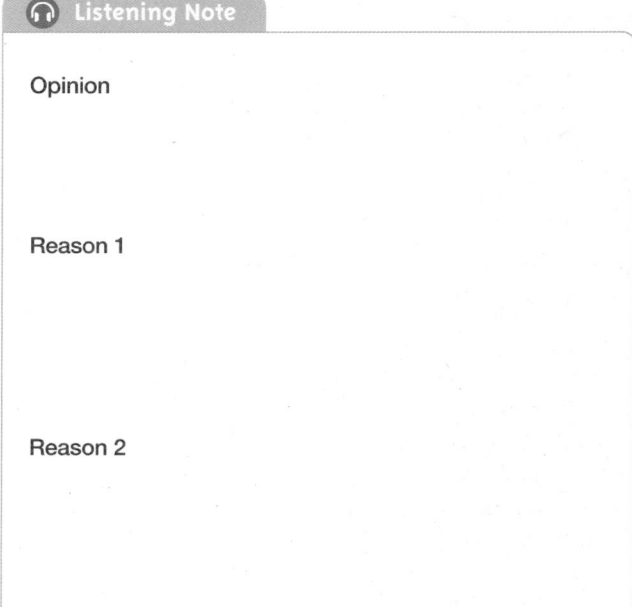

Fit and Explain

- **Speaking Expressions**

  Opinion
  - The man agrees with ...
  - The man disagrees with ...
  - The man approves of ...
  - The man is against ...
  - The man supports ...
  - The man is opposed to ...
  - He shares the view that ...
  - He has a different opinion from ...

  Reason
  - The woman says that ...
  - She also mentions that ...
  - The first reason is that ...
  - The second reason is that ...
  - He points out that ...
  - He comments on ...
  - First,
  - Second,

  Detail
  - For example,
  - So,
  - In other words,
  - What he means is that ...
  - Instead,
  - Especially,
  - That's because ...
  - Since ...

- **Idiomatic Expressions**

  Get a raw deal:
  Having unfair or bad treatment.

  Ex) It's true that children taught in large classes **get a raw deal**.

🎤 My Response

- Opinion

- Reason 1

  - Details

- Reason 2

  - Details

Evaluation		1	2	3	4
Topic Development	Could you complete your response?				
	Is your response coherent and unified?				
	Do you find a sequence in your response?				
Language Use	How is the use of vocabulary?				
	Is the grammatical structure good?				
	How is the use of idiomatic expressions?				
Delivery	Is your response fluent and smooth?				
	Is your pronunciation clear?				
	How is the use of stress and intonation?				

Task 3

6 MP3 97

TOEFL SPEAKING

Reading Time : 45 seconds

Letter to the Editor

I would like to share my opinion of the university's idea to make it mandatory for all senior students to do volunteer mentoring with at least one public school in the community during the summer. Although I am aware that many students are against this idea, I personally welcome the school's decision. I believe this new policy will provide educational help for many children in the community who have difficulty with their studies. Also, this can make our university's commitment to social consciousness more visible in the community, which will lead to creating a better image for our school.

Kate Wilson/ Sophomore

Listening Now listen to two students as they discuss the student's letter.

Question The woman expresses her opinion of the university's policy on its mentoring program. State her opinion and explain the reasons she gives for holding that opinion.

| Preparation time : 30 seconds |
| Response time   : 60 seconds |

Reading Note

Policy

Letter (Agree or Disagree)

Reason 1

Reason 2

Listening Note

Opinion

Reason 1

Reason 2

Fit and Explain

• Speaking Expressions

Opinion

- The man agrees with ...
- The man disagrees with ...
- The man approves of ...
- The man is against ...
- The man supports ...
- The man is opposed to ...
- He shares the view that ...
- He has a different opinion from ...

Reason

- The woman says that ...
- She also mentions that ...
- The first reason is that ...
- The second reason is that ...
- He points out that ...
- He comments on ...
- First,
- Second,

Detail

- For example,
- So,
- In other words,
- What he means is that ...
- Instead,
- Especially,
- That's because ...
- Since ...

🎤 My Response

- Opinion

- Reason 1

  - Details

- Reason 2

  - Details

• Idiomatic Expressions

Groan inwardly:
Feel despair, pain, or distress, but don't express one's emotions.

Ex) When Danny was mistreated by his boss, he just **groaned inwardly**.

Evaluation		1	2	3	4
Topic Development	Could you complete your response?				
	Is your response coherent and unified?				
	Do you find a sequence in your response?				
Language Use	How is the use of vocabulary?				
	Is the grammatical structure good?				
	How is the use of idiomatic expressions?				
Delivery	Is your response fluent and smooth?				
	Is your pronunciation clear?				
	How is the use of stress and intonation?				

Task 3

7 MP3 98

TOEFL SPEAKING

Reading Time : 45 seconds

Residency Period Reduced

The university has decided to reduce the maximum residency period for students. Starting this school year, students will only be given up to five years to finish their four-year degrees, instead of the usual six years. This is being done to promote a better academic environment. A great number of students have maximized their stay in the university for the past ten years, greatly extending student-teacher ratios and creating shortages in dormitory and parking spaces. This has severely affected the quality of education the university offers. All current sophomores and freshmen shall be covered by this new policy.

Listening Now listen to two students as they discuss the article.

Question The man expresses his opinion of the new university policy. State his opinion and explain the reasons he gives for holding that opinion.

| Preparation time : 30 seconds |
| Response time : 60 seconds |

Reading Note

Policy

Reason 1

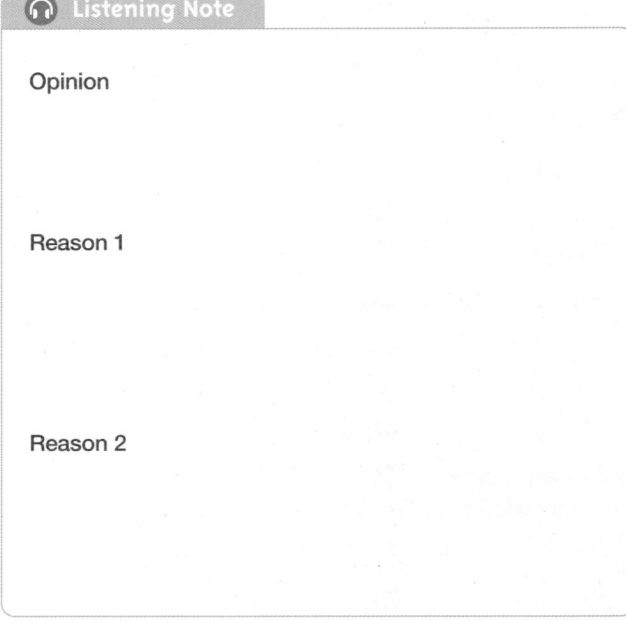

Listening Note

Opinion

Reason 1

Reason 2

Fit and Explain

Speaking Expressions

Opinion
- The man agrees with ...
- The man disagrees with ...
- The man approves of ...
- The man is against ...
- The man supports ...
- The man is opposed to ...
- He shares the view that ...
- He has a different opinion from ...

Reason
- The woman says that ...
- She also mentions that ...
- The first reason is that ...
- The second reason is that ...
- He points out that ...
- He comments on ...
- First,
- Second,

Detail
- For example,
- So,
- In other words,
- What he means is that ...
- Instead,
- Especially,
- That's because ...
- Since ...

Idiomatic Expressions

Weather the storm:
Going through difficulties or hardships successfully.

Ex) Though Alex broke up with his girl friend, he decided to **weather the storm** somehow.

🎤 My Response

- Opinion

- Reason 1

  - Details

- Reason 2

  - Details

	Evaluation	1	2	3	4
Topic Development	Could you complete your response?				
	Is your response coherent and unified?				
	Do you find a sequence in your response?				
Language Use	How is the use of vocabulary?				
	Is the grammatical structure good?				
	How is the use of idiomatic expressions?				
Delivery	Is your response fluent and smooth?				
	Is your pronunciation clear?				
	How is the use of stress and intonation?				

Task 3

8

TOEFL SPEAKING

Reading Time : 45 seconds

Clean Campus Without Student Voice?

I have recently been made aware of the university's policy to have all banners, flags, and other written materials banned on campus premises. That means from now on we cannot see any message-bearing materials hanging from building exteriors, lamp posts, and other school structures. The school said this is for ensuring cleanliness and maintaining campus safety. Clean campus? Good. But do banners and flags really have anything to do with safety? I don't see a clear connection. Moreover, limiting the space where we can post our opinions to a few bulletin boards will seriously reduce the chance for us to express our opinions.

Isabelle Johnson/ Junior

Listening Now listen to two students discussing the student's letter.

Question The man expresses his opinion of the student's letter. State his opinion and explain the reasons he gives for holding that opinion.

Preparation time : 30 seconds
Response time   : 60 seconds

Reading Note

Policy

Letter (Agree or Disagree)

Reason 1

Reason 2

Listening Note

Opinion

Reason 1

Reason 2

Reason 3

Fit and Explain

Speaking Expressions

Opinion
- The man agrees with ...
- The man disagrees with ...
- The man approves of ...
- The man is against ...
- The man supports ...
- The man is opposed to ...
- He shares the view that ...
- He has a different opinion from ...

Reason
- The woman says that ...
- She also mentions that ...
- The first reason is that ...
- The second reason is that ...
- He points out that ...
- He comments on ...
- First,
- Second,

Detail
- For example,
- So,
- In other words,
- What he means is that ...
- Instead,
- Especially,
- That's because ...
- Since ...

🎙 My Response

- Opinion

- Reason 1

  – Details

- Reason 2

  – Details

- Reason 3

  – Details

Idiomatic Expressions

Hot potato:
A controversial issue or matter

Ex) The private issues of celebrities easily become **hot potatoes**.

Evaluation		1	2	3	4
Topic Development	Could you complete your response?				
	Is your response coherent and unified?				
	Do you find a sequence in your response?				
Language Use	How is the use of vocabulary?				
	Is the grammatical structure good?				
	How is the use of idiomatic expressions?				
Delivery	Is your response fluent and smooth?				
	Is your pronunciation clear?				
	How is the use of stress and intonation?				

Task 04 — General / Specific

TOEFL SPEAKING — Sample Question

Reading Time : 45 seconds

Risk Compensation

Risk compensation is a widely accepted ethological term that describes an effect whereby an individual tends to adjust his or her behavior in response to perceived changes in risk. This theory can explain certain situations that are seemingly incomprehensible. According to common sense, if the possibility of risk is reduced, it is expected that the accident rate would decrease too. However, it is the opposite in many cases, because people tend to behave less cautiously when they feel less danger. This shows that when one aspect of a situation makes you feel more secure, you take more risks in other ways.

Listening Now listen to part of a lecture in a psychology class.

Question Explain how the examples of SUVs and bicycle helmets demonstrate the concept of risk compensation.

Preparation time : 30 seconds
Response time : 60 seconds

Reading Note

Topic
Risk compensation

Main Idea
Altering behavior to accommodate perceived risk

Supporting Ideas
1) Safety/security should increase w/ less risk
   - often reverse is true
2) If sense of risk decreases, less cautious behavior increases

Listening Note

Example 1
SUVs
- People feel safe SUVs, so more likely to engage in unsafe behavior while deriving.

Example 2
Bicycle helmets
- cyclists overly confident, not as careful
- benefit of helmet lost

General / Specific

Speaking Expressions

Definition
- A is B
- A refers to B
- A is defined as B
- A is a term that describes B
- A implies that ...
- A occurs when ...
- A is seen where ...
- A illustrates that ...

Citation
- The reading says that ...
- The professor explains ...
- The reading describes ...
- The lecture describes ...
- What he points out is that ...
- According to the professor ...
- According to the lecture ...
- As discussed by the professor ...

Explanation
- He gives an example of ...
- The professor discusses ... to demonstrate ...
- In the first / second example,
- Another example ... is ...
- He illustrates the concept of ...
- He relates the story of ... to ...
- The first / second example shows how ...
- This is seen in the way ...

Sample Response

- Definition

Risk compensation refers to an effect by which individuals behave less cautiously when they feel protected.

- Citation

The professor describes SUV drivers and cyclists to illustrate how risk compensation comes into play.

- Explanation

In the first example, he talks about SUV drivers not wearing seatbelts and talking on cell phones while driving. The second example shows how bicycle helmets may not reduce accidents. Again, the cyclists who are wearing a helmet tend to indulge in more dangerous behavior because they feel safe due to the fact that they are protected by the helmet.

Idiomatic Expressions

(A) comes into play:
(A) is to be an important factor in something.

Ex) Buying a home is one of the biggest decisions a person can make. It requires careful thought and planning, considering the many different factors that **come into play**.

Evaluation		1	2	3	4
Topic Development	Could you complete your response?				
	Is your response coherent and unified?				
	Do you find a sequence in your response?				
Language Use	How is the use of vocabulary?				
	Is the grammatical structure good?				
	How is the use of idiomatic expressions?				
Delivery	Is your response fluent and smooth?				
	Is your pronunciation clear?				
	How is the use of stress and intonation?				

Task 4

2

TOEFL SPEAKING

Reading Time : 45 seconds

Groupthink

When people start to adapt their beliefs or perceptions to that of other people's line of thinking in order to conform to a group or organization, groupthink is in motion. This kind of thinking normally happens due to man's inherent tendency to follow the group consensus, despite his own personal objections. This tendency is justified by the fear of an individual to be singled out due to his or her divergent belief or opinion. As a result, the application of groupthink often results in an unsound decision making process, as each individual silences his or her own objections to conform with the group.

Listening Now listen to part of a lecture on this topic in a social psychology class.

Question Explain how the example presented by the professor illustrates the concept of groupthink.

Preparation time : 30 seconds
Response time   : 60 seconds

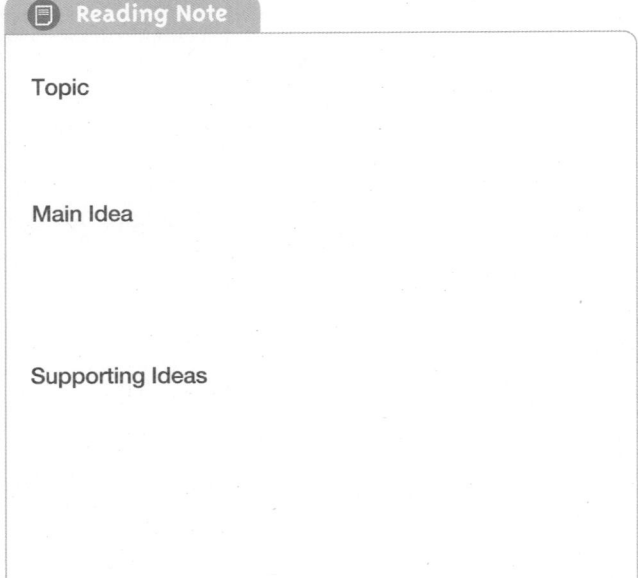

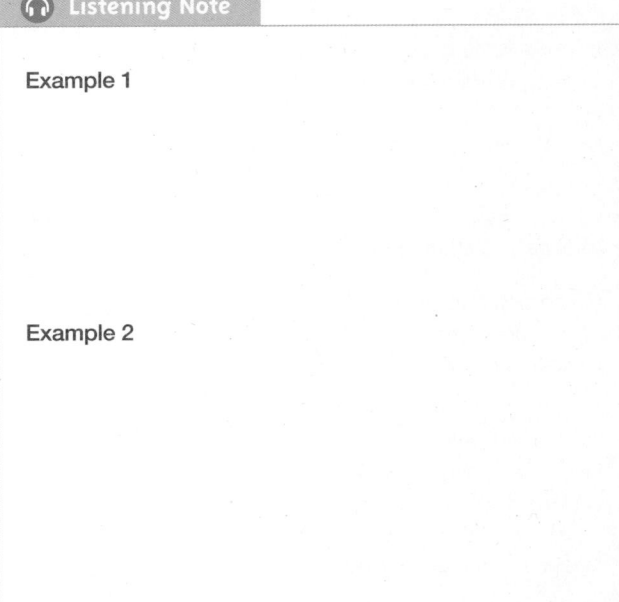

General / Specific

Speaking Expressions

Definition
- A is B
- A refers to B
- A is defined as B
- A is a term that describes B
- A implies that ...
- A occurs when ...
- A is seen where ...
- A illustrates that ...

Citation
- The reading says that ...
- The professor explains ...
- The reading describes ...
- The lecture describes ...
- What he points out is that ...
- According to the professor ...
- According to the lecture ...
- As discussed by the professor ...

Explanation
- He gives an example of ...
- The professor discusses ... to demonstrate ...
- In the first / second example,
- Another example ... is ...
- He illustrates the concept of ...
- He relates the story of ... to ...
- The first / second example shows how ...
- This is seen in the way ...

Idiomatic Expressions

Read between the lines: Try to infer the meaning of something that is not written explicitly.

Ex) People who **read between the lines** enjoy complex literary works. A deeper understanding to see beyond what is on the surface makes them learn more.

My Response

- Definition

- Citation

- Explanation

Evaluation		1	2	3	4
Topic Development	Could you complete your response?				
	Is your response coherent and unified?				
	Do you find a sequence in your response?				
Language Use	How is the use of vocabulary?				
	Is the grammatical structure good?				
	How is the use of idiomatic expressions?				
Delivery	Is your response fluent and smooth?				
	Is your pronunciation clear?				
	How is the use of stress and intonation?				

Task 4

3

TOEFL SPEAKING

Reading Time : 45 seconds

Flow

It is normal for people to be in a mental state where focus is fully centered on one activity. Present is a feeling of intense concentration on the activity at hand, in being completely involved and sensing a kind of accomplishment in doing the activity. When these elements are apparent, the person is engaged in a psychological state of flow. However, it is imperative for the person to have clear goals established and a great deal of concentration toward the particular activity. In addition, for someone to have flow entails a non-disturbing environment, since the slightest distraction may break their concentration.

Listening Now listen to part of a lecture on this topic in a psychology class.

Question The professor talks about two friends of his as examples. Explain how these examples are related to the concept of flow.

Preparation time : 30 seconds
Response time   : 60 seconds

Reading Note

Topic

Main Idea

Supporting Ideas

Listening Note

Example 1

Example 2

General / Specific

Speaking Expressions

Definition
- A is B
- A refers to B
- A is defined as B
- A is a term that describes B
- A implies that ...
- A occurs when ...
- A is seen where ...
- A illustrates that ...

Citation
- The reading says that ...
- The professor explains ...
- The reading describes ...
- The lecture describes ...
- What he points out is that ...
- According to the professor ...
- According to the lecture ...
- As discussed by the professor ...

Explanation
- He gives an example of ...
- The professor discusses ... to demonstrate ...
- In the first / second example,
- Another example ... is ...
- He illustrates the concept of ...
- He relates the story of ... to ...
- The first / second example shows how ...
- This is seen in the way ...

Idiomatic Expressions

Double-edged sword: Something that has both positive and negative consequences.

Ex) We should always be careful of what we say to people because our words can be **a double-edged sword**.

🎤 My Response

- Definition

- Citation

- Explanation

Evaluation		1	2	3	4
Topic Development	Could you complete your response?				
	Is your response coherent and unified?				
	Do you find a sequence in your response?				
Language Use	How is the use of vocabulary?				
	Is the grammatical structure good?				
	How is the use of idiomatic expressions?				
Delivery	Is your response fluent and smooth?				
	Is your pronunciation clear?				
	How is the use of stress and intonation?				

Task 4

4

TOEFL SPEAKING

Reading Time : 45 seconds

Creative Destruction

Innovation has always provided the needed spark to revolutionize industries and economies. One of the results of innovation is creative destruction, a process whereby the creation of new products destroys the market positions of companies producing similar products or using old ways of doing business. Creative destruction was a concept introduced by economist Joseph Schumpeter to explain how innovations caused old inventories, ideas, technologies, skills, and equipment to become obsolete. When old products or old ways of doing business are left unused or abandoned in favor of new products, then it is known as creative destruction.

Listening Now listen to part of a lecture on this topic in a business class.

Question The professor describes the concept of creative destruction by giving examples. Explain how the examples illustrate the concept of creative destruction.

Preparation time : 30 seconds
Response time   : 60 seconds

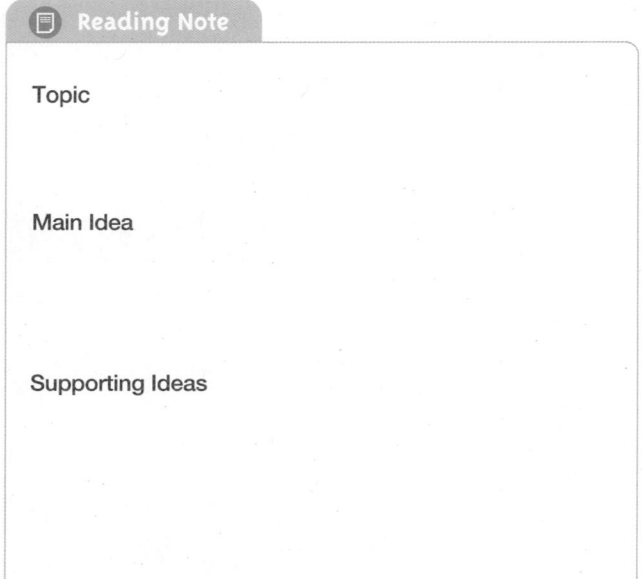

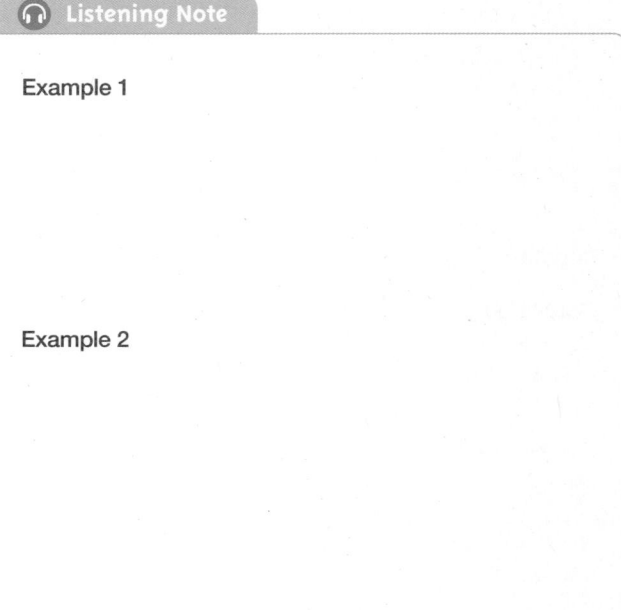

General / Specific

Speaking Expressions

Definition

- A is B
- A refers to B
- A is defined as B
- A is a term that describes B
- A implies that ...
- A occurs when ...
- A is seen where ...
- A illustrates that ...

Citation

- The reading says that ...
- The professor explains ...
- The reading describes ...
- The lecture describes ...
- What he points out is that ...
- According to the professor ...
- According to the lecture ...
- As discussed by the
- professor ...

Explanation

- He gives an example of ...
- The professor discusses ... to demonstrate ...
- In the first / second example,
- Another example ... is ...
- He illustrates the concept of ...
- He relates the story of ... to ...
- The first / second example shows how ...
- This is seen in the way ...

🎤 My Response

- Definition

- Citation

- Explanation

Idiomatic Expressions

Shoot oneself in the foot: Carelessly harm one's own cause.

Ex) He couldn't believe that he had **shot himself in the foot**.

Evaluation		1	2	3	4
Topic Development	Could you complete your response?				
	Is your response coherent and unified?				
	Do you find a sequence in your response?				
Language Use	How is the use of vocabulary?				
	Is the grammatical structure good?				
	How is the use of idiomatic expressions?				
Delivery	Is your response fluent and smooth?				
	Is your pronunciation clear?				
	How is the use of stress and intonation?				

Task 4 |

5

TOEFL SPEAKING

Reading Time : 45 seconds

Convergent Evolution

Convergent evolution is the process by which different species develop similar physical characteristics or abilities. In cases of convergent evolution, the different species are not closely related to each other, but they independently developed their similar physical characteristics or abilities in order to survive in similar environmental conditions. The animals that evolved these traits would eventually dominate in the breeding of their respective species, thus spreading these traits to most other members of the species.

Listening   Now listen to part of a lecture on this topic in a biology class.

Question   The professor discusses why bats and dolphins use echolocation. Explain how this relates to the concept of convergent evolution.

Preparation time : 30 seconds
Response time   : 60 seconds

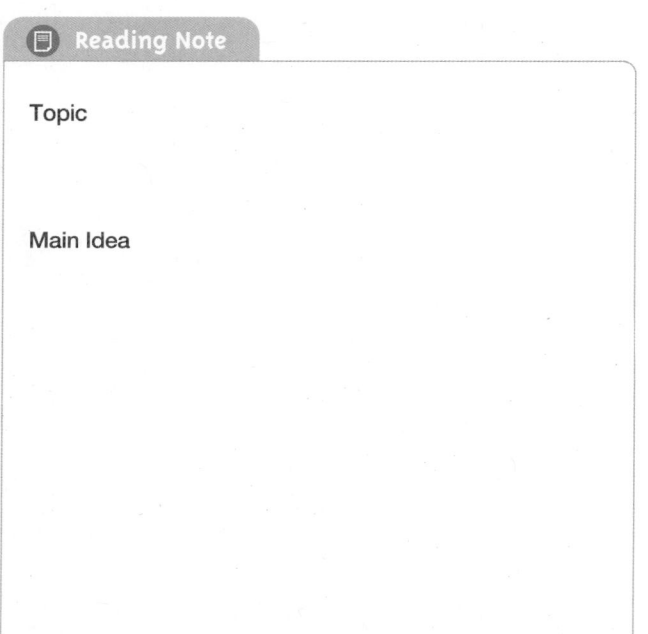

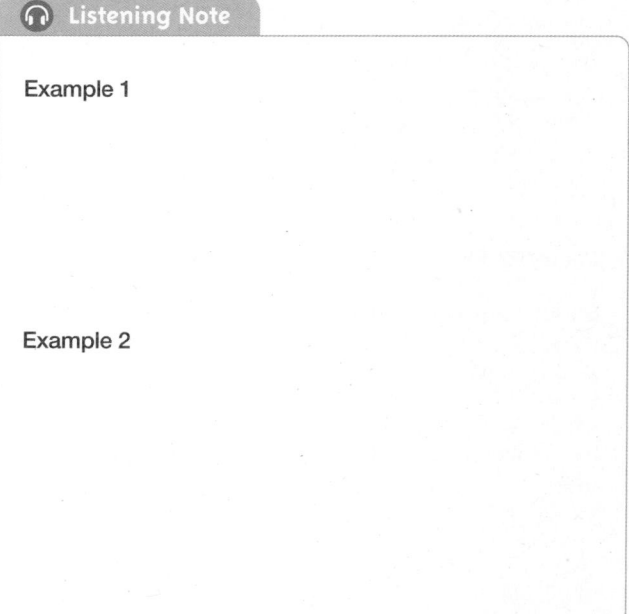

General / Specific

- **Speaking Expressions**

  Definition
  - A is B
  - A refers to B
  - A is defined as B
  - A is a term that describes B
  - A implies that ...
  - A occurs when ...
  - A is seen where ...
  - A illustrates that ...

  Citation
  - The reading says that ...
  - The professor explains ...
  - The reading describes ...
  - The lecture describes ...
  - What he points out is that ...
  - According to the professor ...
  - According to the lecture ...
  - As discussed by the professor ...

  Explanation
  - He gives an example of ...
  - The professor discusses ... to demonstrate ...
  - In the first / second example,
  - Another example ... is ...
  - He illustrates the concept of ...
  - He relates the story of ... to ...
  - The first / second example shows how ...
  - This is seen in the way ...

🎤 **My Response**

- Definition

- Citation

- Explanation

- **Idiomatic Expressions**

  Somebody's trash is someone else's treasure: An object's value can be defined differently according to its owner.

  Ex) Jack, do you know that your trash can be my treasure?

Evaluation		1	2	3	4
Topic Development	Could you complete your response?				
	Is your response coherent and unified?				
	Do you find a sequence in your response?				
Language Use	How is the use of vocabulary?				
	Is the grammatical structure good?				
	How is the use of idiomatic expressions?				
Delivery	Is your response fluent and smooth?				
	Is your pronunciation clear?				
	How is the use of stress and intonation?				

Task 4

6 MP3 105

TOEFL SPEAKING

Reading Time : 45 seconds

The Art of Happening

As art is relative, it is open to various interpretations. In this regard, some people think that art is an event or situation that occurs in actual time, being experienced by both the artist and an audience. Art becomes interactive, instead of still-life. Art that is treated in such a way is called a "happening." It is methodical in the sense that it surely requires the participation of an audience. Simultaneously, it is spontaneous due to the undetermined reaction of the people drawn to the happening.

Listening Now listen to part of a lecture on this topic in an art class.

Question Explain how the two examples given by the professor demonstrate the art of happening.

Preparation time : 30 seconds
Response time   : 60 seconds

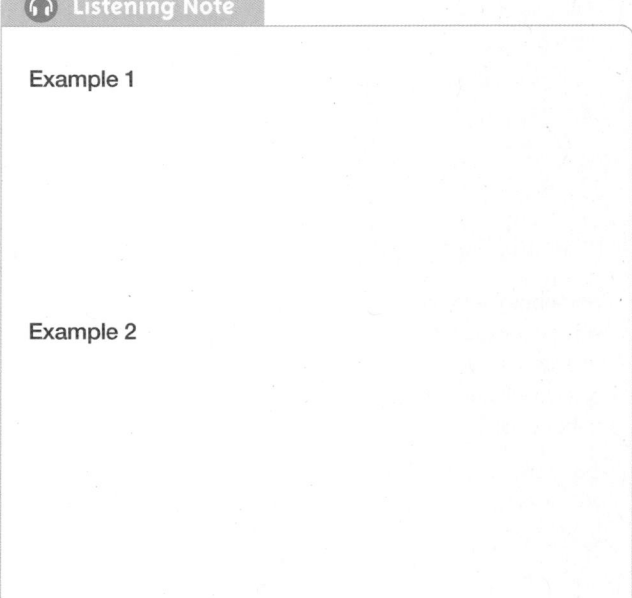

General / Specific

- **Speaking Expressions**

  Definition
  - A is B
  - A refers to B
  - A is defined as B
  - A is a term that describes B
  - A implies that ...
  - A occurs when ...
  - A is seen where ...
  - A illustrates that ...

  Citation
  - The reading says that ...
  - The professor explains ...
  - The reading describes ...
  - The lecture describes ...
  - What he points out is that ...
  - According to the professor ...
  - According to the lecture ...
  - As discussed by the professor ...

  Explanation
  - He gives an example of ...
  - The professor discusses ... to demonstrate ...
  - In the first / second example,
  - Another example ... is ...
  - He illustrates the concept of ...
  - He relates the story of ... to ...
  - The first / second example shows how ...
  - This is seen in the way ...

- **Idiomatic Expressions**

  It takes two to tango:
  When two people have a problem, both people are responsible for the problem.

  Ex) Why do you think it's totally her fault? Don't you think **it takes two to tango**?

🎤 My Response

- Definition

- Citation

- Explanation

Evaluation		1	2	3	4
Topic Development	Could you complete your response?				
	Is your response coherent and unified?				
	Do you find a sequence in your response?				
Language Use	How is the use of vocabulary?				
	Is the grammatical structure good?				
	How is the use of idiomatic expressions?				
Delivery	Is your response fluent and smooth?				
	Is your pronunciation clear?				
	How is the use of stress and intonation?				

Task 4

7 MP3 106

TOEFL SPEAKING

Reading Time : 45 seconds

Suspension of Disbelief

It is not unusual for people to have a suspension of disbelief, a phenomenon that entails a temporary hold on what one considers to be logical or sane, in terms of actual reality. Certain situations require flexibility with perception or acceptance of things happening around us. Improbabilities challenge known beliefs, and yet, a willingness or semi-conscious decision to accept them as fact, so long as consistency and entertainment can be found, cancels any doubts about their verity.

Listening   Now listen to part of a lecture on this topic in a psychology class.

Question   The professor discusses video games and professional wrestling in the lecture. Explain how the two examples relate to the concept of suspension of disbelief.

Preparation time : 30 seconds
Response time   : 60 seconds

Reading Note

Topic

Main Idea

Listening Note

Example 1

Example 2

General / Specific

Speaking Expressions

Definition
- A is B
- A refers to B
- A is defined as B
- A is a term that describes B
- A implies that ...
- A occurs when ...
- A is seen where ...
- A illustrates that ...

Citation
- The reading says that ...
- The professor explains ...
- The reading describes ...
- The lecture describes ...
- What he points out is that ...
- According to the professor ...
- According to the lecture ...
- As discussed by the professor ...

Explanation
- He gives an example of ...
- The professor discusses ... to demonstrate ...
- In the first / second example,
- Another example ... is ...
- He illustrates the concept of ...
- He relates the story of ... to ...
- The first / second example shows how ...
- This is seen in the way ...

🎤 My Response

- Definition

- Citation

- Explanation

Idiomatic Expressions

Go with the flow:
Follow the general opinion.

Ex) Though he had his opinion, he decided to **go with the flow** because he didn't want to cause any conflict.

Evaluation		1	2	3	4
Topic Development	Could you complete your response?				
	Is your response coherent and unified?				
	Do you find a sequence in your response?				
Language Use	How is the use of vocabulary?				
	Is the grammatical structure good?				
	How is the use of idiomatic expressions?				
Delivery	Is your response fluent and smooth?				
	Is your pronunciation clear?				
	How is the use of stress and intonation?				

Task 4

8 MP3 107

TOEFL SPEAKING

Reading Time : 45 seconds

Synergistic Relationships

Synergy is a process through which two objects or events feed into one another's momentum or progress. Synergistic relationships allow objects to work in coordination to attain higher levels of energy than would be possible for either object to attain on its own. In business, synergistic relationships are quite common between products with related technologies. In such cases, advances in the technology of one product help to drive technological advances in the other as well. Synergistic relationships help not only to drive technological advances, but also to increase consumer demand for products.

Listening Now listen to part of a lecture on this topic in an engineering class.

Question The professor discusses the development of flash memory cards and digital cameras. Explain how the development of these technologies demonstrates a synergistic relationship.

Preparation time : 30 seconds
Response time : 60 seconds

Reading Note

Topic

Main Idea

Listening Note

Example 1

Example 2

General / Specific

- **Speaking Expressions**

  Definition
  - A is B
  - A refers to B
  - A is defined as B
  - A is a term that describes B
  - A implies that …
  - A occurs when …
  - A is seen where …
  - A illustrates that …

  Citation
  - The reading says that …
  - The professor explains …
  - The reading describes …
  - The lecture describes …
  - What he points out is that …
  - According to the professor …
  - According to the lecture …
  - As discussed by the professor …

  Explanation
  - He gives an example of …
  - The professor discusses … to demonstrate …
  - In the first / second example, …
  - Another example … is …
  - He illustrates the concept of …
  - He relates the story of … to …
  - The first / second example shows how …
  - This is seen in the way …

🎤 **My Response**

- Definition

- Citation

- Explanation

- **Idiomatic Expressions**

  Same boat: Being in the same situation or condition.

  Ex) My friend enticed me to rob the bank with him. Unfortunately, we were caught and I found out that I was in the **same boat** with him.

Evaluation			1	2	3	4
Topic Development	Could you complete your response?					
	Is your response coherent and unified?					
	Do you find a sequence in your response?					
Language Use	How is the use of vocabulary?					
	Is the grammatical structure good?					
	How is the use of idiomatic expressions?					
Delivery	Is your response fluent and smooth?					
	Is your pronunciation clear?					
	How is the use of stress and intonation?					

Task 05 — Problem / Solution

TOEFL SPEAKING — Sample Question

Listening Listen to a conversation between two students.

Question The students discuss two possible solutions to the woman's problem. Describe the problem. Then state which of the two solutions you prefer and explain why.

Preparation time : 20 seconds
Response time : 60 seconds

Listening Note

Problem

Renovation on free student parking lot
- For the whole semester

Solutions

1) Alternative parking area
   - Located across from the main gates
   - Far from main bldg.
   - Free

2) Paid parking lots
   - Located near main bldg.
   - Saves time / no worry about being late
   - Costs money

   Reasons
   ① Safer
      - Outside → car might be stolen + dangerous to walk to the car
   ② Convenient
      - No need to walk
      - In case of rain

Problem / Solution

• Speaking Expressions

Problem
- The man's problem is that ...
- The man has a problem with ...
- The man is in trouble because ...
- He is having a hard time ... ~ ing ...
- The problem they discuss is that ...
- The man has difficulty with ...
- The man is facing a dilemma.
- He wants to ... , but he isn't able to ...

Solution
- The man suggests two solutions.
- There are two solutions presented.
- He suggests that she either ... or ...
- He suggests that she should ... or ...
- The man advises that she could ...
- The man says that she would ...
- The man tells her to ...
- The man recommends that she ...

Reason
- I think he should ... because ...
- Between the two solutions, I prefer ...
- I think that A is better than B.
- I believe the best way is to ...
- I think the first solution is better.
- I believe the first suggestion is better.
- I suggest he follow the woman's first suggestion for ...
- I consider A to be the most reasonable solution because ...

• Idiomatic Expressions

(A) feels down: Depressed or sad.

Ex) My sister **feels down** because she is pregnant.

🎤 Sample Response

• **Problem**

She feels down because of the parking problem. Her problem is that the school is renovating the free parking lot for students, so she has to find another parking space for her car.

• **Solution**

The man suggests two solutions. The man first suggests that she park outside the campus, where she can park for free; then he suggests using the paid parking venues on campus for a fee.

• **Reason**

I believe the second suggestion, which is to park her car in the paid parking lot, is better. Even if she has to pay for it, parking inside the campus is more secure than parking outside. If she parks outside, her car might get stolen, and maybe it wouldn't be safe for her to walk to her car. It will also be convenient, since she doesn't have to walk far to attend her classes, and if it rains, she'll have easier access to her car.

Evaluation		1	2	3	4
Topic Development	Could you complete your response?				
	Is your response coherent and unified?				
	Do you find a sequence in your response?				
Language Use	How is the use of vocabulary?				
	Is the grammatical structure good?				
	How is the use of idiomatic expressions?				
Delivery	Is your response fluent and smooth?				
	Is your pronunciation clear?				
	How is the use of stress and intonation?				

Task 5

2 MP3 109

TOEFL SPEAKING

Listening   Listen to a conversation between two students.

Question   The students discuss two possible solutions to the man's problem. Describe the problem. Then state which of the two solutions you prefer and explain why.

| Preparation time : 20 seconds |
| Response time   : 60 seconds |

Listening Note

Problem

Solutions

Problem / Solution

- **Speaking Expressions**

  Problem
  - The man's problem is that ...
  - The man has a problem with ...
  - The man is in trouble because ...
  - He is having a hard time ... ~ ing ...
  - The problem they discuss is that ...
  - The man has difficulty with ...
  - The man is facing a dilemma.
  - He wants to ... , but he isn't able to ...

  Solution
  - The man suggests two solutions.
  - There are two solutions presented.
  - He suggests that she either ... , or ...
  - He suggests that she should ... or ...
  - The man advises that she could ...
  - The man says that she would ...
  - The man tells her to ...
  - The man recommends that she ...

  Reason
  - I think he should ... because ...
  - Between the two solutions, I prefer ...
  - I think that A is better than B.
  - I believe the best way is to ...
  - I think the first solution is better.
  - I believe the first suggestion is better.
  - I suggest he follow the woman's first suggestion for ...
  - I consider A to be the most reasonable solution because ...

- **Idiomatic Expressions**

  Any way you cut it: In whatever manner you deal with it, the consequences will not change.

  Ex) Some historians say that we cannot apply our own morals and sensibilities to Roman society, but others say that **any way you cut it**, such behavior is savage and inhuman.

- **My Response**

  - Problem

  - Solution

  - Reason

Evaluation			1	2	3	4
Topic Development		Could you complete your response?				
		Is your response coherent and unified?				
		Do you find a sequence in your response?				
Language Use		How is the use of vocabulary?				
		Is the grammatical structure good?				
		How is the use of idiomatic expressions?				
Delivery		Is your response fluent and smooth?				
		Is your pronunciation clear?				
		How is the use of stress and intonation?				

Task 5 |

3 MP3 110

TOEFL SPEAKING

Listening   Listen to a conversation between two students.

Question   The students discuss two possible solutions to the woman's problem. Describe the problem and two solutions. Then explain what you think the woman should do and why.

| Preparation time : 20 seconds |
| Response time   : 60 seconds |

Listening Note

Problem

Solutions

Problem / Solution

- **Speaking Expressions**

Problem
- The man's problem is that ...
- The man has a problem with ...
- The man is in trouble because ...
- He is having a hard time ... ~ ing ...
- The problem they discuss is that ...
- The man has difficulty with ...
- The man is facing a dilemma.
- He wants to ... , but he isn't able to ...

Solution
- The man suggests two solutions.
- There are two solutions presented.
- He suggests that she either ... or ...
- He suggests that she should ... or ...
- The man advises that she could ...
- The man says that she would ...
- The man tells her to ...
- The man recommends that she ...

Reason
- I think he should ... because ...
- Between the two solutions, I prefer ...
- I think that A is better than B.
- I believe the best way is to ...
- I think the first solution is better.
- I believe the first suggestion is better.
- I suggest he follow the woman's first suggestion for ...
- I consider A to be the most reasonable solution because ...

- **Idiomatic Expressions**

Catch 22: Dilemma

Ex) It's such a **Catch 22** when you can't retrieve your ID inside a building because you need one to get inside.

My Response

- Problem

- Solution

- Reason

Evaluation			1	2	3	4
Topic Development	Could you complete your response?					
	Is your response coherent and unified?					
	Do you find a sequence in your response?					
Language Use	How is the use of vocabulary?					
	Is the grammatical structure good?					
	How is the use of idiomatic expressions?					
Delivery	Is your response fluent and smooth?					
	Is your pronunciation clear?					
	How is the use of stress and intonation?					

Task 5

4

TOEFL SPEAKING

Listening — Listen to a conversation between a student and his art professor.

Question — The speakers discuss two possible solutions to the man's problem. Describe the problem and the two solutions. Then explain what you think the man should do and why.

| Preparation time : 20 seconds |
| Response time   : 60 seconds |

Problem

Solutions

Problem / Solution

- **Speaking Expressions**

  Problem
  - The man's problem is that ...
  - The man has a problem with ...
  - The man is in trouble because ...
  - He is having a hard time ... ~ ing ...
  - The problem they discuss is that ...
  - The man has difficulty with ...
  - The man is facing a dilemma.
  - He wants to ... , but he isn't able to ...

  Solution
  - The man suggests two solutions.
  - There are two solutions presented.
  - He suggests that she either ... or ...
  - He suggests that she should ... or ...
  - The man advises that she could ...
  - The man says that she would ...
  - The man tells her to ...
  - The man recommends that she ...

  Reason
  - I think he should ... because ...
  - Between the two solutions, I prefer ...
  - I think that A is better than B.
  - I believe the best way is to ...
  - I think the first solution is better.
  - I believe the first suggestion is better.
  - I suggest he follow the woman's first suggestion for ...
  - I consider A to be the most reasonable solution because ...

- **Idiomatic Expressions**

  Have one's cake and eat it too: Impossible to get two good things without sacrificing one of them.

  Ex) He tried to **have his cake and eat it too** when he started dating Jennifer while still engaged to Angela.

🎤 **My Response**

- Problem

- Solution

- Reason

Evaluation			1	2	3	4
Topic Development	Could you complete your response?					
	Is your response coherent and unified?					
	Do you find a sequence in your response?					
Language Use	How is the use of vocabulary?					
	Is the grammatical structure good?					
	How is the use of idiomatic expressions?					
Delivery	Is your response fluent and smooth?					
	Is your pronunciation clear?					
	How is the use of stress and intonation?					

Task 5

5 MP3 112

TOEFL SPEAKING

Listening   Listen to a conversation between two students.

Question   The students discuss two possible solutions to the woman's problem. Describe the problem and the two solutions. Then explain what you think the woman should do and why.

| Preparation time : 20 seconds |
| Response time   : 60 seconds |

🎧 Listening Note

Problem

Solutions

Problem / Solution

Speaking Expressions

Problem

- The man's problem is that ...
- The man has a problem with ...
- The man is in trouble because ...
- He is having a hard time ... ~ ing ...
- The problem they discuss is that ...
- The man has difficulty with ...
- The man is facing a dilemma.
- He wants to ... , but he isn't able to ...

Solution

- The man suggests two solutions.
- There are two solutions presented.
- He suggests that she either ... or ...
- He suggests that she should ... or ...
- The man advises that she could ...
- The man says that she would ...
- The man tells her to ...
- The man recommends that she ...

Reason

- I think he should ... because ...
- Between the two solutions, I prefer ...
- I think that A is better than B.
- I believe the best way is to ...
- I think the first solution is better.
- I believe the first suggestion is better.
- I suggest he follow the woman's first suggestion for ...
- I consider A to be the most reasonable solution because ...

Idiomatic Expressions

In the blink of an eye:
Instantaneously or quickly

Ex) The man disappeared **in the blink of an eye**.

🎤 My Response

- Problem

- Solution

- Reason

Evaluation		1	2	3	4
Topic Development	Could you complete your response?				
	Is your response coherent and unified?				
	Do you find a sequence in your response?				
Language Use	How is the use of vocabulary?				
	Is the grammatical structure good?				
	How is the use of idiomatic expressions?				
Delivery	Is your response fluent and smooth?				
	Is your pronunciation clear?				
	How is the use of stress and intonation?				

Task 5

6 MP3 113

TOEFL SPEAKING

Listening Listen to a conversation between two students.

Question The students discuss two possible solutions to the woman's problem. Describe the problem. Then state which of the two solutions you prefer and explain why.

| Preparation time : 20 seconds |
| Response time   : 60 seconds |

 **Listening Note**

Problem

Solutions

Problem / Solution

Speaking Expressions

Problem

- The man's problem is that ...
- The man has a problem with ...
- The man is in trouble because ...
- He is having a hard time ... ~ ing ...
- The problem they discuss is that ...
- The man has difficulty with ...
- The man is facing a dilemma.
- He wants to ... , but he isn't able to ...

Solution

- The man suggests two solutions.
- There are two solutions presented.
- He suggests that she either ... or ...
- He suggests that she should ... or ...
- The man advises that she could ...
- The man says that she would ...
- The man tells her to ...
- The man recommends that she ...

Reason

- I think he should ... because ...
- Between the two solutions, I prefer ...
- I think that A is better than B.
- I believe the best way is to ...
- I think the first solution is better.
- I believe the first suggestion is better.
- I suggest he follow the woman's first suggestion for ...
- I consider A to be the most reasonable solution because ...

Idiomatic Expressions

Bark up the wrong tree:
Aim at a wrong target.

Ex) "Hey, Danny! I know you think that I stole your wallet. But you should know that you are **barking up the wrong tree**."

🎤 My Response

- Problem

- Solution

- Reason

Evaluation			1	2	3	4
Topic Development	Could you complete your response?					
	Is your response coherent and unified?					
	Do you find a sequence in your response?					
Language Use	How is the use of vocabulary?					
	Is the grammatical structure good?					
	How is the use of idiomatic expressions?					
Delivery	Is your response fluent and smooth?					
	Is your pronunciation clear?					
	How is the use of stress and intonation?					

Task 5

7 MP3 114

TOEFL SPEAKING

Listening Listen to a conversation between two students.

Question The students discuss two possible solutions to the man's problem. Describe the problem. Then state which of the two solutions you prefer and explain why.

| Preparation time : 20 seconds |
| Response time   : 60 seconds |

 **Listening Note**

Problem

Solutions

Problem / Solution

Speaking Expressions

Problem

- The man's problem is that ...
- The man has a problem with ...
- The man is in trouble because ...
- He is having a hard time ... ~ ing ...
- The problem they discuss is that ...
- The man has difficulty with ...
- The man is facing a dilemma.
- He wants to ... , but he isn't able to ...

Solution

- The man suggests two solutions.
- There are two solutions presented.
- He suggests that she either ... or ...
- He suggests that she should ... or ...
- The man advises that she could ...
- The man says that she would ...
- The man tells her to ...
- The man recommends that she ...

Reason

- I think he should ... because ...
- Between the two solutions, I prefer ...
- I think that A is better than B.
- I believe the best way is to ...
- I think the first solution is better.
- I believe the first suggestion is better.
- I suggest he follow the woman's first suggestion for ...
- I consider A to be the most reasonable solution because ...

Idiomatic Expressions

Leave the door open: To allow for the possibility that something might happen.

Ex) Although you have **left the door open** for further negotiations, you should know that we are not willing to compromise.

My Response

- Problem

- Solution

- Reason

Evaluation		1	2	3	4
Topic Development	Could you complete your response?				
	Is your response coherent and unified?				
	Do you find a sequence in your response?				
Language Use	How is the use of vocabulary?				
	Is the grammatical structure good?				
	How is the use of idiomatic expressions?				
Delivery	Is your response fluent and smooth?				
	Is your pronunciation clear?				
	How is the use of stress and intonation?				

Task 5

8

TOEFL SPEAKING

Listening   Listen to a conversation between two students.

Question   The students discuss two possible solutions to the woman's problem. Describe the problem. Then state which of the two solutions you prefer and explain why.

| Preparation time : 20 seconds |
| Response time   : 60 seconds |

Listening Note

Problem

Solutions

Problem / Solution

Speaking Expressions

Problem

- The man's problem is that ...
- The man has a problem with ...
- The man is in trouble because ...
- He is having a hard time ... ~ ing ...
- The problem they discuss is that ...
- The man has difficulty with ...
- The man is facing a dilemma.
- He wants to ... , but he isn't able to ...

Solution

- The man suggests two solutions.
- There are two solutions presented.
- He suggests that she either ... or ...
- He suggests that she should ... or ...
- The man advises that she could ...
- The man says that she would ...
- The man tells her to ...
- The man recommends that she ...

Reason

- I think he should ... because ...
- Between the two solutions, I prefer ...
- I think that A is better than B.
- I believe the best way is to ...
- I think the first solution is better.
- I believe the first suggestion is better.
- I suggest he follow the woman's first suggestion for ...
- I consider A to be the most reasonable solution because ...

Idiomatic Expressions

Meet someone halfway:
To compromise and cooperate with others.

Ex) After I discussed the matter with him for several hours, I decided to **meet him halfway**.

🎤 My Response

- Problem

- Solution

- Reason

Evaluation		1	2	3	4
Topic Development	Could you complete your response?				
	Is your response coherent and unified?				
	Do you find a sequence in your response?				
Language Use	How is the use of vocabulary?				
	Is the grammatical structure good?				
	How is the use of idiomatic expressions?				
Delivery	Is your response fluent and smooth?				
	Is your pronunciation clear?				
	How is the use of stress and intonation?				

PART II Practice Test

Task 06 — Summary

MP3 116

TOEFL SPEAKING Sample Question

Listening Now listen to part of a lecture in a biology class.

Question Using points and examples from the talk, explain how the ability to build a resistance to toxins is harmful to humans.

Preparation time : 20 seconds
Response time   : 60 seconds

Listening Note

Topic

Organisms that build up a resistance to toxins

Example 1

- Farmers using pesticides
- Pesticides never kill 100% of the pests
  → The ones that survive build up resistance to pesticides.
  → Farmers have to continuously use more powerful pesticides.

Example 2

- Bacteria and the use of antibiotics
- Bacteria build up a resistance to antibiotics over time
  → It's hard to fight diseases because doctors have to find stronger antibiotics

Summary

Speaking Expressions

Topic
- The lecture is mainly about ...
- The topic of the lecture is ...
- The professor discusses ...
- The professor talks about ...
- According to the professor, A is ...
- According to the lecture, A and B are ...
- According to him, A is defined as
- According to him, A refers to ...

Classification
- The professor gives two types of ...
- There are two factors of ...
- He explains of two definitions of ...
- He demonstrates the concept of ...
- He illustrates this by talking about ...
- He discusses ... as an example of ...
- He gives another example of ...
- He describes ... by giving two examples ...

Detail
- A enabled B
- A paved the way for B
- A caused B
- A resulted in B
- A led to B
- A had a great influence on B
- A occurs mainly because of ...
- According to him, A is the most important factor in ...

Idiomatic Expressions

An old hand: An experienced person.

Ex) Julie is **an old hand** at newspapers, having experience in various different publishing companies.

Sample Response

- **Topic**

The lecture is mainly about all organisms having the ability to build up a resistance to various toxins.

- **Classification**

The professor describes how organisms build up a resistance to toxins by giving two examples.

- **Detail**

First, she says that farmers use pesticides, which are basically toxins, to kill animals and insect pests. But she says that pesticides never kill 100% of pests. The ones that survive build up a resistance to the pesticide. As a result, farmers have to continuously use more powerful pesticides. This is one way that the natural ability of organisms to build a resistance to toxins can be bad for people.

The other example mentioned by the professor involves bacteria and the use of antibiotics. Antibiotics are used to kill bacteria, but bacteria build up a resistance to antibiotics over time. Even an old hand, an experienced doctor, finds it difficult to fight diseases because he always has to find stronger antibiotics.

Evaluation		1	2	3	4
Topic Development	Could you complete your response?				
	Is your response coherent and unified?				
	Do you find a sequence in your response?				
Language Use	How is the use of vocabulary?				
	Is the grammatical structure good?				
	How is the use of idiomatic expressions?				
Delivery	Is your response fluent and smooth?				
	Is your pronunciation clear?				
	How is the use of stress and intonation?				

Task 6

2 MP3 117

TOEFL SPEAKING

Listening   Now listen to part of a lecture in an art class.

Question   Using points and examples from the talk, explain the two examples of artistic imitation presented by the professor.

Preparation time : 20 seconds
Response time   : 60 seconds

Listening Note

Topic

Example 1

Example 2

Summary

- **Speaking Expressions**

  Topic
  - The lecture is mainly about ...
  - The topic of the lecture is ...
  - The professor discusses ...
  - The professor talks about ...
  - According to the professor, A is ...
  - According to the lecture, A and B are ...
  - According to him, A is defined as ...
  - According to him, A refers to ...

  Classification
  - The professor gives two types of ...
  - There are two factors of ...
  - He explains of two definitions of ...
  - He demonstrates the concept of ...
  - He illustrates this by talking about ...
  - He discusses ... as an example of ...
  - He gives another example of ...
  - He describes ... by giving two examples ...

  Detail
  - A enabled B
  - A paved the way for B
  - A caused B
  - A resulted in B
  - A led to B
  - A had a great influence on B
  - A occurs mainly because of ...
  - According to him, A is the most important factor in ...

- **Idiomatic Expressions**

  Vice versa: Conversely.

  Ex) Parents can read their children's minds and not **vice versa**.

🎤 My Response

- Topic

- Classification

- Detail

Evaluation		1	2	3	4
Topic Development	Could you complete your response?				
	Is your response coherent and unified?				
	Do you find a sequence in your response?				
Language Use	How is the use of vocabulary?				
	Is the grammatical structure good?				
	How is the use of idiomatic expressions?				
Delivery	Is your response fluent and smooth?				
	Is your pronunciation clear?				
	How is the use of stress and intonation?				

PART II Practice Test

Task 6

3 MP3 118

TOEFL SPEAKING

Listening Now listen to part of a lecture in a political science class.

Question Using points and examples from the talk, explain how the situations of Presidents Nixon and Bush illustrate the concept of checks and balances.

| Preparation time : 20 seconds |
| Response time   : 60 seconds |

🎧 Listening Note

Topic

Example 1

Example 2

Summary

Speaking Expressions

Topic
- The lecture is mainly about ...
- The topic of the lecture is ...
- The professor discusses ...
- The professor talks about ...
- According to the professor, A is ...
- According to the lecture, A and B are ...
- According to him, A is defined as ...
- According to him, A refers to ...

Classification
- The professor gives two types of ...
- There are two factors of ...
- He explains of two definitions of ...
- He demonstrates the concept of ...
- He illustrates this by talking about ...
- He discusses ... as an example of ...
- He gives another example of ...
- He describes ... by giving two examples ...

Detail
- A enabled B
- A paved the way for B
- A caused B
- A resulted in B
- A led to B
- A had a great influence on B
- A occurs mainly because of ...
- According to him, A is the most important factor in ...

Idiomatic Expressions

Make headway: Making improvement or progress.

Ex) IBM is set to **make headway** in Korea.

My Response

- Topic

- Classification

- Detail

Evaluation		1	2	3	4
Topic Development	Could you complete your response?				
	Is your response coherent and unified?				
	Do you find a sequence in your response?				
Language Use	How is the use of vocabulary?				
	Is the grammatical structure good?				
	How is the use of idiomatic expressions?				
Delivery	Is your response fluent and smooth?				
	Is your pronunciation clear?				
	How is the use of stress and intonation?				

Task 6

4 MP3 119

TOEFL SPEAKING

Listening Now listen to part of a lecture in a music history class.

Question Using points and examples from the talk, explain how the electric guitar and the multi-track recorder illustrate the role of technology in music.

| Preparation time : 20 seconds |
| Response time   : 60 seconds |

Listening Note

Topic

Example 1

Example 2

Summary

Speaking Expressions

Topic
- The lecture is mainly about ...
- The topic of the lecture is ...
- The professor discusses ...
- The professor talks about ...
- According to the professor, A is ...
- According to the lecture, A and B are ...
- According to him, A is defined as
- According to him, A refers to ...

Classification
- The professor gives two types of ...
- There are two factors of ...
- He explains of two definitions of ...
- He demonstrates the concept of ...
- He illustrates this by talking about ...
- He discusses ... as an example of ...
- He gives another example of ...
- He describes ... by giving two examples ...

Detail
- A enabled B
- A paved the way for B
- A caused B
- A resulted in B
- A led to B
- A had a great influence on B
- A occurs mainly because of ...
- According to him, A is the most important factor in ...

Idiomatic Expressions

Get straight to the point: Deal with the main issue without any delay.

Ex) The professor didn't waste time talking about trivial issues and **got straight to the point** in discussing the lesson.

🎤 My Response

- Topic

- Classification

- Detail

Evaluation		1	2	3	4
Topic Development	Could you complete your response?				
	Is your response coherent and unified?				
	Do you find a sequence in your response?				
Language Use	How is the use of vocabulary?				
	Is the grammatical structure good?				
	How is the use of idiomatic expressions?				
Delivery	Is your response fluent and smooth?				
	Is your pronunciation clear?				
	How is the use of stress and intonation?				

Task 6

5 MP3 120

TOEFL SPEAKING

Listening Now listen to part of a lecture on food technology.

Question Using points and examples from the talk, explain how the two methods of lowering temperature and reducing humidity prevent food deterioration.

| Preparation time : 20 seconds |
| Response time   : 60 seconds |

Listening Note

Topic

Example 1

Example 2

Summary

Speaking Expressions

Topic
- The lecture is mainly about ...
- The topic of the lecture is ...
- The professor discusses ...
- The professor talks about ...
- According to the professor, A is ...
- According to the lecture, A and B are ...
- According to him, A is defined as
- According to him, A refers to ...

Classification
- The professor gives two types of ...
- There are two factors of ...
- He explains of two definitions of ...
- He demonstrates the concept of ...
- He illustrates this by talking about ...
- He discusses ... as an example of ...
- He gives another example of ...
- He describes ... by giving two examples ...

Detail
- A enabled B
- A paved the way for B
- A caused B
- A resulted in B
- A led to B
- A had a great influence on B
- A occurs mainly because of ...
- According to him, A is the most important factor in ...

Idiomatic Expressions

Get over it: Overcome.

Ex) It's difficult to **get over** the painful experience.

My Response

- Topic

- Classification

- Detail

Evaluation			1	2	3	4
Topic Development	Could you complete your response?					
	Is your response coherent and unified?					
	Do you find a sequence in your response?					
Language Use	How is the use of vocabulary?					
	Is the grammatical structure good?					
	How is the use of idiomatic expressions?					
Delivery	Is your response fluent and smooth?					
	Is your pronunciation clear?					
	How is the use of stress and intonation?					

6 MP3 121

TOEFL SPEAKING

VOLUME

Listening Now listen to part of a lecture in an art class.

Question Using points and examples from the talk, explain how fragmentation and ambiguity affect the illusion of space in cubist paintings.

Preparation time	: 20 seconds
Response time	: 60 seconds

Listening Note

Topic

Example 1

Example 2

Summary

Speaking Expressions

Topic
- The lecture is mainly about ...
- The topic of the lecture is ...
- The professor discusses ...
- The professor talks about ...
- According to the professor, A is ...
- According to the lecture, A and B are ...
- According to him, A is defined as ...
- According to him, A refers to ...

Classification
- The professor gives two types of ...
- There are two factors of ...
- He explains of two definitions of ...
- He demonstrates the concept of ...
- He illustrates this by talking about ...
- He discusses ... as an example of ...
- He gives another example of ...
- He describes ... by giving two examples ...

Detail
- A enabled B
- A paved the way for B
- A caused B
- A resulted in B
- A led to B
- A had a great influence on B
- A occurs mainly because of ...
- According to him, A is the most important factor in ...

Idiomatic Expressions

Call the shots: Control the situation.

Ex) Alex acts like he is the authority figure, but it's always his mother who **calls the shots**.

🎤 My Response

- Topic

- Classification

- Detail

Evaluation		1	2	3	4
Topic Development	Could you complete your response?				
	Is your response coherent and unified?				
	Do you find a sequence in your response?				
Language Use	How is the use of vocabulary?				
	Is the grammatical structure good?				
	How is the use of idiomatic expressions?				
Delivery	Is your response fluent and smooth?				
	Is your pronunciation clear?				
	How is the use of stress and intonation?				

Task 6

7 MP3 122

TOEFL SPEAKING

Listening   Now listen to part of a talk in an ecology class.

Question   Using points and examples from the lecture, explain how biodiversity is protected and preserved.

| Preparation time : 20 seconds |
| Response time   : 60 seconds |

Listening Note

Topic

Example 1

Example 2

Summary

- **Speaking Expressions**

  Topic
  - The lecture is mainly about ...
  - The topic of the lecture is ...
  - The professor discusses ...
  - The professor talks about ...
  - According to the professor, A is ...
  - According to the lecture, A and B are ...
  - According to him, A is defined as ...
  - According to him, A refers to ...

  Classification
  - The professor gives two types of ...
  - There are two factors of ...
  - He explains of two definitions of ...
  - He demonstrates the concept of ...
  - He illustrates this by talking about ...
  - He discusses ... as an example of ...
  - He gives another example of ...
  - He describes ... by giving two examples ...

  Detail
  - A enabled B
  - A paved the way for B
  - A caused B
  - A resulted in B
  - A led to B
  - A had a great influence on B
  - A occurs mainly because of ...
  - According to him, A is the most important factor in ...

- **Idiomatic Expressions**

  Spot on: Exactly correct!

  Ex) I know that her answer is **spot on**!

🎤 My Response

- Topic

- Classification

- Detail

Evaluation		1	2	3	4
Topic Development	Could you complete your response?				
	Is your response coherent and unified?				
	Do you find a sequence in your response?				
Language Use	How is the use of vocabulary?				
	Is the grammatical structure good?				
	How is the use of idiomatic expressions?				
Delivery	Is your response fluent and smooth?				
	Is your pronunciation clear?				
	How is the use of stress and intonation?				

Task 6

8 MP3 123

TOEFL SPEAKING

Listening Now listen to part of a lecture in a psychology class.

Question Using points and examples from the talk, explain how the two situations presented by the professor exemplify the concept of selective attention.

| Preparation time : 20 seconds |
| Response time   : 60 seconds |

Listening Note

Topic

Example 1

Example 2

Summary

Speaking Expressions

Topic

- The lecture is mainly about …
- The topic of the lecture is …
- The professor discusses …
- The professor talks about …
- According to the professor, A is …
- According to the lecture, A and B are …
- According to him, A is defined as
- According to him, A refers to …

Classification

- The professor gives two types of …
- There are two factors of …
- He explains of two definitions of …
- He demonstrates the concept of …
- He illustrates this by talking about …
- He discusses … as an example of …
- He gives another example of …
- He describes … by giving two examples …

Detail

- A enabled B
- A paved the way for B
- A caused B
- A resulted in B
- A led to B
- A had a great influence on B
- A occurs mainly because of …
- According to him, A is the most important factor in …

Idiomatic Expressions

Out of your depth: Having little or no knowledge about something.

Ex) When he started to talk about politics, I knew it was **out of my depth**.

🎤 My Response

- Topic

- Classification

- Detail

Evaluation			1	2	3	4
Topic Development	Could you complete your response?					
	Is your response coherent and unified?					
	Do you find a sequence in your response?					
Language Use	How is the use of vocabulary?					
	Is the grammatical structure good?					
	How is the use of idiomatic expressions?					
Delivery	Is your response fluent and smooth?					
	Is your pronunciation clear?					
	How is the use of stress and intonation?					

HOOKED ON TOEFL SPEAKING

Actual Test

- Actual Test 1
- Actual Test 2

L·I·N·G·U·A·F·O·R·U·M·H·O·O·K·E·D·O·N·T·O·E·F·L·S·P·E·A·K·I·N·G

PART III

Actual Test 01

Speaking Section Directions

TOEFL SPEAKING

In this section of the test, you will be able to demonstrate your ability to speak about a variety of topics. You will answer six questions by speaking into the microphone. Answer each of the questions as completely as possible.

In questions 1 and 2, you will speak about familiar topics. Your response will be scored on your ability to speak clearly and coherently about the topics.

In questions 3 and 4, you will first read a short text. The text will go away and you will then listen to a talk on the same topic. You will then be asked a question about what you have read and heard. You will need to combine appropriate information from the text and the talk to provide a complete answer to the question. Your response will be scored on your ability to speak clearly and coherently and on your ability to accurately convey information about what you have read and heard.

In questions 5 and 6, you will listen to part of a conversation or a lecture. You will then be asked a question about what you have heard. Your response will be scored on your ability to speak clearly and coherently and on your ability to accurately convey information about what you heard.

You may take notes while you read and while you listen to the conversations and lectures. You may use your notes to help prepare your response.

Listen carefully to the directions for each question. The directions will not be written on the screen.

For each question, you will be given a short time to prepare your response. A clock will show how much preparation time is remaining. When the preparation time is up, you will be told to begin your response. A clock will show how much response time is remaining. A message will appear on the screen when the response time has ended.

Click on Continue to go on.

Actual Test 1

TOEFL SPEAKING   Question 1 of 6

Describe your most memorable birthday and explain why it was memorable. Please include specific details in your response.

| Preparation time : 15 seconds |
| Response time   : 45 seconds |

When grading their students, some university professors focus on the results of exams and term papers, while other professors focus more on the participation of the students in class. Which way of grading do you think is more reasonable and why?

| Preparation time : 15 seconds |
| Response time   : 45 seconds |

Actual Test 1

TOEFL SPEAKING — Question 3 of 6

Reading Time : 45 seconds

Announcement from the Office of the Dean of Academic Affairs

It has come to the attention of the administration that some professors have not been strictly enforcing the university's attendance policy. As this policy is a cornerstone of the university's academic program, all professors have been reminded of their obligation to adhere to this policy, effective immediately. As a reminder to the student body, three unexcused absences from any class will result in failure in that class. For more information regarding what constitutes an unexcused absence, consult your student handbook.

The man expresses his opinion of the attendance policy. State his opinion and explain the reasons he gives for holding that opinion.

Preparation time : 30 seconds
Response time   : 60 seconds

Reading Time : 45 seconds

Environmental Impact Analysis of the Production Process

Environmental impact analysis of the production process is a method of determining the environmental impacts of producing a particular product. In order to determine this, environmental engineers must calculate the total amount of energy required to produce a product, as well as what waste materials are created during production. The objective of environmental impact analysis of the production process is to determine which areas of the production process can be improved to consume less energy or to produce less waste.

The professor describes a study conducted at a winery. Explain how this study demonstrates the methods and applications of environmental impact analysis for the production process.

| Preparation time : 30 seconds |
| Response time   : 60 seconds |

Actual Test 1

TOEFL SPEAKING   Question 5 of 6

The students discuss two possible solutions to the man's problem. Describe the problem. Then state which of the two solutions you prefer and explain why.

Preparation time : 30 seconds
Response time   : 60 seconds

Using points and examples from the talk, explain how eating more meat resulted in higher levels of intelligence in early society.

Preparation time : 30 seconds
Response time   : 60 seconds

Actual Test 02

Speaking Section Directions

TOEFL SPEAKING

In this section of the test, you will be able to demonstrate your ability to speak about a variety of topics. You will answer six questions by speaking into the microphone. Answer each of the questions as completely as possible.

In questions 1 and 2, you will speak about familiar topics. Your response will be scored on your ability to speak clearly and coherently about the topics.

In questions 3 and 4, you will first read a short text. The text will go away and you will then listen to a talk on the same topic. You will then be asked a question about what you have read and heard. You will need to combine appropriate information from the text and the talk to provide a complete answer to the question. Your response will be scored on your ability to speak clearly and coherently and on your ability to accurately convey information about what you have read and heard.

In questions 5 and 6, you will listen to part of a conversation or a lecture. You will then be asked a question about what you have heard. Your response will be scored on your ability to speak clearly and coherently and on your ability to accurately convey information about what you heard.

You may take notes while you read and while you listen to the conversations and lectures. You may use your notes to help prepare your response.

Listen carefully to the directions for each question. The directions will not be written on the screen.

For each question, you will be given a short time to prepare your response. A clock will show how much preparation time is remaining. When the preparation time is up, you will be told to begin your response. A clock will show how much response time is remaining. A message will appear on the screen when the response time has ended.

Click on Continue to go on.

Actual Test 2

TOEFL SPEAKING — Question 1 of 6

Describe what kind of books you like to read and explain why you like those books. Use specific examples and details in your response.

Preparation time : 15 seconds
Response time : 45 seconds

Some people prefer face-to-face communications, while others prefer virtual communications (like the cell phone or the Internet). Which way of communicating with people do you prefer and why?

| Preparation time : 15 seconds |
| Response time   : 45 seconds |

Reading Time : 45 seconds

Announcement from the Dean of Student Affairs

After last semester's alarming rise in alcohol-related incidents on campus, the administration has determined that stiffer penalties for alcohol infractions on campus are called for. Effective immediately, the mandatory period of disciplinary probation following an alcohol violation on campus will be extended from one semester to a full school year. As you know, further violations of the student code while a student is on disciplinary probation can lead to expulsion. Please take note of this policy change, and help us keep our university safe and alcohol≈free.

The woman expresses her opinion of the penalty increase on alcohol violations on campus. State her opinion and explain the reasons she gives for holding that opinion.

Preparation time : 30 seconds
Response time   : 60 seconds

Predatory Loan Practices

Predatory loans are designed to take advantage of consumers, especially consumers who lack knowledge about the financial system. Predatory loans lure customers with the promise of quick cash, but the terms of the loans are highly unfavorable to the customers. Predatory loans often have exceedingly high interest rates or unreasonably long payment periods. Often the true objective of a predatory loan is to get the customer into a situation in which they are unable to pay back the loan, at which point the loan company can repossess property which may have a much higher value than the loan itself.

Explain how mortgage refinancing companies demonstrate the concept of predatory loan practices.

| Preparation time : 30 seconds |
| Response time   : 60 seconds |

Actual Test 2

TOEFL SPEAKING Question 5 of 6

The students discuss two possible solutions to the woman's problem. Describe the problem. Then state which of the two solutions you prefer and explain why.

| Preparation time : 20 seconds |
| Response time   : 60 seconds |

Using points and examples from the talk, explain the term collective switching cost.

Preparation time	: 20 seconds
Response time	: 60 seconds

HOOKED ON TOEFL SPEAKING

Appendix

- Appendix 1 Pronunciation
- Appendix 2 Note-Taking
- Appendix 3 Power Vocabulary

L·I·N·G·U·A·F·O·R·U·M·H·O·O·K·E·D·O·N·T·O·E·F·L·S·P·E·A·K·I·N·G

Appendix 1 Pronunciation

※ 본 Pronounciation 섹션에 대한 사운드 파일은 http://test.linguaforum.com 사이트에서 회원가입 후 자료실에서 다운로드하여 사용하십시오.

Exercise 1 Words with Similar Sounds

들려주는 단어가 둘 중 어떤 단어인지 표시해 보자.

1. ☑ accept
    ☐ except

2. ☐ assess
    ☐ excess

3. ☐ adept
    ☐ adopt

4. ☐ affect
    ☐ effect

5. ☐ aggravated
    ☐ aggregated

6. ☐ casual
    ☐ causal

7. ☐ comprehensible
    ☐ comprehensive

8. ☐ conscious
    ☐ conscience

9. ☐ cooperation
    ☐ corporation

10. ☐ fiscal
    ☐ physical

11. ☐ ideal
    ☐ idle

12. ☐ imitate
    ☐ intimate

13. ☐ pose
    ☐ pause

14. ☐ suit
    ☐ suite

15. ☐ advice
    ☐ advise

16. ☐ assure
    ☐ ensure

17. ☐ farther
    ☐ further

18. ☐ loss
    ☐ loose

19. ☐ expand
    ☐ extend

20. ☐ disburse
    ☐ disperse

21. ☐ ingenious
    ☐ ingenuous

22. ☐ emigrate
    ☐ immigrate

23. ☐ persecute
    ☐ prosecute

24. ☐ censor
    ☐ censure

25. ☐ bibliography
    ☐ biography

26. ☐ overdo
    ☐ overdue

27. ☐ personal
    ☐ personnel

28. ☐ principal
    ☐ principle

29. ☐ stationary
    ☐ stationery

30. ☐ hostel
    ☐ hostile

Exercise 2 Commonly Mispronounced Words

다음 제시된 단어들은 한국인들이 흔히 잘못 발음하기 쉬운 단어들이다. 단어를 스스로 소리내어 읽고 녹음한 후 다시 들어보자. 그리고 나서 원어민의 발음을 듣고 자신의 발음과 비교하여 보자. 발음이 비슷하게 될 때까지 이 과정을 반복하도록 한다.

1. allergy
2. label
3. neon
4. Atlantic
5. athlete
6. athletic
7. charisma
8. missile
9. amateur
10. Asian
11. oxygen
12. chaos
13. mortgage
14. Caribbean
15. conservative
16. close *(adj.)*
17. closer *(adj.)*
18. closely
19. disease
20. February
21. acid
22. hierarchy
23. short-lived
24. ascertain
25. gauge
26. bury
27. executive
28. parallel
29. caramel
30. buffet
31. Styrofoam
32. aesthetic
33. Mediterranean
34. debt
35. barbecue
36. vinyl
37. pamphlet
38. pajamas
39. scenario
40. theme
41. margarine
42. ballet
43. accurate
44. genome
45. report
46. resume *(noun)*
47. mayonnaise
48. carnivorous
49. harass
50. genuine

Exercise 3 Word Stress

🎧 다음 단어들을 강세의 위치에 따라 분류하여 보자.

antonym	popularity	photography	statistics
mischievous	maintain	feature	landlord
nuclear	analyze	presentation	economic
prerogative	analysis	interfere	disappoint
photograph	committee	compromise	photographic
comfortable	fatigue	pervade	recommend
academic	genuine	mistakenly	participate
resource	photographer	discuss	illustrate
economy	engineer	educational	manufacture

| 첫째 음절 |

antonym

| 둘째 음절 |

prerogative

| 셋째 음절 |

academic

Exercise 4 Weakened Sound

들려주는 단어가 둘 중 어떤 단어인지 표시해 보자.

1. ☑ account
   ☐ count

2. ☐ alive
   ☐ live

3. ☐ approve
   ☐ prove

4. ☐ assign
   ☐ sign

5. ☐ assure
   ☐ sure

6. ☐ attain
   ☐ obtain

7. ☐ custom
   ☐ accustom

8. ☐ division
   ☐ vision

9. ☐ enrich
   ☐ rich

10. ☐ estate
    ☐ state

11. ☐ around
    ☐ round

12. ☐ aside
    ☐ side

13. ☐ apart
    ☐ part

14. ☐ return
    ☐ turn

15. ☐ pit
    ☐ spit

16. ☐ forgive
    ☐ give

17. ☐ illogical
    ☐ logical

18. ☐ irrelevant
    ☐ relevant

19. ☐ preserve
    ☐ reserve

20. ☐ remind
    ☐ mind

21. ☐ retired
    ☐ tired

22. ☐ sphere
    ☐ fear

23. ☐ ready
    ☐ already

24. ☐ because
    ☐ cause

25. ☐ irrational
    ☐ rational

26. ☐ abnormal
    ☐ normal

27. ☐ unable
    ☐ able

28. ☐ resolution
    ☐ solution

29. ☐ abound
    ☐ bound

30. ☐ immoral
    ☐ moral

Exercise 5 Sound Comparison

A 들려주는 단어가 둘 중 어떤 단어인지 표시해 보자.

1	☐ tin	☑ thin	13	☐ etch	☐ edge
2	☐ nipple	☐ nibble	14	☐ dare	☐ their
3	☐ cap	☐ cab	15	☐ cede	☐ seethe
4	☐ crammer	☐ grammar	16	☐ deadly	☐ deathly
5	☐ define	☐ divine	17	☐ zoo	☐ Jew
6	☐ wag	☐ whack	18	☐ thorn	☐ torn
7	☐ proof	☐ prove	19	☐ array	☐ allay
8	☐ zest	☐ jest	20	☐ rhyme	☐ lime
9	☐ face	☐ phase	21	☐ leak	☐ league
10	☐ composer	☐ composure	22	☐ suit	☐ shoot
11	☐ teeth	☐ teethe	23	☐ though	☐ dough
12	☐ buzz	☐ budge	24	☐ choke	☐ joke

B 밑줄 친 모음 중 나머지 셋과 다르게 발음되는 하나를 골라보자.

1. tr<u>a</u>sh, <u>A</u>frica, n<u>a</u>p, (b<u>a</u>ll)
2. dr<u>ea</u>m, p<u>eo</u>ple, n<u>ee</u>d, l<u>i</u>ved
3. fr<u>ie</u>nd, <u>a</u>ngel, h<u>ea</u>vy, spr<u>ea</u>d
4. <u>aw</u>ful, d<u>au</u>ghter, r<u>o</u>pe, h<u>a</u>ll
5. p<u>oo</u>l, r<u>oo</u>m, b<u>oo</u>ts, g<u>oo</u>d
6. w<u>a</u>nder, f<u>o</u>ssil, b<u>o</u>ttle, <u>a</u>vid
7. n<u>i</u>ght, r<u>i</u>ght, dr<u>ou</u>ght, ps<u>y</u>cho
8. l<u>i</u>ke, r<u>i</u>ce, w<u>i</u>de, <u>i</u>mpossible
9. c<u>e</u>de, b<u>e</u>nd, st<u>e</u>m, t<u>e</u>nder
10. m<u>ai</u>d, l<u>ei</u>sure, <u>ei</u>ght, s<u>a</u>fe
11. s<u>ui</u>t, c<u>oo</u>l, <u>oo</u>ze, bl<u>oo</u>d
12. min<u>u</u>te, b<u>ui</u>lding, l<u>i</u>tter, f<u>ie</u>ld
13. c<u>ow</u>, c<u>oa</u>ch, d<u>ou</u>bt, ar<u>ou</u>se
14. c<u>a</u>lm, f<u>a</u>rm, c<u>au</u>se, b<u>a</u>rk
15. sl<u>a</u>ve, w<u>ei</u>ght, sk<u>a</u>te, ch<u>e</u>ss
16. l<u>ie</u>, th<u>igh</u>, sl<u>igh</u>t, l<u>i</u>t
17. c<u>ou</u>ntry, s<u>oa</u>p, c<u>o</u>ke, p<u>o</u>stage
18. h<u>u</u>g, <u>o</u>ther, bl<u>oo</u>d, beh<u>a</u>lf
19. w<u>a</u>nt, <u>o</u>bject, b<u>o</u>mb, m<u>o</u>ther
20. r<u>e</u>cipe, th<u>e</u>se, <u>e</u>dge, d<u>e</u>bt
21. st<u>a</u>lker, cl<u>o</u>thes, acr<u>o</u>ss, f<u>au</u>lt
22. p<u>ee</u>r, p<u>ea</u>r, f<u>ea</u>r, g<u>ea</u>r
23. s<u>i</u>de, p<u>ie</u>, r<u>i</u>sen, l<u>i</u>ce
24. r<u>a</u>ke, l<u>a</u>tter, ch<u>a</u>se, m<u>ai</u>nly

Exercise 6 Pronounced or Not?

🎧 다음 각 문장에 밑줄친 단어들은 묵음이 있는 단어들이다. 발음되지 않는 부분에 O로 표시한 후 녹음된 문장을 듣고 정확한 발음을 확인해 보자.

1. He knelt down and asked Fiona if there was any doubt in her mind.
2. The plumber kept knocking on the door, hearing several voices talking, but got no answer.
3. He fastened his seat belt and hastened to the hospital immediately.
4. She often takes a walk in her neighborhood, listening to music.
5. The mountain was so high that we couldn't get to the top within the day; we climbed all day, though.
6. He'd bought a birthday present for his eight-year old daughter, and just finished wrapping it up.
7. Matthew took out a knife from the cupboard and cut the doughnut in half to share with his younger brother.
8. They conducted a signature-collecting campaign opposing nuclear bomb tests, and thousands of people signed their names.
9. I was struck dumb by the grand scale of the castle, but it is unknown who designed it.
10. When Jessica sat the baby on her knee, she couldn't feel the weight of it.

Exercise 7 Sentence Stress

🎧 다음 문장을 읽고 강세가 와야 할 단어에 밑줄을 쳐 보자. 그리고 나서 녹음된 문장을 들으면서 강세가 바르게 표시되었는지 확인해 보자.

1. This guy in the newspaper is saying that the policy is fantastic!
2. That way, you won't have to worry about paying for your tuition.
3. Have you heard about the issue with the sculpture purchases?
4. I think it's really unfair to scrap the teams after what they have done for the school.
5. Telling freshmen that they can't bring a car to school won't help them settle in school.
6. My schedule has been crazy ever since I heard about that stupid policy.
7. Students who want to work aren't limited to finding jobs at the computer labs.
8. The woman is upset because she hasn't gotten into a class that she needs to graduate.
9. Her problems with finances will be more manageable with a full scholarship.
10. The woman says that he could ask his friends to move his things for him.

Appendix 2 — Note-Taking

*i*BT 토플의 가장 큰 변화는 노트필기가 가능하다는 것이다. 모든 내용을 기억력에 의존할 수 없으므로 새로이 시행되는 *i*BT 토플은 시험 내내 제공되는 종이에 노트필기가 허용된다. 다양한 유형의 문제에 대해 제한된 짧은 시간 내에 생각을 정리하고 답변을 해야 하는 Speaking에서는 노트필기의 필요성이 더욱 절실하다. 효과적인 노트 필기를 이용한 고득점 전략을 세워보는 것이 좋겠다. 다음의 사항들에 유의하여 자신만의 노트 필기 방법을 만들어 가며 연습을 하도록 하자.

자신만의 형식을 만들자.

☐ 빠르고 간단하며 효과적으로 노트를 하지 못한다면 노트 필기를 하는 의미가 없다. 이를 위해 자신만의 방식으로 노트 필기를 할 필요가 있다. 노트 필기를 하는데 정해진 규칙이 있는 것은 아니다. 스스로에게 익숙하고 편한 방식을 찾을 필요가 있다.

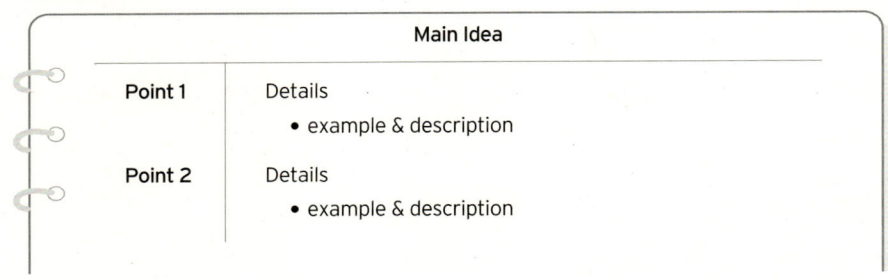

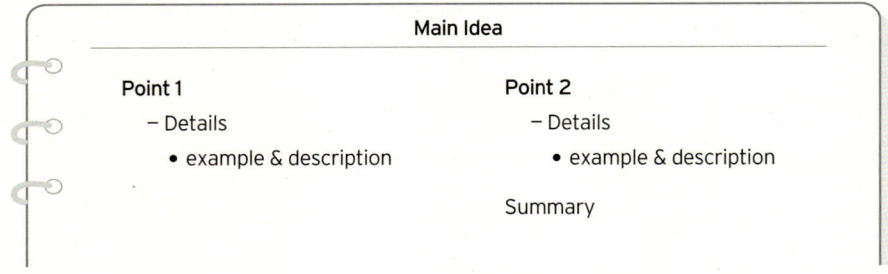

2 시간을 절약하자.

❏ 제한된 시간 내에 생각을 적거나, 독해지문을 읽고 청취지문을 듣는 동안 내용을 기록해야 하기 때문에 긴 단어나 문장을 그대로 옮겨 적기는 쉽지가 않다. 기호나 약어 등을 이용하면 노트 필기를 하는데 드는 시간을 절약 할 수 있을 뿐 아니라, 필기를 짧고도 효과적으로 하는데 도움이 된다.

❏ 기호(Symbol)
- 기호를 사용하여 언급된 내용들간의 관계를 표시하자. 빠르게 노트필기를 할 수 있을 뿐 아니라 한눈에 내용을 파악하기 쉬워 응답을 하는데 많은 도움을 준다. 자기만 알아보는 기호를 사용하는 것도 중요하지만 공통적으로 많이 사용되는 기호들을 사용한다면 내용파악을 하는데 혼동을 줄일 수 있을 것이다.

- 기호(Symbol) 사용의 예

Symbol	Meaning	Example
→	lead to, cause, mean	smoking → cancer
←	come from, because of	field trip canceled ← rain
↓	decrease	unemployment ↓ labor market
↑	increase	profit ↑ April
@	at	dinner @ French restaurant
&	and	Smith & Jones' Attorneys
/	per	hours / day
∴	therefore	I think ∴ I am
∵	because	actions ∵ policy

- Mathematical Symbols

Symbol	Meaning	Example
+	plus, in addition, also	ride bike + skate board
=	is equal to, to be	Seoul = largest city in Korea
≠	is not same, not to be, false	diet drink ≠ real
#(#s)	number (numbers)	Q 4 answer → #2
X	times	5 x increasing
〉	greater than, more important	5 〉π
〈	less than	my salary 〈 Tony
~	approximately, more or less	sum ~ 300
$	cost, price, dollars	Price = $50,000
≒	almost same	a ≒ b

❏ 약어(Abbreviation)의 사용
- 영어의 단어를 그대로 적기 보다는 단어의 철자를 줄여서 일부만 적는다면 노트필기 하는 시간을 절약할 뿐 아니라 필기를 짧게 하는데 도움이 된다. 하지만 약어를 사용할 때 글자를 너무 많이 줄이면 나중에 어떤 단어를 적은 것인지 구분 할 수 없게 될 수 있으므로 주의 해야 한다.

- 보통 첫 음절 이후에 나오는 모음을 생략하거나, 모음을 생략하고 자음으로만 발음 구분이 가능한 범위 내에서 약어를 만드는 경우가 많다. 약어를 만드는 정해진 규칙이 있는 것이 아니므로 자신만의 약어를 만드는 방법을 찾아서 연습할 필요가 있다.

- 약어 사용의 예

Abbreviation	Meaning	Example
w/	with	degree w/ distinction
w/o	without	Available w/o charge
s.th	something	s.th happens
i.e.	that is, in other words	courses, i.e. studies
cf.	compare	cf. original text
e.g.	example	Mammals e.g. whales
etc.	et cetera, and so on	insects, scorpions etc.
b/c	because	high prices b/c high wages
esp.	especially	employees esp. clerks
min.	minimum	yield min. 100 units
max.	maximum	max. 1000 units
ASAP	As soon as possible	Send data ASAP
re.	reference	re. August sales figures
yr.	year	Average from yr.
b/4	before	to yr.work b/4 leisure
Co.	company	the firm of Smith & Co.
comm.	communication	refer comm. department
gov't	government	gov't offices
prof.	professor	Pro. Wilson
btw	between	btw 15 & 30 kg
info	information	info society

Appendix 3 — Power Vocabulary

1 Campus-Related

Office Hours

absence note	결석계
academic advisor	지도 교수
academic warning	학사 경고
accreditation	허가, 인가
advance registration	조기 수강 신청
advanced course	상급 과정
alumni association	동문회
application	신청, 응용
assistantship	조교직
audit	청강하다
certificate	증명서
community college	지역 전문 대학
conditional admission	조건부 입학
course syllabus	강의 계획안
cram	(벼락치기로) 공부하다
credit	학점
credit system	학점 단위제
deadline	마감일
criterion	기준
dean	학장
dean's list	장학생 명단
dissertation	(박사) 논문
doctorate	박사 과정의
donation	기부금
drop	수강을 철회하다
dropout	중퇴
elective course	선택 과정
evaluation	평가
extension	연장
faculty	학과, 교수진
field trip	현장 학습
flunk	낙제하다
footnote	주석
graduation requirement	졸업 필수 과목
grant	장학금
lecturer	강사
matriculate	입학을 허가하다
mentor	지도교수
plagiarism	표절
preliminary	예비의
prerequisite	전제조건
probation	근신 기간, 수습 기간
proficiency	숙달
proofread	교정하다
quote	인용하다
recommendation	추천장
reference book	참고 도서
register / sign up for	등록하다
remedial	보충의
repeater	유급생
required course	전공 필수 과정
skip	월반하다
spring semester	봄 학기
student council	학생 자치 위원회
submit	제출하다
transcript	성적 증명서
transfer	학점을 교환하다
tuition fee	학비
tuition waiver	수업료 면제

Service Encountrers

☐ accommodation	숙박시설	☐ loan	대출
☐ account number	예금 구좌	☐ maintenance office	관리 사무실
☐ auditorium	강당	☐ maturity	만기
☐ bibliography	도서 목록	☐ medical excuse	질병 사유서
☐ brochure	소책자	☐ off campus	교외
☐ call number	도서 정리 번호	☐ paperback	염가 도서
☐ career center	취업 정보실	☐ parking permit	주차 허가증
☐ carrel	개인 열람석	☐ past due notice	반납 요청서
☐ charity bazaar	자선 바자회	☐ postgraduate	대학원생
☐ checkbook	수표책	☐ prospective	지망생, 예비생
☐ circulation desk	대출계	☐ qualify	자격을 주다
☐ commencement	학위 수여식	☐ resident assistant	기숙사 조교
☐ deposit	보증금	☐ school directory	학교 편람
☐ deposit slip	예금 전표	☐ signboard	게시판
☐ dormitory(=dorm)	기숙사	☐ sorority	여학생 동호회
☐ extracurricular activities	과외 활동	☐ sports facilities	스포츠 시설
☐ field	(연구, 활동) 분야	☐ student council	학생 자치회
☐ fraternity	남학생 동호회	☐ student identification	학생증
☐ furnished	가구가 딸려 있는	☐ student union	학생 회관
☐ GPA(grade point average)	성적 평균점	☐ subscription	예약 구독
☐ gymnasium	체육관	☐ utility fee	공과금
☐ infirmary	학교 부설 진료소	☐ vacancy	결원
☐ inter-library loan	타 도서관 대여 제도	☐ varsity	대학 대표팀
☐ job fair	취업 박람회	☐ vending machine	자판기
☐ late fee	연체료	☐ workshop	강습

2 Academic

Psychology

☐ acquisition	습득, 획득	☐ apathetic	무관심한, 냉담한
☐ aggression	공격성	☐ assimilation	동화
☐ altruistic	이타적인	☐ attribution	특성, 속성
☐ amnesia	기억상실증	☐ catharsis	정화, 카타르시스
☐ analysis	분석	☐ cognition	인지, 인식력
☐ compliance	응낙, 순종	☐ conation	의욕, 능동
☐ compulsion	강박현상	☐ conform	순응하다

delusion	망상	invariant	불변
disillusion	환상을 깨우치다	manifest	(감정을) 표명하다
dissonance	불일치, 부조화	motivation	동기부여
egocentric	자기 중심의	norm	표준, 전형
enthusiasm	의욕, 열중	observe	관찰하다, 주시하다
extroversion	외향성	operant	자발적인
fallacy	허위, 착오	plasticity	적응성
frustration	욕구 불만	panic	공황
habituate	길들이다	perception	지각
hostile	적대적인	perversion	성도착, 남용
hypnosis	최면(술)	phobia	공포
hypothetical	가설의	puberty	사춘기
illusion	환각, 환영	receptive	감수성이 풍부한
impulse	충동	regress	퇴보하다
incubation	부화, 보육	reinforce	강화하다
inference	추론	resentment	분노
insanity	광기, 정신이상	retrieval	회복, 복구
internalization	내면화	self-awareness	자각, 자기 인식
introversion	내향성	self-esteem	자존심, 자부심
intuition	직관, 직감	stimulus	자극, 격려

Biology

absorb	흡수하다, 빨아들이다	circulation	순환하다
adapt	적응하다, 순응하다	clone	복제하다
aerobic	유산소의	cohesion	점착, 결합
algae	해조류	compound	합성물
amphibian	양서류	conjugation	접합
anabolism	동화작용	deciduous	낙엽성의
anatomy	해부학	digest	소화하다
antibody	항독소	diversity	다양성
antigen	항원	dominance	우월, 군림
breed	양육하다	duplication	복제, 복사
capture	포획하다	ecosystem	생태계
carbohydrate	탄수화물	embryo	태아
carbon dioxide	이산화탄소	endangered	멸종위기에 처한
carnivore	육식 동물	enzyme	효소
catabolism	분해작용	eradicate	박멸하다
chlorophyll	엽록소	eugenics	우생학

☐ extinct	멸종된, 절멸한	☐ microbe	미생물의
☐ ferment	발효, 발효시키다	☐ molar	어금니
☐ fertilization	수정, 수태	☐ mortality	사망률
☐ gene	유전자	☐ multiply	번식시키다
☐ germ	세균	☐ mutate	돌연 변이하다
☐ gland	내분비샘	☐ parasite	기생충
☐ habitat	서식지, 자생지	☐ respiration	호흡
☐ heredity	유전	☐ retina	망막
☐ host	숙주	☐ scope	범위
☐ hybrid	잡종	☐ secretion	분비 작용
☐ immune	면역성의	☐ solidify	응고하다
☐ inherit	유전	☐ trait	특징
☐ internal	체내의	☐ unicellular	단세포의
☐ metabolism	물질대사, 신진대사		

Business/Economics

☐ accumulation	축적	☐ downsizing	기구 축소
☐ agent	대리인	☐ drastically	과감하게
☐ asset	자본	☐ expenditure	지출, 소비
☐ auction	경매	☐ feasible	가능한
☐ bankruptcy	파산, 부도	☐ GDP	국민 소득
☐ barter	물물 교환	☐ impose	(세금 등을) 부과하다
☐ budget	예산	☐ inflation	물가 상승
☐ capitalism	자본주의	☐ interest	이자
☐ cartel	기업연합	☐ invest	투자하다
☐ census	인구조사	☐ labor union	노동조합
☐ commodity	필수품	☐ liquid capital	유동 자본
☐ consume	소비하다	☐ lucrative	돈이 벌리는, 유리한
☐ contract	줄어들다	☐ manufacturing	제조업의
☐ corporation	회사, 법인	☐ minimum wage	최저 임금
☐ currency	통화	☐ monopoly	전매, 독점
☐ deflation	통화 수축	☐ mortgage	저당
☐ demand	수요	☐ opportunity cost	기회 비용
☐ depression	불경기	☐ patent	특허
☐ devaluation	평가 절하	☐ penalty	위약금
☐ devastation	황폐	☐ profitability	수익성, 이윤

□ privilege	특권, 혜택	□ stock market	주식 시장
□ prosperity	번영	□ subsidize	보조금을 지급하다
□ quota	분담액	□ substitution	대체, 대용
□ recession	경기 후퇴	□ surplus	잉여
□ reimbursement	비용 상환	□ tariff	관세
□ revenue	소득액, 세입	□ thrifty	검소한
□ sanction	재가, 인가	□ transaction	거래, 매매
□ speculate	투기하다	□ utilities	공익 시설
□ stabilize	안정시키다	□ welfare	복지, 후생
□ statistics	통계		

Art & Literature

□ abridge	요약하다	□ dialect	방언, 사투리
□ absurd	부조리한	□ diffusion	전파, 확산
□ adhere	부착하다	□ dimension	치수, 넓이, 차원
□ aesthetic	미적인	□ distort	왜곡하다
□ allegory	우화	□ diversification	다양화
□ allusion	암시, 언급	□ draft	초안
□ ambiguous	모호한	□ empathy	감정이입
□ ambivalence	모순, 반대 감정 병존	□ epic	서사시
□ anonymous	익명의	□ erratic	산만한, 엉뚱한
□ apex	극치	□ evoke	불러 일으키다
□ applied art	응용 미술	□ excerpt	발췌, 인용구
□ appreciate	감상하다, 식별하다	□ explicit	명백한, 명시적인
□ assertive	단정적인	□ exposure	노출
□ authenticity	진정성	□ fictional	꾸며낸
□ calligraphy	서예	□ flamboyant	현란한
□ censorship	검열	□ heritage	유산, 전통
□ colloquial	구어체의	□ inspire	영감을 불어넣다
□ commentary	주석, 설명	□ limpid	투명한, 명쾌한
□ contemporary	현대의	□ linear	선적인, 선의
□ continuity	촬영 대본	□ literate	글을 읽고 쓸 줄 아는
□ contour	외곽	□ manipulate	솜씨 있게 처리하다, 교묘하게 다루다, 조종하다
□ cynical	냉소적인		
□ denotation	표시, 상징, 명시적 의미	□ manuscript	원고, 초고
□ density	농도	□ metaphor	은유, 암유
□ depict	묘사하다	□ monologue	독백

motif	주제, 테마	rendering	표현
ornament	꾸밈, 장식	resurrect	부활시키다
paradox	역설	rhyme	각운
personification	의인화	sarcasm	비꼼, 빈정거림
perspective	원근법, 전망	satire	풍자
pigment	안료, 색소	scaffold	발판
plagiarize	표절하다	scale	음계
plausible	진짜 같은, 그럴 듯한	solemn	장엄한
plot	줄거리	sturdy	튼튼한
projection	투사, 돌출	subsequent	후속의
prominent	탁월한	symmetry	대칭
proportion	균형, 비율	tangible	실체적인
prose	산문	transition	변화, 변이
quote	인용하다	transparent	투명한
recite	낭독하다	verse	운문, 시

Technology

abacus	주판	detect	탐지하다
abrasion	(물리적) 부식	device	장치
accelerate	촉진하다	durability	내구성
all-purpose	다목적의	elastic	신축적인
arithmetic	산수의, 계산상의	enlargement	확대한 것, 확장, 확대
assembler	부호 번역기	equivalent	~에 해당하는
bandwidth	전송 용량	executable	실행할 수 있는
binary	이진법의	gravity	중력
breakthrough	돌파	infect	감염시키다
capability	용량	interface	접속하다, 연결하다
circuit	회로	inverted	거꾸로 된
compatible	호환성이 있는	luminous	빛을 내는
complexity	복잡성	magnify	확장하다
compression	압축	mainframe	본체
computation	연산, 계산	malfunction	기능장애
conductor	전도체	manually	수동으로
configuration	(시스템의)환경 설정	mechanism	장치, 구조
corrosion	(화학적) 부식	obsolete	쓸모 없이 된
coverage	적용 범위	optical	광학상의, 빛의
CPU(central processing unit)	중앙 처리 장치	particle	미립자

☐ peripheral device	주변 장치	☐ sphere	원
☐ pilot	시험적인	☐ strain	변형
☐ pixel	화소	☐ supplant	밀어내다
☐ portable	휴대할 수 있는	☐ terminal	단말기
☐ probability	확률	☐ throughput	처리량
☐ propel	추진하다	☐ transistor	증폭 장치
☐ prototype	시제품	☐ transmission	전송, 송신
☐ reinforcing	강화	☐ transmit	전송하다
☐ retrieval	검색	☐ velocity	속도
☐ sequence	순서	☐ via	경유로, ~을 거쳐

HOOKED ON TOEFL SPEAKING

Orientation

I. TOEFL *i*BT/ Next Generation TOEFL

II. 점수 환산 기준

I. TOEFL *i*BT/Next Generation TOEFL

2005년 9월을 기점으로 1998년 미국에서부터 시행된 TOEFL CBT은 인터넷을 기반으로 하는 TOEFL *i*BT 체제로 바뀌었다. 일부에서는 새롭게 시행되는 토플에 한국인들이 특히 강한 문법이 없어지고 한국인들이 상대적으로 약한 Speaking이 추가되어 이제 토플로 고득점을 획득하기는 어려울 것이라 생각하는 경우가 있는 것 같다. 하지만 새로운 토플을 면밀히 분석하여 그에 맞는 공부 방법으로 철저히 대비한다면 *i*BT에서도 고득점을 얻는 것이 충분히 가능하다.

1. TOEFL이란?

TOEFL (Test of English as a Foreign Language)은 영어가 모국어가 아닌 사람(EFL학습자 또는 nonnative speakers of English)이 미국, 캐나다 등 영어 사용권 국가의 대학이나 대학원에 입학할 경우 치러야 하는 영어 사용 능력 검정시험이다. TOEFL시험은 미국 New Jersey주의 Princeton에 본부를 둔 ETS (Educational Testing Service)의 주관으로 전세계적으로 시행되고 있으며 5,000여 대학이나 교육기관에서 공인시험으로 인정하고 있다.

❋ **What is ETS?**
ETS는 Educational Testing Service의 약자다. ETS는 1947년에 설립된 미국 북동부의 New Jersey에 위치한 국가공인 시험 전문 비영리기관(Nonprofit Institution)이다. ETS는 TOEFL 등 영어에 대한 시험뿐만 아니라 미국의 고등학교, 대학교, 대학원 입학에 관련된 영어, 수학, 논리, 전공에 대한 시험을 주관한다. ETS에서 주관하는 대표적인 시험으로는 SAT (미국 대학 입학 능력 평가), GRE (미국 대학원 입학 능력 평가), GMAT (미국 경영대학원 입학 능력 평가), LSAT (미국 법대 입학 능력 평가) 등이 있다. 합격 또는 불합격에 대한 판정은 하지 않으며 단지 해당 시험 분야에 대한 능력만을 평가한다.

2. TOEFL *i*BT란?

2006년부터 전세계적으로 새롭게 시행되고 있는 인터넷 기반의 새로운 토플 시험을 Next Generation TOEFL (차세대 토플) 또는 TOEFL *i*BT (Internet-based Test) 라고 한다.

❋ TOEFL *i*BT는 2005-2006년에 걸쳐 순차적으로 전세계적으로 시행되었다.
  ✓ 2005년 9월 – 미국에서 시행
  ✓ 2005년 10월 – 캐나다, 독일, 프랑스, 이탈리아 등 4개국에서 시행
  ✓ 2006년 – 한국을 포함, 전세계적으로 시행(한국에서는 2006년 9월 시행)

❋ TOEFL *i*BT는 인터넷을 기반으로 ETS에서 지정한 날짜(주로 금요일과 토요일)에 연중 30-40회 정도 시행이 되며, 시험장소가 대폭 확대되어 가까운 곳에서 편리하게 시험을 볼 수 있다.

❋ TOEFL *i*BT의 시험 등록은 인터넷, 메일, 전화 등 다양한 매체를 통해 가능하며, 비용은 $140~$170이다.

3 TOEFL iBT의 주요 변화

❏ **문법(Structure)이 없어지고 Speaking이 추가**

새로운 토플에서는 기존의 structure 평가영역이 사라지고 실제 의사소통 기능을 갖는 통합형 평가 방식 위주의 speaking이 보강되었다.

✱ 이는 문법이나 영어구조에 대한 학습은 중요하지 않고 speaking이 더 중요하다는 의미는 아니다. 우리와 같이 제한된 시간에만 영어에 노출되어 있는 EFL환경에서는 문법과 어휘 등 언어구조에 대한 학습이 필수적이라는 인식에는 이견이 없다. 따라서 새로운 토플 체제하에서도 문법학습은 여전히 중요하다고 할 수 있다.

❏ **통합형 문제(Integrated Tasks)의 도입**

영어를 사용하는 실제 환경의 구현을 위해 [읽고+듣고+쓰기]와 같은 실제 의사소통 기능을 갖는 통합형 평가 방식(Integrated-Skills Approach)의 문제가 출제된다. 새롭게 도입된 통합형 문제 유형은 다음과 같다.

Read / Listen / Speak
Listen / Speak
Read / Listen / Write

❏ **Core Academic Skills Assessment 강화**

기존의 영어시험이 제시된 영어문장의 이해도를 주로 평가하는 것이라면 새로운 토플은 note taking, paraphrasing, synthesizing, summarizing 등과 같은 영어로 수업을 진행하는데 필요한 실질적인 능력(Core Academic Skills)을 요구하고 있다.

❏ **Reading과 Listening의 난이도는 현재의 CBT와 같은 수준**

외형상 새로운 토플에 많은 변화가 있기는 하지만 Reading과 Listening은 대부분 기존에 익숙한 CBT 문제 유형을 그대로 사용하고 있다. 또한 새로운 토플에 등장하는 문장의 구조나 어휘범위, 토픽 범위, Writing Topics 등이 기존의 CBT와 동일한 수준이다.

4 TOEFL iBT의 각 영역별 개요

	Reading (독해)	Listening (청취)	Speaking (말하기)	Writing (작문)

구성	• 총 지문 수: 3-5개
	• 총 문제 수: 36-70개
	• 각 지문 당 문제 수: 12-14개
	• 각 지문 당 단락 수: 4-8개
	• 각 지문 당 어휘 수: 약 700단어
		• Conversation: 2-3개
		• Lecture: 4-6개 (Interactive Lecture 2-3개; Academic Lecture 2-3개)
		• Conversation은 2-3분 정도 (400-500단어의 길이), Lecture는 4-5분 정도 (600-800단어의 길이)
		• 2-3개의 Conversation (각 5문제씩)과 4-6개의 Lecture (각 6문제씩)에서 총 34-51문제 출제
			• Independent Speaking (개별 말하기): 2문제
			• Integrated Speaking (통합형 말하기시험): 4문제 (읽고 듣고 말하기 2문제; 듣고 말하기 2문제)
			• Integrated Speaking의 독해 지문은 75-100단어 수준으로 45초의 읽기시간이 주어진다.
			• Integrated Speaking의 듣기 지문은 150-280단어 수준으로 1-2분 정도의 길이다.
			• 총 6문제 출제
				• Integrated Writing (통합형 작문): 1문제(20분 동안 150-225단어 정도 작성)
				  - Integrated Writing의 독해 지문은 230-300단어 수준으로 3분의 읽기시간이 주어진다.
				  - Integrated Writing의 듣기지문은 230-300단어 수준으로 2분 정도의 길이다.
				• Independent Writing (개별 작문): 1문제(30분 동안 최소한 300단어 이상 작성)
				• 총 2문제 출제

시간	총 60-100분 (각 지문당 20분씩)	대략 60-90분 정도(듣는 시간을 제외하고 실제 문제를 푸는데 걸리는 시간은 20-30분)	대략 20분	대략 50분 (Integrated Writing: 20분; Independent Writing: 30분)
문제 유형	(1) Vocabulary Questions (2) Reference Questions (3) Sentence Simplification Questions (4) Factual Information Questions (5) Negative Fact Questions (6) Inference Questions (7) Rhetorical Purpose Questions (8) Insert Text Questions (9) Prose Summary Questions (10) Classifying, Categorizing, and Organizing Information Questions	(1) Main Idea Questions (2) Supporting Detail Questions (3) Organization Questions (4) Organization-Rhetorical Connection Questions (5) Content-Identifying Relationship Questions (6) Content-Linking Questions (7) Stance / Attitude Questions (8) Function-Purpose Questions	(1) Independent Speaking Personal Preference (2) Independent Speaking Paired Choice (3) Reading / Listening / Speaking Campus Situation Topic (4) Reading / Listening / Speaking Academic Course Topic (5) Listening / Speaking Campus Situation Topic (6) Listening / Speaking Academic Course Topic	(1) Reading / Listening / Writing Academic Course Topic (2) Independent Writing based on Experience & Knowledge
특징	• Glossary (어휘사전) 제공: 단어를 클릭하면 해당 단어의 설명이 나타난다. • Review (복습) 기능: 체크한 답과 그렇지 않은 답의 상태를 알 수 있어 그냥 지나간 문제를 확인할 수 있다. • 각 지문의 제목이 제시된다. • 문제는 보통 지문의 순서대로 주어지며, 문제가 왼쪽에, 지문이 오른쪽에 제시된다.	• Note Taking (받아적기) 가능: 듣는 동안에 요점을 종이에 쓸 수 있다. • 강의의 핵심 구문을 모니터 상에 제시한다. • 들은 내용을 그대로 다시 들려주고 푸는 Replay Item을 도입했다.	• Note Taking을 이용해 효율적으로 Speaking Task의 답변을 준비할 수 있다. • Independent Speaking은 일상 생활의 경험에 관한 질문 등 매우 익숙한 토픽에 대한 질문이다. • Integrated Speaking은 읽고 들은 내용을 바탕으로 Speaking Task가 주어진다. • 각 문제당 15-30초 정도의 답변 준비 시간이 주어지고 실제 답변 시간은 45초 또는 60초다.	• Note Taking을 이용해 효율적으로 Writing Task의 답변을 준비할 수 있다. • Independent Writing의 주제는 기존의 CBT TOEFL의 185 Writing Topics와 거의 동일하다. • Integrated Writing은 읽고 들은 내용을 바탕으로 Writing Task가 주어진다.

5 TOEFL iBT의 점수체계

❏ Next Generation TOEFL Scores

Four skill scores

Reading: 0 – 30
Listening: 0 – 30
Speaking: 0 – 30
Writing: 0 – 30
Total score: 0 – 120

* 각 영역별(Reading, Listening, Speaking, and Writing)로 0-30의 scale로 할당되며 total 120 scale이 만점이다. 또한 성적통지표에는 4개의 영역 점수(four skill scores)와 더불어 total score난이 별도로 표기된다.

* Score Report는 테스트 후 15일 이후에 온라인에서 확인하거나 우편으로 받아볼 수 있다.

❏ 각 영역별 배점체계

	Reading (독해)	Listening (청취)	Speaking (말하기)	Writing (작문)
구 성	• 보통 문제당 1점의 원점수가 주어진다. • Prose Summary Questions나 Classifying, Categorizing, and Organizing Information Questions 문제 유형은 부분 점수가 부여되는 Partial-Credit Item으로 0-4점 사이의 원점수가 부여된다. • 모든 원점수를 합하여 30점 만점으로 환산한다.	• 보통 문제당 1점의 원점수가 주어진다. • 일부 Supporting Detail Questions 문제의 경우 2점의 원점수가 주어질 수 있다. 이 경우, 해당 문제에 점수기준이 명시되어 있다. • 모든 원점수를 합하여 30점 만점으로 환산한다.	• Scoring Rubrics를 바탕으로 각 문제당 0-4점 사이의 원점수가 주어진다. • 6명의 human raters에 의해 채점된다. • 모든 원점수를 합하여 30점 만점으로 환산한다.	• Scoring Rubrics를 바탕으로 각 문제당 0-5점 사이의 원점수가 주어진다. • 2명의 human raters에 의해 채점된다. • 모든 원점수를 합하여 30점 만점으로 환산한다.
문제 수	36-70	34-51	6	2
환산점수	0-30	0-30	0-30	0-30

* 한국인의 토플 평균 점수는 200-210점(CBT기준)으로 추산된다. 이는 링구아 토플시리즈의 *i*-TOEFL단계에 해당하는 수준으로 약 5,000-6,000단어 정도의 어휘력을 갖는 것으로 추정하며, 이를 링구아 토플 중급학습자로 분류한다.

* 보통 미국 대학에서 요구하는 토플 점수는 213점(CBT기준)으로 TOEFL *i*BT 80점에 해당하는 점수이다.

II. 점수 환산 기준

TOEFL Total Score Comparison

Internet-based Total	Computer-based Total	Paper-based Total
120	300	677
120	297	673
119	293	670
118	290	667
117	287	660-663
116	283	657
114-115	280	650-653
113	277	647
111-112	273	640-643
110	270	637
109	267	630-633
106-108	263	623-627
105	260	617-620
103-104	257	613
101-102	253	607-610
100	250	600-603
98-99	247	597
96-97	243	590-593
94-95	240	587
92-93	237	580-583
90-91	233	577
88-89	230	570-573
86-87	227	567
84-85	223	563
83	220	557-560
81-82	217	553
79-80	213	550
77-78	210	547
76	207	540-543
74-75	203	537
72-73	200	533
71	197	527-530
69-70	193	523
68	190	520
66-67	187	517
65	183	513
64	180	507-510
62-63	177	503
61	173	500
59-60	170	497
58	167	493
57	163	487-490
56	160	483
54-55	157	480
53	153	477
52	150	470-473
51	147	467
49-50	143	463
48	140	460
47	137	457
45-46	133	450-453
44	130	447
43	127	443
41-42	123	437-440
40	120	433
39	117	430
38	113	423-427
36-37	110	420
35	107	417
34	103	410-413
33	100	407
32	97	400-403
30-31	93	397
29	90	390-393
28	87	387
26-27	83	380-383
25	80	377
24	77	370-373
23	73	363-367
22	70	357-360
21	67	353
19-20	63	347-350
18	60	340-343
17	57	333-337
16	53	330
15	50	323-327
14	47	317-320
13	43	313
12	40	310
11	37	310
9	33	310
8	30	310
7	27	310
6	23	310
5	20	310
4	17	310
3	13	310
2	10	310
1	7	310
0	3	310
0	0	310

Range Comparison

Internet-based Total	Computer-based Total	Paper-based Total
111-120	273-300	640-677
96-110	243-270	590-637
79-95	213-240	550-587
65-78	183-210	513-547
53-64	153-180	477-510
41-52	123-150	437-473
30-40	93-120	397-433
19-29	63-90	347-393
9-18	33-60	310-343
0-8	0-30	310

Converting Rubric Scores to Scaled Scores
Speaking Section of the New TOEFL *i*BT Test

Speaking Rubric Mean	Scaled Score
4.00	30
3.83	29
3.66	28
3.50	27
3.33	26
3.16	24
3.00	23
2.83	22
2.66	20
2.50	19
2.33	18
2.16	17
2.00	15
1.83	14
1.66	13
1.50	11
1.33	10
1.16	9
1.00	8
	6
	5
	4
	3
	1
	0

Final iBT

http://www.finalibt.co.kr

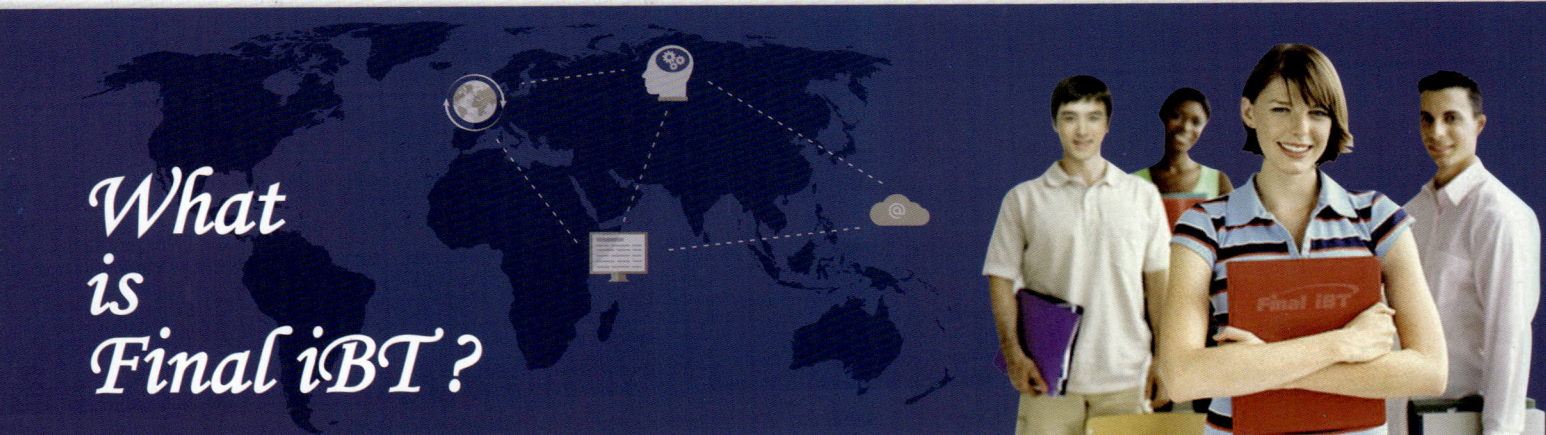

What is Final iBT?

 1

Final iBT는 TOEFL 시험을 준비하는 학습자를 위한 완벽한 준비 도구로서 실제 IBT시험을 치르는 것과 같은 full-length의 연습테스트를 제공합니다. 지난 시험들을 통해 철저히 분석된 문제들을 연습하게 되며 48시간 이내에 점수를 받아볼 수 있습니다.

 2

시험을 마친 후 상세한 그래프와 함께 자신의 점수를 분석할 수 있습니다. 또한 자신이 풀었던 문제와 답뿐만 아니라 Reading, Listening, Speaking, Writing의 스크립트를 제공받아 철저한 복습이 가능합니다.
Final iBT는 토플 모의 시험으로써 토플 준비를 위한 완벽한 학습 자료가 될 것입니다.

시험 구성

: 시험 구성은 다음과 같습니다.

Level	Test Version	Questions (문항)			
		Reading	Listening	Speaking	Writing
고급	Full	39~42	34	6	2
	Short	14~28	17	3	1
	Half (R/L)	39~42	34	X	X
	Half (S/W)	X	X	6	2
초급	Short	21~24	13	2	1

* 총 40회분의 시험이 제공됩니다.

http://www.finalibt.co.kr

고득점으로 가는 최적의 토플 iBT 종합서
NEW EDITION
HOOKED ON
TOEFL
SPEAKING

Answer Key & Explanations

- 고득점을 위한 세분화된 Speaking 연습
- 각 유형별 핵심 전략 제시
- 최다 실전 문제 수록
- MP3 파일 다운로드
- 실전과 동일한 시험환경 제공

LinguaForum

HOOKED ON TOEFL SPEAKING

Answer Key
& Explanations

Contents

PART I	Task Types	**A** 3
PART II	Practice Test	**A** 44
PART III	Actual Test	**A** 87
Appendix		**A** 95

PART I Task Types

TASK 01 Personal Preference

Pre-Speaking p14

STEP 1 • Basic Outlining

2

Topic	Park Ji-Sung	
Reason 1 Humility		**Reason 2** He is good at what he does.
Details • Humble despite his pre-eminence • No exaggeration & Never get overexcited • Focus on doing his best		**Details** • Continues to strive for excellence. • Honest effort made him the best.

3

Topic	Organic farm	
Reason 1 Taste a lot of fruit for free		**Reason 2** Taste different kinds of fruits
Details Organic farm in Seoul • Fresh Fruit Festival		**Details** Organic farm in Seoul • Fresh Fruit Festival

4

Topic	Learn to ski	
Reason 1 Race on the snow		**Reason 2** Feel healthy
Details Snow ski game • Downhill Skiing Competition.		**Details** Used to catch a cold. • No cold medicine taken • Good workouts

5

Topic	Play violin	
Reason 1 Receive attention and applause		**Reason 2** Have something to be proud of
Details Musicians get the sense of admiration.		**Details** Music Scholarship in college and other opportunities.

6

Topic: Watch a movie or a play

Reason 1	Reason 2
An ice breaker for conversation.	Find out each other's opinions
Details	**Details**
Have something in common. Nothing to talk about is awkward.	Get to know more.

7

Topic: My happiness depends on me

Reason 1	Reason 2
Learn to be independent	More matured
Details	**Details**
Realized that I shouldn't depend on others	Seek self-satisfaction.

8

Topic: Love

Reason 1	Reason 2
Without love, can't teach for a long time.	Can't improve the quality of education
Details	**Details**
My teacher quit- stress from students	Taught the same materials over and over. No interest in her profession.

Vocabulary

hangout 밖에 나가 시간을 보내다　　workout 운동, 체조　　applause 박수 갈채, 칭찬
have something to be proud of 무엇인가에 대해 자긍심을 갖다　　admiration 칭찬, 감탄　　have something in common 무엇인가 공통점을 가지다
awkward 어색한, 불편한, 서투른　　independent 독립적인　　self-satisfaction 자기 만족　　profession 직업

STEP 2 • Speaking

Topic -- p17

2 Without a doubt, the famous person that I admire as my hero is Park Ji-Sung.

3 I would say that my visit to an organic farm was my favorite hangout.

4 As far as I'm concerned, the most enjoyable activity I did last year was to learn to ski.

5 I think I would go back to the time I was starting out with the violin if I could travel back in time.

6 I believe I would like to watch a movie or a theatrical performance on my date.

7 My best friend moved to another state, and it seems to me the most valuable lesson I learned from this is that my happiness solely is and should be up to my own self; that I shouldn't anchor my happiness to other people.

8 In my opinion, the most important quality of a good teacher is love.

Reason -- p19

2 ❶ One of the reasons why I chose Park Ji-Sung is because of his humility. ❷ The other reason is that he is extremely good at what he does.

3 ❶ One reason why I love this farm is because I could taste a lot of fruit for free. ❷ I like the farm also because I could taste various different kinds of fruit.

4 ❶ First, it's so exciting to race on the snow. ❷ Second, I felt healthier than ever before.

5 ❶ First, I want to be in the center of attention and be applauded by people. ❷ Second, I would then have something to be proud of that's not so common.

6 ❶ What I like about watching a movie or a play is that it can serve as an ice breaker for our conversations throughout the date. ❷ The other reason is that this will also lead us to finding out about each other's point of view, personal opinions and such.

7 ❶ One of the reasons why I consider this experience to be valuable is because I learned to be independent as I go through this harsh experience of parting. ❷ Another reason is that I could become a more fulfilled person as I go through this experience.

8 ❶ One reason why I consider love to be important is because teachers can't teach for a long time unless they have genuine love for students. ❷ Another reason is that teachers can't improve their quality of education if they don't have love for their profession.

Detail -- p22

2 ❶ For example, he is always humble despite his pre-eminence. He doesn't exaggerate his ability or get overexcited even when performing his best. He just persistently focuses on doing his best. ❷ I mean he never settles down and he continues to strive for excellence. This honest effort enabled him to be one of the finest soccer players in the world. For this reason, he is my role model and hero.

3 ❶ To give you a specific example, I will talk about my experience of having much fruit for free at an organic farm. I went to a small organic farm located in Seoul, and they held an event called the Fresh Fruit Festival. On this day, I could try various fruits for free. ❷ To illustrate, I not only had a lot of fruit for free, but also tasted various different kinds of fruits including apples, grapes, peaches, and pears. It definitely was my favorite hangout and became an enjoyable memory.

4 ❶ What I am saying is that I was so thrilled skiing in the mountains. Last year I enjoyed participating in a snow ski game called the Downhill Skiing Competition. Once again, I realized that skiing is a fascinating sport. ❷ In other words, I could enjoy the winter and didn't have to take cold medicine and rest in bed doing nothing. In fact, I didn't even catch a cold this winter as I constantly did the skiing exercises and workouts.
I am so thankful that I not only had enjoyable activities but also felt healthier than ever before this winter.

5 ❶ When looking at those who can play a musical instrument very well, to give a specific example, the sense of admiration people give them is irreplaceable. ❷ What I am saying is that I have a regret in letting my own opportunity pass me by. If I'd continued with it, I could have tried out for a music scholarship in college that would've aided me financially.

6 ❶ I mean it will give us the chance to have or talk about something in common. We can avoid awkward moments having nothing to talk about in particular. ❷ I mean experiencing something together will allow us to know each other on a more personal level.

7 ❶ I got really depressed for a few days when my best friend moved to another state. But I find this experience valuable because it taught me to stand by myself without depending on others. ❷ In other words, I learned that I have to do things that are geared toward my own welfare instead of that of others first.

8 ❶ For instance, my high school teacher quit her job because she got too much stress from students. She couldn't understand the students' situations and embrace them when troubles occurred among students. ❷ To illustrate, my teacher taught the same materials over and over. She didn't even think about improving the quality of her teaching materials due to her lack of interests in her profession. She didn't love what she was doing. Thus, love is the most important quality to be a good teacher.

Practice Questions

1

Sample Outlining

Topic	Rainy weather	
Reason 1		**Reason 2**
Feel the sense of peace		Cleansing effect
Details		**Details**
It drowns out noise -the sounds of car, bus, etc • helps me sleep		Smog and chemicals are washed away • fresh air, good for health

Sample Response

I like rainy weather because of the sound of the rain. I feel a sense of peace hearing the falling rain on the streets and rooftops. It drowns out the rest of the bustling noise. I won't have to bear the sound of the cars and buses, and if I'm at home, it helps me sleep more peacefully. Another reason is the cleansing effect of the rain. Our air suffers from all sorts of pollution. Whenever it rains, the smog and other chemical buildup in the air are washed away. This gives us fresher air to breathe, which is better for our health.

2

Sample Outlining

Topic	Alfredo	
Reason 1 Makes jokes		**Reason 2** He is always there when needed
Details Become the ladies' favorite duo in class		**Details** Borrowed some money.

Sample Response

I have a friend named Alfredo, who is quite special to me. Alfredo is the same age as I. We were classmates in high school, and have been best friends ever since. He's kinda special because he makes the biggest jokes, and makes all the girls laugh, you know. And because of that we have become the ladies' favorite duo in class. Another thing is that he's always there when I need him. He is someone I can depend upon. I remember that when I badly needed some cash, he willingly helped me, although he was also short of money.

3

Sample Outlining

Topic	July	
Reason 1 My birthday		**Reason 2** Outdoor activities
Details Good weather Relatives and people I love gather together		**Details** Spend the days with friends

Sample Response

My favorite month is July, since my birthday falls in this month and because of the summer weather around this time of the year. I get to spend time with most of the people I care about every July because my relatives and friends celebrate my birthday with a party. I also enjoy the weather in July that allows me to engage in outdoor activities more. I get to spend the days with friends who are also on summer break.

Vocabulary

cleansing effect 깨끗하게 하는 효과   smog 스모그 (공기 오염 물질)   chemicals 화학 제품 [약품]   drown out ~을 떠내려 보내다   bustling noise 떠들썩한 소음, 웅성거리는 소리   suffer from ~로부터 고통 당하다   breathe 숨을 쉬다   make jokes 농담하다   duo 2인조, 같은 종류의 2쌍으로 되어 있는 것   willingly 자진해서, 쾌히   relatives 친척, 인척, 동족   outdoor activity 야외활동   fall in ~안에 들어가다, 빠지다   celebrate 경축하다, 축하하다   engage in 참여하다   get to spend (시간이나 돈) 사용할 수 있다   summer break 여름 방학

TASK 02 Paired Choice

Pre-Speaking   p28

STEP 1 • Basic Outlining

2

Topic	Shopping w/ friends	
Reason 1	**Reason 2**	
More enjoyable	Helpful	
Details	**Details**	
Good way to spend time with friends	Get honest opinions about things to buy	

3

Topic	No plastic surgery	
Reason 1	**Reason 2**	
Inside is more important than appearance	Dangerous	
Details	**Details**	
Don't agree with the social value	Failure in surgery, infection Natural face is more appealing	

4

Topic	Adult supervision	
Reason 1	**Reason 2**	
Dangerous without adult supervision	Quality time	
Details	**Details**	
Might get lost Strangers	Heart-to-heart conversation Learn more about their children	

5

Topic	Study group	
Reason 1	**Reason 2**	
Encourage one another to study harder	Share notes and useful information	
Details	**Details**	
Many people come up with different opinions	Borrow notes when missing class, etc.	

6

Topic: Actual books

Reason 1
Reliability

Reason 2
Don't need to have a computer.

Details
False information is found online very often

Details
Convenient

7

Topic: Strict rules

Reason 1
Not much experience - can't make responsible decisions

Reason 2
Grow wild

Details
Don't think about consequences

Details
Rules teach them to care for others' needs
No harm

8

Topic: A part-time job

Reason 1
Learn to be under someone else's supervision

Reason 2
No safe feeling

Details
Ready for full-time work

Details
No special treatment

Vocabulary

plastic surgery 성형 수술   infection 전염, 감염   supervision 보호, 감시   quality time 사랑하는 가족이나 친구와 보낸 귀중한 시간
heart-to-heart conversation 마음이 통하는 대화, 진솔한 대화   reliability 신뢰할 수 있는, 믿음직한   convenient 편리한
responsible decision 책임 있는 결정, 책임을 져야 할 결정   full-time work 전임 근무, 정규직

STEP 2 • Speaking

Topic — p31

2 I think going to the mall with friends is better than going there by myself.

3 I'd rather keep my untouched face than have plastic surgery.

4 I would say that having adult supervision is more advisable than not to have any supervision.

5 Personally, there are a couple of reasons why I prefer studying in a group to studying alone with a private tutor.

6 In my opinion, it's better to use actual books than online materials.

7 The way I see it, children are not mature enough to make their own decisions, and for this reason they need to be guided by adults with strict rules.

8 As I see it, it's better to get a part-time job rather than to work for my parents to earn some cash.

Reason — p33

2 ❶ One of the reasons why I prefer going to the mall with friends is because I can spend time with my friends. ❷ Another reason is that it's more helpful to be with friends when making decisions.

3 ❶ One reason is that plastic surgery reinforces the idea that physical appearance is more important than what is on the inside. ❷ The other reason is that it can be very dangerous, or even fatal.

4 ❶ First, it's too dangerous for children to go to school by themselves without adult supervision. ❷ Second, parents can spend quality time with their children on the way to school.

5 ❶ One reason is that group members often encourage each other to study harder. ❷ The other reason is that group members can share notes and useful information with one another.

6 ❶ That's because actual books are more reliable than online materials. ❷ Furthermore, using books doesn't require me to have a computer just to access any information for my research work.

7 ❶ One of the reasons why I believe children should be guided by adults is because they don't have much life experience to make responsible decisions. ❷ Another reason is that children will grow up thinking it's OK for them to do whatever they want.

8 ❶ Firstly, being an employee will allow me to get a taste of what it feels like to be under someone else's supervision. ❷ Secondly, a part-time job would also curb my tendency to be complacent.

Detail — p36

2 ❶ I mean my friends and I are too busy to see each other often, so spending a few hours together at the mall is a great opportunity to chat and catch up on news. ❷ Also, you can't always trust salespeople, but your friends will tell you if the clothes you're trying on don't look good or if the MP3 player you want isn't a good value, and so on.

3 ❶ In fact, our society values looks too much, and frivolous surgery only reinforces this. ❷ Every year, people die when the simple procedure they went in for is performed incorrectly or causes an infection some time later. In contrast to having a natural face, it would be more appealing to have a fixed face. But I definitely do not agree that it's worth risking one's life for.

4 ① That is to say, children wouldn't know how to behave when they get lost or strangers approach hem. ② In other words, it would be an awesome chance to have a heart-to-heart conversation with their children. As they walk to school with their children, they would be able to learn more about them.

5 ① It means that everyone wants to understand the class materials and do well in the course. For example, if there's something I don't understand, there are several people who can explain it to me. It's helpful to hear the same idea expressed differently. ② What I mean is that if someone missed the class or wasn't able to take notes, the people in the group can borrow their notes.

6 ① I mean online materials are more open to false information because anyone can put information online without going through the same process as for publishing actual books. ② Also, it is more convenient because I can practically bring them anywhere, even without computer access.

7 ① In fact, they can't understand the long-term consequences of their actions. ② In contrast to having no rules, children raised with strict rules always learn to care for others' needs and never try to do anything to harm others.

8 ① That is to say, it will be a good learning experience for me and possibly aid me when the time comes for me to work full-time after college. ② In other words, I will be judged by what I do simply because I won't be given any special treatment when I do something wrong or right, since I have no filial association to my employer.

Practice Questions

p39

1

Sample Outlining

Topic: Familiar foods

Reason 1	Reason 2
You're used to it	Comfortable

Details	Details
No disappointment	No worry of ingredients that might make you sick.

Sample Response

I prefer to eat familiar foods. I mean, you already know what they taste like, so you will not be disappointed about the taste or the kind of cooking done. Sometimes, you can try exotic or unusual foods, but they may not taste so good, and you may choose not to eat them, or they might even make you sick. But with familiar foods, you are quite comfortable, and you will not eat ingredients which might trigger your allergies or some other problems.

2

Sample Outlining

Topic	Women should have any jobs	
Reason 1	**Reason 2**	
Performing work effectively is irrelevant to sex	Create inequality in wealth between sexes.	
Details	**Details**	
Nurses	Firefighters	

Sample Response

I believe that professions shouldn't be exclusive to any gender. This is because the ability to perform work effectively doesn't necessarily depend on whether you're a man or a woman. If I run a clinic, I don't want to hire a female applicant as a nurse instead of a male applicant just because she is a woman. Another reason is that if employers exclude a particular sex from getting a job, it can lead to poverty for the sex that is excluded. For example, if only men are chosen as firefighters, rejected female applicants who were trained to become firefighters won't have money to support their families.

3

Sample Outlining

Topic	With family	
Reason 1	**Reason 2**	
Reminds me of my childhood	Need to spend time with my brother	
Details	**Details**	
Camping in the mountains with family	Pleasant and relaxed atmosphere to spend time with family.	

Sample Response

Although it's fun to spend holidays with friends, I enjoy spending my vacation with my family. One reason for this is that it reminds me of when I was little, and my parents would take my brothers and me camping in the mountains. Another reason is that now that my brothers and I are older, we don't really spend much time together as a family. Going on vacation together allows us to get caught up on each other's news in a pleasant and relaxed atmosphere. We always have a great time and look forward to doing it each year.

Vocabulary

disappointment 실망, 낙담, 기대에 어긋남   ingredient 성분, 요소, 원료   exotic 외래의, 외국산의, 이국풍의
trigger (사건, 행동, 폭소)등을 일으키다. 유발하다 (감정) 자극하다   comfortable 안정된   allergy 알레르기, 반감, 거부감   perform 수행하다
effectively 효과적으로   irrelevant 관련성이 없는, 타당하지 않은   inequality 불평등   exclusive 배타적인, 배제적인, 독점적인
necessarily 반드시, 부득이, 할 수 없이   poverty 가난, 빈곤   childhood 어린 시절, 유년 시대   pleasant 즐거운, 기쁜   atmosphere 분위기
look forward to ~ing ~하기를 기대하다

TASK 03 Fit & Explain

Sample Question

|지문해석|

공고: 다음 학기부터 청강 수업 신청 인원을 최대 3명으로 제한할 예정이니 양지하시기 바랍니다. 이는 수용 공간의 부족과 강의의 효과적인 경영을 위한 학교의 노력에 따른 것입니다. 매년 학생의 인원이 증가하고 있는 상황에서 학교는 학생들의 학문적인 목표를 도달하는데 필요한 양질의 교육을 제공하기 위한 최선의 노력을 하고 있습니다. 더 자세한 사항을 아시려면 교무처에 문의하시기 바랍니다.

|Script|

W: Jesse, you seem really happy today ... Did anything happen that I should know about?

M: Finally, the school's come up with a good plan for us ...

W: Oh, did you mean the cap on audit courses? Why, aren't you a fan of audit students?

M: It's not that at all. I'm just glad that students who actually need to attend those classes and pass the course will be prioritized. I mean, audit students don't have the same things at stake, like passing the course exams or submitting major papers and requirements. Like me, I won't have to worry about not getting into a class because someone wants to just sit in class ... know what I mean?

W: Well, audit students also want to learn ...

M: I understand where they're coming from ... it's just that putting a limit on the number of students does give everyone a chance at a better learning environment. I mean, the professor won't have to sacrifice his lecture time trying to figure out how to be heard clearly by everyone ...

|Script 해석|

여자: 제시, 너 오늘 정말 기분 좋아 보인다. 내가 알아야 할 무슨 일이 있었던 거야?

남자: 마침내 학교가 우리에게 유익한 계획을 발표했어.

여자: 오, 청강 수업에 관한 제한 말이야? 왜? 너 청강생들 좋아하지 않니?

남자: 전혀. 나는 정말로 이 수업을 듣고 수료해야 하는 학생들에게 우선권이 주어진다는 게 기뻐. 내 말은 청강생들은 시험을 통과해야 한다든지 중요한 레포트나 과제물을 내야 한다든지 하는 절박한 것이 없잖아. 수업 시간에 앉아있기만 하고 싶은 사람 때문에 나 같은 사람이 수업을 못 들을 걱정도 없고 말이야. 무슨 뜻인지 알겠어?

여자: 흠, 청강생들도 마찬가지로 배우고 싶어하는 건데?

남자: 나도 그들이 왜 오는지는 알아. 다만 청강생 수에 제한을 두면 결국은 모든 사람에게 더 나은 학습환경이 주어지는 거야. 내 말은 교수님도 강의 시간에 어떻게 하면 모두가 다 들을 수 있는지 고민하느라 시간을 낭비하지 않아도 된다고.

Vocabulary

- **audit course** 청강 과목 **shortage** 부족 **availability** 이용할 수 있음, 유용성 **effective** 효과적인 **quality education** 질 좋은 교육
- **prioritize** ~에 우선 순위를 매기다 **summit** 제출하다 **requirement** 요구조건 **learning environment** 학습 환경
- **figure out** ~을 이해하다, ~을 해결하다, ~을 생각해내다

Pre-Speaking

p45

STEP 1 • Basic Outlining

1

|지문해석| **도서관 자료 대출 정책에 대한 변화**: 더욱 더 경쟁력 있고 진보적인 학습 환경을 추구하는 학교 당국의 목표와 도서관 내 소중한 자료 보존에 대한 염려가 증가하고 있는 추세로 인해 도서 대출 기한을 기존의 30일에서 주말을 포함한 7일로 줄이게 되었습니다. 대여 기간이 초과한 도서에 대해서는 하루 1달러씩의 벌금이 부과됩니다. 이 새 정책은 다음 학기부터 실시 될 예정이며 교수 요원을 제외한 모든 직원과 각 단과 대학에 등록한 모든 학생에게 적용됩니다. 모든 관계자는 엄격하게 실행할 예정입니다.

|Script|
M: Hey, Marissa ...
W: Hi, Ryan.
M: You angry about something? You seem kind of mad.
W: I am. I just came from the library. Have you heard about the new policy on the library books? It's just stupid.
M: Oh, you mean the thing about having only a week for keeping borrowed books? Well, yeah ... what's wrong with it?
W: Are you serious? We can only keep books for a week? How do they expect me to read a book in a week? That's too little time for me. I don't read and retain info that fast. You know what I mean? Plus, it's not as if I only have one class to think about.
M: The school's just probably concerned about reading materials getting lost ... you know, people lose things after a while ... they just want to prevent any more additional expenses ...
W: Well, how about my expenses? Money doesn't exactly grow on trees in my household. One dollar doesn't seem like a lot, but if you add 'em up, that's a lot of money. Plus, when I'll have to photocopy most of the pages I need ... that costs money too, and I'm on a budget as it is.

|Script 해석|
남자: 안녕, 마리사
여자: 제시, 라이언
남자: 무슨 안 좋은 일 있어? 화난 것 같은데.
여자: 응. 지금 막 도서관에서 오는 길이야. 도서관 책에 관한 새로운 정책에 대해 들었니? 정말 어리석은 정책이야.
남자: 아. 대여한 도서를 일주일 안에 반납해야 한다는 것 말이야? 응, 그런데 뭐가 잘못됐니?
여자: 진심이야? 대출 기간이 일주일이라니? 어떻게 일주일안에 책 한 권을 읽으라고 할 수 있지? 너무 촉박해. 난 그렇게 짧은 시간에 책을 읽고 정보를 얻을 수 없어. 무슨 말인지 알겠니? 게다가 신경 써야 할 과목이 한 개만 있는 것도 아니고
남자: 학교는 아마 도서 자료들이 없어지는 것에 대해서만 신경을 쓰니까 그럴 거야. 사람들이 시간이 지나면 쉽게 뭔가를 잃어 버리는 것을 너도 알잖아. 학교는 그렇게 해서 돈이 더 드는 것을 막고 싶어하는 거겠지.
여자: 흠. 내 돈이 드는 건 어쩌고? 나도 돈이 나무에서 그냥 열리는 건 아니잖아. 일 달러가 별 것 아닌 것처럼 보여도 그게 모이면 대단한 양이 된다고. 게다가 내가 필요한 부분을 모두 복사해야 하면 그것도 돈이 드는 일이잖아. 나도 예산을 세워야 한단 말이야.

Vocabulary
competitive 경쟁의, 경합하는   preservation 보존   valuable contents 귀중한 자료, 소중한 자료   compliance (명령, 요구 등에) 따르기, 순종
additional expenses 추가 비용, 부가적인 지출   money doesn't grow on trees 돈 벌기 쉽지 않다   photocopy 복사하다   budget 예산

2

|지문해석| **편집장님께:** 대학교 조각상 구입 계획에 대해서 씁니다. 전 그 구입이 학교 예산의 낭비라고 굳게 믿습니다. 저는 작년보다 15%나 증가한 학비와 기숙사 비용이 교육에 있어서의 더 나은 발전이 아닌 부분에 사용되기를 원치 않습니다. 게다가 학교 광장은 체육과 여가 활동의 장소로써 많은 학생이 이용하고 있는 곳입니다. 저와 친구들도 광장에서 축구를 하는데, 조각으로 광장이 어지럽혀진다면 더 이상 못하게 될 것입니다. 저는 대부분의 학생들이 학교의 미관보다 좋은 여가 시설을 더 중요하게 여길 것이라고 생각합니다.

조쉬 스미스 / 4학년

|Script|
M: Have you heard about the issue with the sculpture purchases? It seems not everyone's all too happy about the school buying them. I just read this letter in the paper today ... Look here ...
W: Let me see that ... really? I think it's a fabulous idea. Whoever wrote that is just plain silly, if you ask me.
M: What makes you say that? This Josh guy seems to have raised some good points ... don't you think so?
W: Well, for starters, the school budget won't be used to buy the sculptures. It'll be coming from an anonymous donor. So, he shouldn't be complaining about part of his fees being used for this move by the school to make the grounds look more appealing.
M: Maybe the university just needs to clarify that point ... so, they won't get such complaints.
W: No ... I think what's really bugging him is the fact that the sculptures will be located on the quad and he plays soccer there. If the school buys the pieces, he'll have to find a different place to play soccer, that's all. But big deal, there's plenty of places on campus to play.

|Script 해석|
남자: 조각상 구입에 대한 얘기 들었니? 모두가 다 좋아하는 것 같지는 않아. 나도 신문에 난 이 편지를 지금 방금 읽었는데, 이 부분을 봐봐.
여자: 어디 보자. 정말? 난 좋은 생각인 것 같은데. 내 생각엔 누가 썼는지 모르지만 이걸 쓴 사람 정말 멍청하다.
남자: 왜 그렇게 말하는 거지? 이 조쉬라는 남학생이 좋은 지적을 한 것 같은데, 그렇게 생각 안 하니?
여자: 우선, 학교 예산으로 조각상을 구매하는 것이 아니야. 무명의 기부자가 낸 돈으로 사는 거야. 그러니까 자신이 낸 학비의 일부가 학교 정원을 꾸미기 위해 사용된다고 불평해서는 안돼.
남자: 그러면 학교 차원에서 다시 명확하게 밝혀야겠네. 그런 불평이 안 생기게 하려면 말이야.
여자: 아니야 … 내 생각에 이 남학생의 진짜 문제는 그 조각상이 놓이는 장소에서 자신이 축구를 하기 때문인 거 같아. 만약 학교가 그 조각상을 산다면 축구 할 다른 장소를 찾아봐야 하니까. 그게 다야. 그렇지만 뭐가 문제야! 학교 안에 축구 할 장소는 무척 많은데 말이야.

Reading Note

Policy
Purchasing sculptures for the campus

Letter (Agree or (Disagree))

Reason 1
• Waste of school budget

Reason 2
• Campus quad
 - for athletic & recreational activities

Listening Note

Opinion
Doesn't agree

Reason 1
Money will come from a donor
• not from school budget

Reason 2
The student is complaining b/c he can't play soccer there
• there are other places to play

Vocabulary
- athletics and recreational activities 체육과 여가활동
- be cluttered with 어지럽혀지다
- facility 시설, 기관
- fabulous 굉장히 좋은
- anonymous 익명의, 작자불명의
- bug 괴롭히다, 골탕 먹이다
- pay for ~을 위해 지불 되었다

3

|지문해석| 대학 대표팀 해체: 학교 대표팀 해체 건에 대한 학교 회의가 확정되었다. 인터뷰에서 체육 팀 담당인 맥과이어 박사는 학교가 대학 팀을 임시적으로 최소 2년간 해체할 것이라고 밝혔다. 박사는 학교간 시합을 위해서 팀을 개발하는데 필요한 예산을 학교가 더 이상 감당하지 못한다고 말했다. 그러나 맥과이어 박사는 2년의 기간 후에 재정적인 상황이 좋아진다면 다시 조직될 수 있다는 것을 암시했다. 이 보도가 학생들과 교수진 그리고 스포츠에 열광적인 동문들에게 어떤 영향을 미칠지 주목된다.

|Script|
M: Good morning, Christina! Going jogging today?
W: Hi, Rob. Yeah, sort of ... just to take out some stress I'm having ...
M: Why? What's up?
W: Haven't you read the school paper? They're scrapping the varsity teams ... and for two years ... that means no games and no championships for that long ... the news is true, after all ...
M: Oh, I can't believe it ... not this university ...
W: This is totally unfair! Just two years ago they were celebrating our NCAA basketball championship ... we were all over the news ... even Dr. McGuire was all smiles while holding the trophy ... I think it's really sick to scrap the teams after what they have done for the school ...
M: Yeah, I agree ...
W: It's also unfair for the students, you know ... because we're known as a premier university ... Hmmm ... I think this will send the wrong signal to the whole academic community – that our school is way below par ... I mean ... this is what the other students will think about us. I'm sure student applicants will have second thoughts about enrolling in our school from now on ...

|Script 해석|
남자: 안녕, 크리스티나! 조깅하러 가니?
여자: 안녕 롭. 응 비슷해. 스트레스 좀 풀까 하고.
남자: 왜? 무슨 일이야?
여자: 학교 신문 안 읽었어? 대학 팀을 해체한대. 2년 동안은 경기나 선수권 대회도 없을 거란 얘기지. 사실이더라고 …
남자: 믿을 수가 없어 … 우리 학교만은 안 되는데.
여자: 너무 불공평해. 2년 전만 하더라도 전국 대학 리그에서 종합 우승한 것을 축하했는데 말이야. 우리 모두 그 소식에 열광했잖아. 맥과이어 박사도 트로피를 들고선 내내 웃었는데 말야. 그 동안 학교에 세운 공을 생각하면 해체하는 건 너무하다고 생각해.
남자: 응, 네 말이 맞아.
여자: 너도 알다시피 학생들에게도 불공평한 거야. 우리는 일류 대학으로 알려져 있는데. 흠 … 이 일을 통해 전체 대학 사회에 우리가 수준 이하라는 안 좋은 이미지가 생길 거야. 내 말은 다른 학생들이 우리에 대해서 그렇게 생각할 거라는 것이지. 이제부터 우리 학교를 오려고 했던 지원자들이 등록을 재고해볼 거라고 확신해.

Reading Note

Policy
Suspending varsity teams at least for 2 years.

Reason 1
Can't bear the budget
- may be organized again if the financial problems are solved

Listening Note

Opinion
Against

Reason 1
Unfair to the team
- considering what they did for school 2 years ago

Reason 2
Unfair to the students
- will hurt school's reputation

Vocabulary
temporarily 일시적으로   competition 경쟁   financial prospect 재정 상황   alumni 동문들   reputation 명성

4

|지문해석| 신입생 차량 운행 금지: 다음 학기부터 대학 당국은 공기 오염을 줄이고 학내의 교통 혼잡을 완화할 목적으로 신입생의 차량 반입을 금지할 것입니다. 학생수가 매년 꾸준히 증가함에 따라 학내의 차량 수와 인구 유동량 또한 증가하고 있습니다. 특별 허가를 받은 차량만이 이 규정에서 제외될 것입니다. 현재 재학생은 이번 학기가 끝나기 전 새로운 차량 허가증을 획득하십시오. 이 규정에 해당되는 학생을 위해 무료 셔틀 서비스가 제공될 것입니다. 승차 지점과 시간에 대해서는 추후에 공고하겠습니다.

|Script|
M: Hey, Tina. Isn't your little sister gonna be a freshman here next semester? What's she think about this new policy?
W: Yeah, she is ... but she doesn't know how to drive anyway ... so, I don't think she'll have a problem with this car ban ...
M: Well, I don't think this is such a good idea. I mean, telling freshmen they can't bring a car to school in their first year won't help them settle in school. If the university wants to help save the environment, just try to get everyone to drive a bit less. Singling out freshmen seems unfair to me ...
W: But we do need to do something about campus traffic ... and they did say they will provide shuttle service ...
M: Even if they offer free rides, not everyone has a flexible schedule. What if the service schedule doesn't fit with the students' schedules? You're going to have a lot of late students ... And some of them might live far from school. They can't just leave their cars off campus that easily ...
W: Oh, well, let's just hope for the best, then ...

|Script 해석|
남자: 안녕, 티나. 다음 학기에 네 여동생이 입학하지 않니? 학교의 새 정책에 대해서 그 애는 어떻게 생각해?
여자: 응, 다음 학기에 입학해. 그런데 내 동생은 어차피 운전할 줄 몰라서 자동차 금지 정책이 문제가 될 것 같지는 않아.
남자: 글쎄, 난 별로 좋은 생각 같지 않아. 내 말은 신입생에게 차를 가지고 오지 말라고 하는 것이 학교에 빨리 적응하도록 돕지 못할 거라는 거야. 학교가 환경 문제에 도움이 되고 싶으면 모두가 조금씩 덜 타게 하도록 하면 되잖아. 신입생만 못 타게 하는 것은 불공평한 것 같아.
여자: 그래도 학교 교통 문제를 위해서 뭔가를 해야 할 필요는 있어. 그리고 셔틀 버스를 운행한다고도 했고.
남자: 차비를 받지 않는다고 해도 모두가 셔틀 버스를 이용하기는 어려울 거야. 운행 시간과 수업 시간이 맞지 않으면 어떻게 해? 많은 학생이 지각을 할거야. 그리고 멀리 사는 학생도 있을 거고. 차를 캠퍼스 밖 멀리 놓고 오는 것이 그렇게 쉽진 않을 거야.
여자: 그러게. 아무튼 최선의 결과를 기대하자.

Reading Note

Policy
Car ban for 1st year students

Reason 1
- Traffic increase
  - Free shuttle service will be provided

Listening Note

Opinion
Against

Reason 1
Won't help freshmen settle in school
- Why freshmen → Unfair!

Reason 2
Shuttle service may not fit every student's schedule
- Students will be late for class
- Some students live far from school

Vocabulary
- decongest 혼잡함을 완화하다 steadily 꾸준하게 exempt 면제하다 permit 인가, 허가증 drop-off 하차
- flexible 변형 가능한, 유연한 prohibit 금지하다 inconvenience 불편함 fit 잘 맞다

STEP 2 • Speaking

Opinion — p50

2 a genius
→ The woman supports his opinion that the school's plan to purchase sculptures is a waste of school finances.

3 I think this is fair. / an unavoidable consequence
→ The woman shares the view that the university's plan to scrap the varsity teams is reasonable.

4 I don't think this is a good idea.
→ The man disagrees with the university's policy to enforce a vehicle ban for all incoming freshmen.

Reason — p53

2 an anonymous donor / bugging him
→ Her reasons for holding that opinion are twofold. Firstly, she explains that the school budget won't be used to buy the sculptures. Secondly, she thinks that the real reason the student is opposed to buying the sculptures is that he wants to play soccer in the quad.

3 celebrating our overall championship / we're known as a premier university
→ There are two reasons why she disagrees with the university's plan. The first reason is that the varsity teams joined the championship at the National College League two years ago. The second reason is that it's is also unfair for the students because people will think that the university has low standards.

4 not everyone has a flexible schedule
→ He provides two reasons for holding his opinions. First, he believes it won't do any good to the freshmen who are still trying to get settled in their new school. Second, the ban will inconvenience a lot of students, since the shuttle service schedule may not fit with the students' schedule.

Detail — p56

2 won't be used / shouldn't be complaining about
→ The woman, however, points out that this is not true. In reality, they are actually being paid for by a donor.

3 they were celebrating / we were all over the news
→ What she means is that it's unfair to the varsity teams because they brought success to the school with their championship years back.

4 leave their cars off campus
→ He believes it is unfair to single out just freshmen. Instead, he thinks the school should urge every member of the university to drive less.

Practice Questions

p 58

1

|지문해석| **가급제 기간 변경**: 대학 내의 학업적 탁월성을 증가시키고 학생의 교내 기강을 개선하는 목적으로, 평균 학점 2.0 이하이거나 가급제 기간인 학생은 교외 활동에 참여할 수 없게 됩니다. 이는 다음 학기부터 실행되며 가급제 기간의 학생은 평균 학점이 학교의 요구 수준에 도달할 때까지 운동 활동이나 해외 교환 프로그램에 참여할 수 없습니다. 가급제 기간 후에도 학업적 수준을 향상시키지 못한 학생은 학업적 목표를 재검토하기 위해 한 학기 휴학을 해야 합니다.

|Script|
M: Why the long face, Trish? Hmm ... let me guess, you're ecstatic about the new policy concerning yourself?
W: Yes, I am very much concerned, for your information. If I didn't know any better, I would think my parents penned this policy ...
M: Well, honestly, focusing on academics should be a basic part of student life. I mean, failing is way more serious than missing out on sports for a while ... don't you think? Besides, it's just a matter of getting your priorities straight ... because if you think about it, flunking out won't help you with your extra-curricular activities either.
W: I just think it's a bit harsh, that's all. What makes the school so sure that crippling our social life would help improve our grades?
M: Sure, it's no guarantee. But what would happen if the school let people just continue on with bad grades and they flunked out after, like, three years or something? Then they'd owe a lot of money too. At least this way, they have to stop for a while and think about their school work. It could save people a lot of trouble in the long run.

|Script 해석|
남자: 트리쉬, 왜 그렇게 기분이 안 좋은 거야? 흠, 내가 맞춰볼까, 너랑 관련된 새 정책 때문에 그런 거지?
여자: 참고로 말한다면, 그래 너무 신경 쓰여. 내가 잘 몰랐다면 이 정책을 부모님이 썼다고 생각 했을 거야.
남자: 음, 사실 말이야, 수업에 초점을 맞추는 것은 학생 생활의 가장 기본적인 것이 되야 하잖아. 내 말은 낙제하는 건 운동을 얼마 동안 못하는 것보다 더 심각한 일이라고, 그렇게 생각하지 않니? 게다가, 이건 단지 우선 순위를 다시 잡는 문제야. 왜냐면, 생각해봐, 낙제하는 것은 학과 외 활동을 위해서도 별로 좋지 않아.
여자: 난 단지 좀 가혹하다고 생각하는 것뿐이야. 학교는 어째서 우리가 사회 생활을 중단하면 성적이 오를 거 라고 확신하는 걸까?
남자: 물론, 보장은 못하지. 그래도 성적이 나쁜 학생들을 그냥 내버려 두어서 그들이 3학년쯤 마치고 낙제생으로 쫓겨 나면 어떻게 되겠어? 그렇게 된다면 많은 빚도 지게 되는 거야. 이렇게 함으로써 최소한 잠깐 동안이라도 멈춰서 학업을 생각해 보겠지. 그리고 결국에는 많은 문제를 막아줄 수도 있고 말이야.

Reading Note
Academic probation
Students having GPA below 2.0

1) Improve the academic excellence
   • can't participate in extra-curricular activities

Listening Note
Agree
1) Education is more important
   • learn to take their academics seriously
2) Help students improve their academic standing.
   • no waste of money and no risk of being kicked out.

|Sample Respone| The university is trying to impose some discipline on students under probation by prohibiting them from participating in extra-curricular activities, like athletic activities and foreign exchange programs. The man agrees with the policy, saying that education is more important than extra-curricular activities, so the students must learn to take their academics more seriously. Also, the policy states that those who fail to improve their standing will be forced to take a leave of absence to review their academic goals. The man thinks that the policy will actually help the students improve their academic standing, lest they extend for another term and waste more money and time, or risk being kicked out of the college.

Vocabulary
- academic excellence 학업의 탁월성
- ecstatic 무아지경의, 황홀한
- pen 쓰다
- cripple 손상시키다
- guarantee 보증
- impose (의무을) 부과하다
- kick out 쫓아내다

2

|지문해석| **독자 의견**: 연극 동아리 예산을 삭감하겠다는 대학의 결정에 분개함을 느낀다는 의견을 표명하는 바입니다. 연극 동아리는 수년 동안 학교 내의 문화적 예술적 생활의 핵심 요소였습니다. 학교 학생들과 예술계 모두가 연극 동아리의 작품을 감상해왔습니다. 학교 내에서 동아리가 차지하는 중요성을 생각한다면 예산 삭감이 아닌 예산 증가를 해주어야 합니다. 게다가 학교 당국은 이 결정이 학교 명성에 어떤 영향을 미칠지에 대해서 생각해보지 않았음이 분명합니다. 학교에 제대로 지원을 받는 연극 동아리가 없다는 것을 알면 지원자들이 어떻게 생각할까요?

연극을 사랑하는 학생으로부터

|Script|
M: This girl is so full of herself!
W: Huh? What girl is that? Oh, you're reading that editorial about the drama club's budget?
M: Yeah, what a joke!. She goes on and on about how important the drama club is to the cultural life of the school and to the students. Let me ask you something. Have you ever been to a play that they've put on?
W: Well ... no.
M: Exactly! No one goes, so who cares if the school cut the budget? In fact, I'm glad they did it. They should take that money and use it for something that we're actually interested in.
W: Yeah, I guess so. There are a lot of other programs that are a lot more popular.
M: And that garbage about it hurting the reputation of the school? Come on. Not a single person cares what kind of drama club we have. The only thing that kids look at when they pick a school is the ratio of boys to girls, the sports teams, and maybe the academic programs. Cutting the drama club's budget isn't going to hurt the school's reputation one bit.

|Script 해석|
남자: 이 여자애 너무 자기중심적인데!
여자: 어? 누군데? 아, 연극 동아리 예산에 관해서 쓴 논설 보고 있구나?
남자: 응, 정말 웃겨. 이 여자애는 연극 동아리가 학교와 학생의 문화 생활에 얼마나 중요한지 늘어놓고 있어. 뭐 하나만 묻자. 너 그 동아리가 하는 연극 본 적 있어?
여자: 음 … 아니.
남자: 바로 그거야. 아무도 안 가잖아. 학교가 예산을 줄인다고 누가 걱정하겠어? 사실 줄인 건 잘 한 거야. 그 돈을 우리가 정말로 더 좋아하는 부분에 사용해야 한다고.
여자: 응, 나도 그렇게 생각해. 더 인기 있는 프로그램도 많으니깐.
남자: 예산 삭감이 학교의 명성에 피해를 준다는 허풍? 이봐. 우리 학교에 어떤 연극 동아리가 있는지 아무도 신경쓰지 않는다구. 신입생이 학교를 선택 할 때는 남, 여학생 비율이나 스포츠팀이나 아니면 학술 프로그램 같은 거야. 연극 동아리 예산을 삭감 했다고 해서 학교 명성에 조금도 피해 주지 않아.

Reading Note

Slashing the budget of the drama club
Against
1) An element of cultural and artistic life on campus for a long time
2) Impact the reputation of the school

Listening Note

Doesn't agree
1) Drama club is not important
 • No one goes to see the performances
2) Doesn't hurt school's reputation
 • Students only care for the ratio of boys to girls, sports teams, & academic programs.

|Sample Respone| The man does not take the student's letter very seriously. In fact, he basically seems to be laughing at her. He does not agree with her claim that the drama club is important to students. He says that most students have probably never even been to a play put on by the drama club. He says that the school should cut the drama club's budget and use the money for something that is more important to the students. He also doesn't believe that cutting the drama club budget will hurt the reputation of the school. He says that most incoming freshmen probably don't even know that there is a drama club. According to him, the only things that new students care about are the numbers of boys and girls at the school, the sports teams, and the academic programs.

Vocabulary
- slash 인하(삭감)하다
- decently 상당히, 꽤, 제법
- editorial 사설, 논설
- reputation 평판, 명성
- academic program 학습 프로그램

TASK 04 General / Specific

Sample Question

|지문해석| **근접 발달 영역**: 근접 발달 영역은 러시아의 심리학자 레브 비고츠키에 의해 처음 도입된 교육학적 개념이다. 비고츠키에 의하면 독립적으로 문제를 해결함으로써 결정되는 실제의 발달 수준과 어른의 지도 아래, 또는 보다 유능한 또래와의 협력 하에서 문제를 해결할 때 결정되는 잠재적 발달 수준 사이에는 늘 격차가 있다. 격차가 너무 크면 학습자는 새로운 내용을 배우지 못하고 좌절하게 된다. 격차가 너무 작으면 학습자는 그 과제가 너무 쉽다고 생각하고 흥미를 잃게 된다.

|Script| OK, when you put students into pairs for group assignments, you need to think about how you pair students up very carefully. Uh, it's not just matching up the students' personalities so that you avoid arguments ... you need to, uh, consider their ability levels as well. Ideally, you want to place students of slightly different levels together. This way the more capable students can help guide those who are less capable. This works out well for both students. The less capable student receives the support of the better student, and therefore finds the assignment within his range of ability ... uh, and the better student is challenged because he has to help teach the less capable student. But you need to be careful in doing this ... uh, don't place the best student in the class with the worst student in the class. Their ability levels are too different. The worst student just isn't ready to function at the level of the best student ... uh, even with help, it's just not within his range of ability yet. Such a pairing will only lead to frustration and discouragement.

|Script 해석| 자, 그룹 과제를 위해 학생들 짝을 지어줄 때에는 어떻게 할 것인지 주의 깊게 생각해야 합니다. 학생의 성격을 고려해서 짝을 나눠 논쟁을 피하는 것만이 전부가 아닙니다. 여러분은 학생의 능력도 고려해야 합니다. 이상적으로는 수준이 조금씩 다른 학생을 한 조로 묶고 싶을 것입니다. 이렇게 하면 좀 더 잘하는 학생이 조금 부족한 학생을 도와줄 수 있을 테니까요. 이 방법은 양쪽 모두에게 도움이 됩니다. 수준이 낮은 학생은 잘하는 학생의 도움을 받으면서 과제가 자신이 할 수 있는 범위 내의 것이라는 사실을 알게 되고, 잘하는 학생은 못하는 학생을 도와야 하기 때문에 도전이 되죠. 그렇지만 이렇게 할 때 조심할 필요가 있습니다. 반에서 가장 우수한 학생과 가장 성적이 낮은 학생을 한 조로 넣지 마세요. 능력 수준이 너무 다릅니다. 성적이 낮은 학생은 우수한 학생의 수준에 맞출 준비가 되어있지 않습니다. 도움을 받는다고 해도 능력 밖의 문제입니다. 그렇게 조를 편성하면 마찰과 낙담이라는 결과만을 얻게 됩니다.

Vocabulary

- collaboration 협동, 협조
- capable peer 유능한 동료(친구)
- frustrate 좌절시키다
- match up 짝짓기
- slightly 약간, 조금
- function 기능, 작용, 역할
- frustration 좌절
- discouragement 낙담, 낙심

Pre-Speaking

STEP 1 • Basic Outlining

1

|지문해석| **동물의 눈속임**: 생존은 다양한 생물체에게 있어 자연적 진보이다. 그 중에서도 동물은 같은 지역에서 어슬렁거리며 돌아다니는 천적으로부터 스스로를 보호하거나 그들을 훼방 놓기 위해 특정한 특징과 습성에 적응하고 보여준다. 눈속임은 방어기제로써, 자신의 생명에 위협이 된다고 간주하는 다른 동물들로부터 벗어나기 위한 근본적인 적응 능력이다. 어떤 동물은 신체적인 외양에서 닮은 다른 종에 속하는 것처럼 가장하기도 하고, 다른 동물은 생명이 없는 물체로 가장하여 배경의 일부인 것처럼 보이게도 한다.

|Script| Looking more closely into the ways animals adapt and survive to their environment, it is not uncommon for them to use deceit as a means to divert predators' attention away from themselves. Some animals are able to deceive potential predators through mimicry. This means they are able to copy, or mimic, the behavior, movements, or sounds of another animal. For example, some animals are able to replicate the sound of a larger, more threatening animal. When a predator comes by, they are able to scare it away by mimicking the sound of this larger animal. Another way that animals sometimes deceive predators is to pretend to be injured. The objective here is to lure the predator away from the animal's young, or from its den. A good example of this would be some bird species. In some bird species, the female will pretend to have a broken wing in order to divert the attention of a predator away from her nest and her young. This draws the predator away from the nest ... and once it is a safe distance away, the mother flies away to safety.

|Script 해석| 동물이 환경에 적응하고 살아남는 방식을 자세히 들여다보면 주의를 다른 곳으로 돌리게 하기 위해 속임수를 쓰는 것은 드문 일이 아닙니다. 어떤 동물들은 흉내내기를 통해 천적을 속일 수도 있습니다. 이 말은 다른 동물들의 행동이나 동작 혹은 울음 소리를 따라 하거나 흉내를 낸다는 뜻이죠. 예를 들어 어떤 동물들은 몸집이 더 크고 위협적인 동물의 울음 소리를 흉내 낼 수 있습니다. 천적이 가까이로 오면 더 큰 동물의 울음소리를 흉내 냄으로써 겁을 먹고 도망가게 할 수 있습니다. 또 다른 방식은 부상을 입은 것으로 가장하여 천적을 속이는 것입니다. 이 방식의 목적은 주로 자신의 새끼나 동굴로부터 천적을 멀어지게 하려는 것입니다. 새 종류에서 좋은 예를 발견 할 수 있습니다. 어떤 새 종류는 암컷이 둥지와 새끼로부터 천적의 주의를 돌리게 하기 위해서 날개가 다친 것처럼 가장합니다. 천적은 둥지로부터 주의를 돌리게 되고 안전할 정도로 둥지로부터 거리가 멀어지면 어미 새는 다시 돌아 옵니다.

Vocabulary

- natural progression 자연적인 과정   predatory 약탈하는, 포식의   defense mechanism 방어기제   deception 속임수   adaptive ability 적응능력   resemble ~을 닮다   physical appearance 신체적(물리적) 외관   pretend ~인 체하다, 가장하다   injure 해치다, 손상하다
- divert 주의를 딴 데로 돌리다, 전환하다   deceive 속이다, 현혹시키다   mimic 흉내내다   replicate ~을 모사 (복제)하다   threaten 위협하다

2

|지문해석| **습곡 산맥**: 지각은 지구의 가장 바깥 층이다. 지각은 플레이트라고 하는 암석층으로 이루어져 있다. 열과 압력이 주어지면 플레이트는 서로에게 압력을 가하면서 움직여 지각이 변형된다. 이 압력과 그에 따른 지각 일부의 상향 운동은 그 부분을 뒤틀고 구부리거나 주름지게 만들 수 있으며 그 결과 능선과 계곡 같은 주름진 지형이 생성된다. 지각 안에 특정한 암석이 존재할 때만 일어나는 이 변형의 과정을 습곡이라고 한다.

|Script| We know that mountains are identified based on how they are formed, right? So today, I would like to discuss with you the principle of mountain building through a process called folding. Imagine that the surface of the earth is a rug. We'll identify both ends of the rug as plates. Now, try pushing together both ends of the rug with your fingers, which we'll identify as "forces." What happens? It crumples and wrinkles, right? Now, the more pressure you apply on both ends of the rug, the more wrinkles and crumples you produce. This same action can be seen in the movement of the earth's crust. Now, in order for folding to occur, rocks must have the ability to deform under pressure and heat. Imagine that a rock is like a piece of plastic. When you heat plastic, it bends and deforms easily, but when it cools, it takes a rigid form again. Some rocks are the same way and thus susceptible to mountain folding. Others, which don't have this property of plasticity, just shatter when they are subjected to heat and pressure, and the mountains they form are markedly different.

|Script 해석| 산은 형성된 방식에 따라 분류된다는 것을 알고 있죠? 그래서 오늘은 습곡이라고 알려진 과정을 통해 산이 생성되는 원리에 대해서 이야기를 해보려고 합니다. 지구의 표면을 양탄자라고 생각해봅시다. 양탄자의 양쪽 끝은 플레이트라고 볼 수 있습니다. 자, 여러분의 손가락으로 양탄자의 양끝을 밀어봅시다. 우리는 이것을 '압력'이라고 부릅니다. 어떻게 됐죠? 구겨지고 주름이 생기죠? 자, 양 끝에 더 많은 힘을 줄수록 더 많은 구김과 주름이 생겨납니다. 이와 같은 일이 지구 표면에서도 일어납니다. 습곡이 생기기 위해서는 암석이 압력과 열에 의해 변형될 수 있어야 합니다. 암석을 플라스틱이라고 생각해봅시다. 플라스틱에 가열을 하면 쉽게 구부러지고 변형이 되지만, 식은 후에는 다시 단단한 형태를 취합니다. 몇몇 종류의 암석은 이와 같은 특징을 가지고 있어서 습곡을 형성하기에 적당합니다. 플라스틱의 특징을 가지고 있지 않은 다른 암석들은 열과 압력을 받으면 그냥 부서져버리고, 그렇게 형성된 산은 매우 다른 모양을 가지게 됩니다.

Reading Note

Topic
Folded mountains

Main Idea
- Folding process - heat & pressure

Details
→ move plates against each other
→ deform the crust
→ create wavelike ridges & valleys
- ccurs only w/ certain types of rock

Listening Note

Example 1
Earth = rug
- plates = both ends of the rug
- push both ends → the rug wrinkles

Example 2
Rocks must have plasticity (able to deform under pressure & heat)
- other rocks shatter when heated & pressed
- form mountains w/ different shapes

Vocabulary

outermost 가장 바깥의   **crust** 외피, 표면   **deform** ~을 변모시키다   **wrinkle** 주름지게 하다   **wavelike formation** 물결 같은 모양

fold 접다, 포개다   **crumple** 구겨지다   **susceptible** 영향(작용)을 받기 적당한   **rigid** 딱딱한, 고정된   **plasticity** 유연성, 가소성

3

|지문해석| **일탈 행위**: 사회는 법을 만들고 바람직하고 이상적이라고 생각되는 것을 토대로 법과 그에 부합하는 처벌 규정을 만든다. 그리고 구성원이 그 규범에 순응하기를 기대한다. 사회 규범의 위반으로 보이는 것을 일탈 행위라고 하며, 이 행위는 비교적 사소한 것부터 사회적 문제로 간주되는 것까지 다양하다. 문화마다 규범이 다르기 때문에 일탈 행위는 상대적 개념이다. 한 문화에서 올바르다고 간주되는 것이 다른 사회에서는 수용되지 않을 수도 있다.

|Script| Today, we're going to discuss the relativity of deviant behavior. You see, people make judgments based on their own experiences, so saying that someone departs from the norm varies from one culture to another. For example, divorce, while considered a legal and normal way of dissolving a marriage in most cultures, is still frowned upon in other conservative societies ... say, a Catholic society. So, if you are a Catholic, seeking a divorce may be seen as deviant, but in many Protestant communities, divorce is accepted, or at least not as frowned upon as it is in the Catholic Church. So if you lived in a Protestant society, divorce might be seen as a less deviant course of action. Deviance can also be relative from one generation to another. Take the teens of the 1960s, for example. They had, uh, to say the least, quite different social norms than those of their parents' generation. So the actions of teens, uh, wearing unusual clothing, experimenting with drugs, or whatever... it seemed highly deviant to the older generation but perfectly acceptable to the teens themselves.

|Script 해석| 오늘은 일탈 행동의 상대성에 대해서 이야기해 보겠습니다. 알다시피 사람은 자신의 경험을 토대로 판단을 내리기 때문에 어떤 사람이 기준에서 벗어났는지에 대해 말하는 것은 문화마다 다릅니다. 예를 들어, 대부분의 문화권에서 이혼은 결혼 관계를 그만두는 합법적이고 정상적인 방식이지만, 가톨릭 사회 같은 보수적인 사회에서는 눈살을 찌푸리는 일입니다. 그렇기 때문에 만약 여러분이 가톨릭 신자라면 이혼을 하는 것은 일탈 행동으로 보일 수 있지만, 많은 개신교 사회에서는 이혼을 인정하며 적어도 가톨릭 교회에서처럼 눈살 찌푸리는 일이 아닙니다. 그래서 여러분이 개신교 사회에서 산다면 이혼이 일탈 행동으로 보일 가능성은 줄어듭니다. 일탈 행동은 세대마다 다를 수도 있습니다. 1960년대의 십대를 예로 들어보죠. 그들은 말하자면, 부모 세대의 사회 기준과는 많이 다른 기준을 가지고 있었습니다. 평범하지 않은 옷을 입거나 마약을 하거나 하는 등의 십대들의 행동은 당시 어른에게는 무척 이상한 행동으로 보였지만 십대 스스로는 자연스럽게 받아들였습니다.

Reading Note

Topic
Deviant behavior

Main Idea
The relativity of deviant behavior (recognized violation of social norms)

Details
- varies from culture to culture

Listening Note

Example 1
According to the culture
Ex) divorce
- Catholic → deviant
- Protestant → acceptable

Example 2
According to the generation
Ex) teens of 60s
- Different social norms from parents' generation.

Vocabulary
- correspond 일치하다, 부합하다
- sanction 제재, 처벌
- desirable 적합한, 바람직한
- deviant (규범에서) 벗어난, 비정상적인
- relatively 비교적, 상대적
- trivial 사소한
- relativity 상대성
- judgment 판단, 판정
- dissolve 녹이다, 용해시키다
- frown upon 눈살을 찡그리다
- conservative 보수적인

4

|지문해석| **인지적 편향**: 사람은 대개 자신의 경향과 선입견에 근거하여 다른 사람을 인식한다. 이를 사회적 편향, 혹은 심리학 용어로 인지적 편향이라고 하며 이 개념은 우리의 일상적인 사회적 상호작용에 영향을 준다. 이 중에 후광 효과라고 하는 것이 있는데, 이는 한 사람의 한 가지 특성에 대한 좋은 평가가 다른 특성에 대한 평가에 영향을 미치는 것이다. X라고 하는 특징을 가지고 있는 사람은 Y라고 하는 점 또한 가지고 있을 것이라고 생각하는 것이다. 비록 이 두 가지 특징이 서로 연관이 없어도 말이다. 매력적이거나 훌륭한 솜씨를 가지고 있는 사람은 종종 평균적인 외모나 능력을 가진 사람보다 더 경쟁력이 있다는 평가를 받는다.

|Script| Okay ... so we learned that many of the judgments we make are not as logical as we believe, because they are influenced by the halo effect. The halo effect often occurs at job interviews, where the interviewer may be influenced by the appearance of the interviewee. If the interviewee is physically attractive, the interviewer may ignore his/her other weaknesses. This is because the interviewer presumes that the other qualities of that person are as good as his/her looks, although there is no proof that supports this presumption. The halo effect is also often observed in the business area, and companies try to use this effect for marketing their products. The best-known example would be the "iPod halo effect." During recent years, Apple's sales of desktops and laptops have soared, and many people believe that this sudden sales increase is largely owing to the iPod, the portable media player made by Apple, which has gained a huge following all over the world. This theory was advanced by Apple and those who have studied Apple's business and marketing strategies. According to the theory, people who are satisfied with the use of their iPods come to be aware of the existence of other Apple products, become interested in them, and finally decide to purchase those products because they believe they are as good as the iPod.

|Script 해석| 자 … 우리는 후광 효과에 영향을 받기 때문에, 우리가 내리는 많은 판단은 우리가 믿는 것만큼 논리적이지 않다는 점을 배웠습니다. 후광 효과는 면접관이 면접을 받는 사람의 외모에 영향을 받을 수 있는 구직 인터뷰에서 종종 발생합니다. 면접 받는 사람이 매력적이면 그의 다른 약점을 쉽게 지나치게 될 수도 있습니다. 이는 상대방이 외모만큼이나 다른 면도 좋을 것이라고 면접관이 가정하기 때문입니다. 비록 이 가정을 뒷받침할 근거가 없더라도 말입니다. 후광 효과는 비즈니스 분야에서도 종종 나타나며, 기업은 상품 판매에 이 효과를 이용하려 노력합니다. 가장 잘 알려진 것이 'iPod 후광 효과' 라고 할 수 있습니다. 최근 몇 년 동안 애플사의 데스크톱 컴퓨터와 노트북 컴퓨터의 판매가 눈에 띄게 증가했고, 많은 사람들은 이런 급격한 증가가 iPod 때문이라고 믿습니다. iPod는 최근 전세계적으로 많은 팬들을 확보한 애플사의 휴대용 미디어 플레이어지요. 이 이론은 애플사와 애플사의 영업과 판매 전략을 연구하는 사람들에 의해 발전되었습니다. 이 이론에 따르면 iPod 제품에 만족한 사람들이 애플사의 다른 제품도 알게 되고 관심을 갖게 되며 마침내는 구입을 결정하게 되는데, 왜냐하면 iPod만큼 다른 제품들도 좋을 것이라고 믿기 때문입니다.

Reading Note

Topic
The halo effect

Main Idea
High evaluation of one quality affects the judging of other qualities

Details
(quality x → quality y) there is no relation

Listening Note

Example 1
Job interviews
- attractive applicants → other qualities are regarded as good as their looks

Example 2
The iPod halo effect
- a good appreciation of the iPod → buy other Apple products as well.

Vocabulary

- **predisposition** 경향, 성질
- **bias** 성향, 선입관
- **psychological term** 심리학 용어
- **competence** 능력, 역량
- **interviewer** 면접관
- **presume** 가정(간주)하다
- **presumption** 추정, 가정
- **portable media player** 휴대용 미디어 플레이어
- **strategy** 전략
- **purchase** 구입하다

STEP 2 • Speaking

Definition — p68

2 Folding occurs when two of the earth's plates meet and push against each other.

3 Deviant behavior is any recognized violation of the norms accepted by society.

4 The halo effect occurs when a particularly good quality of a person becomes the basis of how we view that person's other possible qualities or abilities.

Citation — p71

2 ability to deform under pressure and heat
- The professor describes this by stating that some rocks function like plastics when they are put under heat and pressure.

3 normal way of dissolving a marriage / conservative societies / any Protestant communities
- According to the professor, while divorce is seen as acceptable in many cultures, it is still seen as highly deviant within a Catholic culture.

4 the appearance of the interviewee
- The professor says that this effect is often seen during an interview, where the interviewer might be attracted to the interviewee's appearance and believe other qualities of that applicant are as good as his looks.

Explanation — p74

2 susceptible to mountain folding / markedly different
- The professor illustrates the concept of mountain folding. Some rocks are susceptible to mountain folding and others don't do this; they just shatter, and so they won't form folded mountains.

3 quite different social norms / highly deviant to the older generation
- The professor discusses the teenagers in 1960s. They had a very different set of values than their parents. They felt that wearing strange clothing and experimenting with drug were acceptable forms of behavior, but people in their parents' generation found these actions to be highly deviant.

4 supports this presumption
- The first example shows how one's appearance affects a job interview.

Practice Questions

1

| 지문해석 | **최상위 포식자의 취약성**: 최상위 포식자란 먹이사슬 제일 상위에 있으면서 다른 동물에게 잡아 먹히지 않는 동물을 의미한다. 이 사실 때문에 사람들은 최상위 포식자는 곧 힘이 센 동물과 동일시 된다. 그러나 사실 최상의 포식자의 생명 주기는 굉장히 연약하며 파괴되기 쉽다. 이는 먹이가 되는 종에게 영향을 미치는 어떤 것이든, 최상위 포식자에게 궁극적으로 영향을 주기 때문이다. 그러므로 최상위 포식자는 다른 동물 종보다 더 많은 환경적 스트레스를 받게 된다.

| Script | OK, today we are going to talk about the American bald eagle, a predatory bird that lives at the top of its food chain. Now, in the 1970s and 1980s, the American bald eagle was on the brink of extinction ... uh, despite the fact that it is the national bird of the United States and therefore protected by law. What was really damaging the populations of the bald eagle was not hunting or the destruction of its habitat. It was the use of a pesticide called DDT, which was widely used by American farmers. DDT is a highly toxic chemical, and it tends to remain in the body for a very long time. Anyway, farmers used DDT on their fields, and the mice and small rodents that lived in those fields absorbed the DDT into their bodies, but not in high enough concentrations to really harm them. But a bald eagle might eat hundreds of mice over the course of a year, so DDT became much more concentrated in the bodies of the bald eagles. DDT poisoning didn't kill the bald eagles, but it made many of them sterile, and this was the reason for their population decline.

| Script 해석 | 네, 오늘은 먹이 사슬의 제일 위에 있는 육식성 조류인 미국 대머리 독수리에 대해서 이야기해 봅시다. 1970년대와 1980년대에 미국 대머리 독수리는 거의 멸종 위기에 처했습니다. 미국의 국조라서 법의 보호를 받는데도말이죠. 이 새의 수를 정말로 감소시켰던 것은 사냥이나 거주지 감소의 위험이 아니었습니다. 당시 미국 농부들이많이 사용 했던 DDT라는 살충제가 바로 그 원인입니다. DDT는 독극 화학물질이며 체내에 오랜 시간 남아 있습니다. 어쨌든 농부들이 자신의 밭에다가 DDT를 뿌립니다. 그리고 밭에 사는 쥐같이 작은 설치류들이 체내에 이 DDT를 흡수합니다. 그들에게 해를 끼칠 정도로 많은 양이 축적 되는 것은 아니지만, 대머리 독수리는 일 년 동안 수 백 마리의 쥐를 잡아 먹고 DDT가 체내에 축적되는 양이 더 많아 집니다. DDT 중독은 대머리 독수리를 죽이지 않았지만 불임 상태로 만들었습니다. 그리고 이것이 개체수가 감소하게 된 이유였습니다.

Reading Note

Apex predators
- the life cycles of apex predators are remarkably fragile
  → apex predators are affected by anything that impacts their prey species
  → apex predators are subject to far greater environmental stress than other animal species

Listening Note

1) the American bald eagle was on the brink of extinction
   - farmers used DDT and mice absorbed the DDT
   - a bald eagle eats hundreds of mice in a year.
   - DDT poisoning didn't kill the bald eagles
     → but it made them sterile and was the reason for the population decline.

| Sample Response | According to the professor, the population decline of the American bald eagle was due to the use of a pesticide called DDT. DDT was absorbed into the bodies of mice and small rodents, but not in large enough amounts to kill them. Bald eagles, however, ate hundreds of these small animals, and so the DDT levels in their bodies rose to levels high enough to make them sterile. Thus DDT has a greater effect on the populations of bald eagles than on other animals because bald eagles are apex predators and the toxins build to higher levels in their bodies. This demonstrates the sensitivity of apex predators to environmental problems.

Vocabulary

- synonymous 동일한, 뜻이 같은　environmental stress 환경적 스트레스　extinction 멸종　destruction 파괴　pesticide 살충제　toxic chemical 독성이 있는 화학물질　rodent 설치류 동물
- absorb 흡수하다　concentration 농축, 응축　DDT 디디티(살충제)　demonstrate 입증, 증명하다　sensitivity 민감한　environmental problems 환경적인 문제들

2

|지문해석| **처벌과 강화**: 처벌과 강화는 행동을 수정하려는 노력의 일환으로 사용하는 두 가지 방법이다. 처벌은 바람직하지 않은 행동을 그만두게 하기 위해 사용된다. 바람직하지 않은 행동을 하면 불쾌한 자극을 더하거나 유쾌한 자극을 줄임으로써 벌을 받는다. 강화는 바람직한 행동을 보상함으로써 격려하는 것이다. 보상은 유쾌한 자극을 더해주거나 부정적인 것을 소멸함으로써 주어진다. 대개 강화가 행동 수정에 있어서 더욱 효과적인 형태인데, 이는 바람직한 행동을 바로 격려하기 때문이다. 반면에 처벌은 반드시 바람직한 행동을 하게 하지 않는다.

|Script| OK, one of the biggest challenges for new parents is toilet training their child. The best way is to praise the child for progress. Uh, let's say that you have a young son, and he comes and tells you that he has to go to the bathroom, instead of just going in his diaper. Well, then after you take him to the bathroom, you praise him and tell him what a "big boy" he is. Uh, you can also use longer term goals. For example, you can promise the child that when he is fully potty trained, he will get to wear "big boy's pants." That way the child has a goal to work towards. This works really well because there is a specific behavior the child must engage in to get praise, i.e. he must not soil his diaper. Scolding the child for soiling his diaper would be far less effective. Here, the child does not learn that using the bathroom like an adult is "good." He only learns that soiling his diaper is "bad." As a result the child may not learn to go to the bathroom. Instead, he may, uh, simply learn not to tell his parents when he has soiled his diaper in order to avoid being scolded.

|Script 해석| 자, 막 부모가 된 사람들에게 있어서 가장 큰 도전 중 하나는 아이의 용변 교육입니다. 가장 좋은 방법은 잘 한 일에 대해서 칭찬을 하는 것입니다. 아들이 한 명 있다고 해봅시다, 그리고 그 아이가 와서 화장실에 가고 싶다는 말을 합니다, 기저귀에다가 볼일을 보지 않고 말이죠. 음, 그렇다면 여러분은 아이를 화장실로 데리고 간 뒤에 아이를 칭찬해주고 '다 큰 아이' 라고 말해줍니다. 더 장기적인 목표를 사용할 수도 있습니다. 예를 들어, 아이에게 기저귀를 완전히 떼고 나면 '큰 아이가 입는 바지' 를 입을 수 있게 된다는 약속을 할 수 있습니다. 이렇게 함으로써 아이에게는 이루어야 할 목표가 생기는 것입니다. 이는 아이가 칭찬을 받기 위해서 해내야 할 특정한 행동 – 다시 말하면, 기저귀를 더럽히지 않는 것 – 이기 때문에 큰 효과를 볼 수 있습니다. 기저귀를 더럽혔다고 아이를 꾸짖는 것은 훨씬 효과가 없습니다. 이렇게 하면 아이들은 화장실을 어른들처럼 사용하는 행동이 '좋은 것' 이라는 사실을 배우지 못합니다. 아이는 단지 기저귀를 더럽히는 것이 '나쁜 일' 이라는 것만을 배웁니다. 결과적으로 화장실을 사용하는 법을 배우지 못합니다. 대신에 아이는 혼나지 않으려고 기저귀가 더럽혀졌을 때에도 부모에게 말하지 않게 됩니다.

Reading Note

Punishment & reinforcement
Used to modify behavior
→ Punishment is used to discourage a behavior
→ Reinforcement works to encourage a behavior

Listening Note

1) Praise the child for progress.
   - praise him and tell him what a "big boy"
2) Scold the child for soiling his diaper
   - less effective
   - does not learn that using the bathroom like an adult is "good," but only learns that soiling his diaper is "bad."

|Sample Response| The professor talks about the different methods a parent can use to toilet train a child. The professor says that one way is to praise or reward the child. For example, the professor says that the parent can reward the child verbally by telling the child that he is a "big boy" or with a material reward like letting him wear "big boys' pants." This would be an example of using reinforcement to encourage a desired behavior. The professor also says that the parent could scold the child when he soiled his diaper, which would be a form of punishment. But she says this is generally less effective than praising the child because the child may only learn not to tell his parents when he soils his diaper. This demonstrates the concept that reinforcement is more effective than punishment as a form of behavior modification.

Vocabulary
- unpleasant stimulus 불쾌한 자극
- reinforcement 강화
- toilet-train 변기 사용법 훈련
- scold 꾸짖다
- effective 효과적인
- verbally 언어적으로
- modification 수정, 변경, 조절

TASK 05 Problem / Solution

Sample Question

| Script 해석 | 여자: 왜 이젠 토요일마다 체육관에서 네가 안 보이는 거지? 요즘 다른 일이 있는지 바빠 보이네.
남자: 오, 그런 거 아냐, 믿어줘. 요즘 '의미 있는' 일자리를 찾느라 체육관에 못 갔어. 아버지가 언젠가 가게 하나를 물려주시려고 하거든. 그런데 내가 준비가 안됐다고 생각하셔. 그래서 내가 미래에 대해서 진지해지고 직업을 구해봐야 한다고 하셨어. 그게 내 인격을 쌓게 해준다나. 너도 알잖아 부모님들이 어떠신지.
여자: 그래. 나도 학교 근처에 있는 경영 회사에서 임시직으로 일하고 있어. 그냥 사무직이야. 인사과에서 항상 아르바이트생을 구하고 있던데, 한번 지원해보는 게 어때? 만약 들어온다면 회사가 어떻게 직원들을 관리하는지 배울 수 있을 텐데. 근사하지 않니? 용돈도 모을 수 있고 말이야.
남자: 응, 좋아 보인다. 실제로 봉급을 받는 직업이라. 그 일자리가 나한테 맞는지는 잘 모르겠지만 말이야.
여자: 아 그럼, 아버지 가게에서 일할 수 있는지 여쭤보는 건 어때? 경영 부분에서는 아직 신뢰하시지 못하더라도 상자같은 것을 쌓고 재고 정리를 하거나, 뭐 고객들을 맞이하는 사람으로 고용할 수도 있잖아. 급여를 주지는 않으실지도 몰라. 하지만 분명히 네가 언젠가 스스로 그 가게를 운영할 준비를 해줄 거야.
남자: 음, 다시 한번 살펴볼게. 어쩌면 다시 체육관에서 보자. |

Pre-Speaking
p81

STEP 1 • Basic Outlining

1

| Script | W: I can't seem to get a break with my schedule. I'm about to graduate, and this is what I get ...
M: Oh, you're having problems getting into your required courses, huh?
W: You got it. I need to take this course to graduate ... and now they tell me the course isn't offered this semester. My graduation is on the line here, and I have no idea how I'll be able to get through this.
M: It's not really the end of the world, you know. If you really have to, you could take the course taken by the graduate students. It's probably harder than your typical course, but you'll be able to graduate if you pass it.
W: Well, there is that ... and it is going to be harder than my usual level ...
M: Or you can try cross-registering to our affiliate college for the same course. It's a long distance from our school, but you'll have the exact course you need in order to graduate. So, what do you think?
W: I think I need to think about this very carefully. I don't want to regret choosing one over the other. Thanks for the advice, though! |

| Script 해석 | 여자: 내 시간표는 너무 빡빡해. 곧 졸업인데 내 상황은 왜 이럴까?
남자: 아, 필수 과목 때문에 문제가 생긴 거야?
여자: 맞아. 졸업을 하려면 이 과목을 들어야 하는데 이번 학기에 개설이 안 된다는 거야. 졸업을 못할 수도 있단 말이야. 어떻게 해야 할지 도무지 모르겠어.
남자: 이봐, 세상이 끝난 건 아니잖아. 정말 들어야 한다면 대학원 수업을 들으면 되잖아. 정규 과목보다야 좀 어렵겠지만 통과만하면 졸업할 수 있어.
여자: 글쎄, 그렇지만 내 수준보다 더 어려울 텐데.
남자: 아니면 우리 학교와 결연을 맺은 학교에 학점 교류 신청을 해서 같은 과목을 들을 수도 있어. 거리가 좀 멀긴 하지만 졸업하기 위해 들어야 하는 그 과목을 들을 수 있어. 어떻게 생각해?
여자: 신중하게 생각해봐야겠다. 잘못 선택해서 후회하고 싶지는 않거든. 어쨌든 조언 고마워. |

Vocabulary
management 경영, 처리, 조작   clerical staff 사무직원   personnel department 인사과   promising 유망한   stack 쌓아 올리다
inventory work 재고정리 업무   typical course 정규과목   affiliate college 결연대학   get through 헤쳐나가다, 극복하다
cross-registering 학점교류신청

2

| Script |

M: Hey, Alice, what's up with all those forms?

W: Oh these? I'm just weighing my options; that's all. I got offers from two grad schools. I'm trying to figure out which one's the best for me ...

M: Well, what are they offering, anyway? There's got to be something you like ...

W: Here's the thing. One's offering me a full scholarship, but it is three hours away from home and where I'm working right now ... the other one's only given me a partial scholarship, but it's just a stone's throw away from my apartment ... And you know I can't afford the tuition or lose my part-time job ...

M: Don't you think it's better to accept the partial scholarship, since as you said, it's near your apartment and all? You don't have to travel all the way just to get to school, and you can use your extra time for your part-time job.

W: That seems logical ... still, I'm not sure about the school expenses...

M: Well ... then take the full scholarship. That way, you won't have to worry about paying for your tuition. Not a lot of people get offers like yours. And if it's the job you're worried about, you could start looking for jobs within the school area ... that way, you won't have to worry about not having one.

W: Thanks for the input. I'll think it over this weekend.

| Script 해석 |

남자: 안녕, 앨리스, 이 서류는 다 뭐야?

여자: 아 이거? 내가 선택할 수 있는 것을 두고 생각하고 있는 중이야. 대학원 두 군데에서 입학 허가를 받았거든. 어떤 것이 제일 나은지 알아보는 중이야.

남자: 흠, 어떤 제안인데 그래? 네가 원하는 게 반드시 있을 거야.

여자: 뭐냐 하면, 한 곳에서는 전액 장학금을 준대. 그런데 우리 집과 내 직장에서 세 시간이 걸려. 다른 곳은 부분 장학금을 주지만 내 아파트에서 무척 가까워. 너도 알잖아 학비를 다 낼 수도 아르바이트를 그만 둘 여유도 없다는 것을 말이야.

남자: 네 말처럼 그 부분 장학금 주는 학교를 가는 게 낫지 않겠어? 너희 집에서 가까운 곳에 있잖아. 학교에 가기 위해서 오래 걸리지 않아도 되고 남는 시간에 아르바이트를 할 수도 있잖아.

여자: 그게 맞는 것처럼 보이지만 학비가 얼마가 더 들어갈지 잘 모르겠어.

남자: 그럼 전액 장학금을 선택해. 그렇다면 학비 걱정은 하지 않아도 될 테니. 모두가 이런 제안 받을 수 있는 것은 아니잖아. 그리고 일자리가 걱정 된다면 학교 근처에서 찾아봐도 되고. 그렇게 하면 일자리를 잃는 문제는 걱정할 필요 없잖아.

여자: 의견 고마워. 주말 동안 한번 생각해볼게.

Listening Note

Problem Choosing a grad school to attend

Solutions

1) One offering a full scholarship
   - far from her home & workplace
   - need the job to pay for tuition
   - not a common opportunity
   - could look for a job there

2) One offering a partial sch.
   - very close
   - can keep her part-time job

Reasons
① More helpful to her finances -no worry about tuition 'til graduation
② Can get another job near the school -part-time jobs are easy to find

Vocabulary

figure out 계산하다, 생각해 내다   a stone's throw away 지척지간, 매우 가까운 거리   partial scholarship 부분적인 장학금
school expenses 학비

3

| Script |

W: Whoa! Hold it ... those boxes look heavy. Let me help. Where you off to?

M: Oh, thanks. I'm starting to move some of my stuff over to my cousin's place ... just two blocks away from here. My lease won't expire 'til after next month, but my landlord wants me out by next week. I forgot that I forfeited my last month's stay the last time I renewed my lease ... I just don't know how I'll manage to get all my stuff out on time ...

W: Why? What do you mean?

M: I mean I don't have the time this week because I have to be out of town ... part of my internship with Prof. Miller. I missed the last two sessions. I can't afford to miss another one.

W: Oh, I see ... that's a tough one ... hmmm, well, why don't you ask some of your close friends to do the moving for you while you're away? See if one of them has a truck you could use to make it easier ...

M: Well, yeah, I could probably ask them ... but I was also thinking of just paying a couple of professional movers to do the job. They'll know what to do with my stuff ... what do you think?

W: That's actually up to you ... why don't you weigh your options and then decide, hopefully by tomorrow morning ... see what works for you?

M: Right. I should think about this first before I do anything ... Thanks for the help!

| Script 해석 |

여자: 왜! 잠깐만, 이 상자들 무거워 보인다. 도와줄게. 어디로 가져가는 거야?

남자: 아, 고마워. 사촌 집으로 옮겨다 놓으려고. 여기서 두 블록 떨어져있거든. 임대가 다음 달이 되야 끝나는데 집주인이 다음 주에 방을 빼달래. 지난 번에 재계약 하면서 마지막 달에 살지 않기로 한걸 잊어버리고 있었어. 내 물건을 시간 안에 다 옮길 수 있을지 모르겠다.

여자: 왜? 무슨 뜻이야?

남자: 내 말은 밀러 교수님이랑 하는 인턴쉽 때문에 이번 주에 어딜 좀 가야 하거든. 지난 두 번도 모두 못해서 이번에는 안하면 안돼.

여자: 아, 무슨 말인지 알겠어. 어려운 일이네. 그럼 친한 친구들한테 너 없는 사이에 물건 옮기는걸 좀 도와달라고 하면 어때? 더 쉽게 이사 할 수 있게 누구에게 트럭이 있는지도 알아보고.

남자: 흠, 그래 부탁해 볼 수 있겠다. 그렇지만 이사 대행업체를 알아볼까 생각해 보기도 했거든. 어떻게 하는지 잘 알 것 같아서, 어떻게 생각해?

여자: 네 판단에 달린 문제네. 선택할 수 있는걸 잘 생각해 보고 어떤 것이 더 나을지 내일 아침쯤 결정하는 것이 어때?

남자: 맞아. 생각해보고 결정해야겠다. 도와줘서 고마워!

Listening Note

Problem   Moving his stuff to his cousin's place
Solutions
1) Ask his friends for help
   Reasons
   ① More reliable
     • prof. movers might not be careful
   ② Costs less
     • prof. movers are expensive

2) Hiring professional movers
   • they do the job well

Vocabulary

stuff 물질, 물건   forfeit ~을 잃다, 박탈 당하다   professional movers 이사 대행업체   hopefully 원컨대

4

| Script |

M: Hey, do you know anyone taking the Geology class this coming summer?
W: No, I don't think so ... Why, what's up? Aren't you attending the same class?
M: Yeah, I am. Thing is ... I'm having a hard time taking notes in class lately. Ever since I sprained my hand, my writing's been slower. And if I push too hard, it gets really painful.
W: Hmmm. Well, maybe you could just borrow someone else's notes for the day and photocopy them or something ... It'll help take the stress off your hands trying to keep up with the lectures on the board ... you could ask your seatmate or someone close to you for the day's lecture notes.
M: That seems simple enough ... though, I'm not too sure about it.
W: Well, maybe you could just bring a tape recorder to class. You could try and sit at the front or near the professor so that the audio will be clear enough to listen to afterwards. Later, you can have someone transcribe the tape for you. You can borrow my recorder, if you want.
M: Well, you've definitely given me something to think about. Thanks!

| Script 해석 |

남자: 안녕, 이번 여름에 지질학 수업 듣는 사람 누구 아니?
여자: 글쎄, 모르겠는데. 왜, 무슨 일 이야? 지금 그 수업 듣고 있는 거 아니야?
남자: 맞아. 문제는 요즘 수업 때 노트 필기하는 것이 어려워서. 손목을 삔 뒤로 글 쓰는 속도가 느려졌거든. 세게 힘을 주면 너무 아파.
여자: 흠, 그럼 다른 사람 것을 빌려서 복사 같은 걸 하면 되잖아. 수업 시간에 칠판 내용을 노트 필기하는 수고를 덜어줄 수 있을 거야. 옆에 앉은 사람이나 가까운 데 앉은 사람한테 그 날 수업한 노트 필기를 빌려 달라고 부탁해 봐.
남자: 보기엔 간단한 일이지만, 자신이 없어.
여자: 흠, 그럼 녹음기를 가지고 가봐. 교수님이랑 가까운 앞 쪽에 앉으면, 나중에 들을 수 있을 정도로 목소리가 깨끗하게 녹음이 될 거야. 나중에 다른 사람한테 부탁해서 받아 적어 달라고 할 수도 있고 필요하면 내 녹음기를 빌려 줄게.
남자: 음, 생각해 봐야겠다. 고마워!

Listening Note

Problem Having a hard time taking notes in class

Solutions

1) borrow some else's notes - ask your seatmate or someone close to you for lecture notes

2) bring a tape recorder to class
   - sit near the professor so that the audio will be clear enough to listen
   - can have someone transcribe the tape

Reasons
① It is simpler - Borrow notes and photocopy them
② Recording is expensive - He has to buy a blank tape and then pay someone to transcribe it to paper.

Vocabulary

geology 지질학   painful 고통스러운, 힘든   take off 없애다, 줄이다   transcribe 필기하다   definitely 명확히, 확실히
seatmate 옆 친구, 동석자   photocopy 복사하다

STEP 2 • Speaking

Problem ---------- p86

2 I am just weighing my options.
→ The woman is having a hard time deciding which scholarship offer to accept due to her financial situation and work.

3 Where you off to? / I am starting to move some of my stuff / I can't afford to miss another one.
→ The man's problem is that he has to move out of his apartment, but he doesn't have much time because he has to go out of town for his internship.

4 anyone taking the Geology class/ I am having a hard time taking notes
→ The problem they discuss is that the man's injured hand makes it hard for him to take notes in class.

Solution ---------- p89

2 One's offering me a full scholarship / a partial scholarship / That seems logical / Not a lot of people get offers like yours.
→ There are two options presented. The first option is receiving a full scholarship from the school that is far away from home. The other option is to receive a partial scholarship from the school that is near her home and work.

3 just paying a couple of professional movers / Why don't you weigh your options
→ The woman advises that he could ask some of his friends to move his things for him. The man says that he could do that or that he could hire professional movers.

4 you could just borrow someone else's notes / It'll help take the stress off your hands / you could just bring a tape recorder to class / someone transcribe the tape for you
→ The woman suggests that he could borrow lecture notes from one of his classmates or bring a tape recorder and record the lecture.

Reason ---------- p92

2 And you know I can't afford the tuition or lose my part-time job / and you can use your extra time for your part-time job / paying for your tuition
→ Between the two solutions, I prefer to take the full scholarship. That way she doesn't need to worry about school fees until she graduates. Her financial problems will be more manageable with a full scholarship. And she can always look for another job that's nearer the school to save her more time.

3 They will know what to do with my stuff / Why don't you weigh your options and decide
→ I think asking his friends for help is better than hiring professional movers. First, if there is nobody there to watch over them, they might not be very careful when they move his things. His furniture might get damaged. Plus, it would be expensive to hire movers. If he asks his friends, they will probably be happy to do this favor for him.

4 It'll help take the stress off your hands trying to keep up with the lectures on the board / You could try and sit at the front or near the professor
→ I believe the best way is to borrow lecture notes and photocopy them. It will be as good as if he had taken notes himself. Recording is also more expensive because he has to buy a blank tape, and then pay someone to transcribe it to paper.

Practice Questions

p94

1

| Script |

W: Hey, Mike. Oh, is something wrong? You look worried.

M: Yeah ... There is a problem that keeps bugging me ... this contemporary history course is one of my favorite courses this semester.

W: Oh, what's the problem with that course?

M: Well, here's the problem. You know I work every night in a bar, and this job pays me well. The problem is, I keep missing the class in the early morning because I can't get up early after all the work at night ...

W: I see ... But you do know that your studies are more important than anything else right now, right? Missing any more of your early class will greatly affect your standing. You need to get a job with an earlier schedule. You're not going to get good grades at this rate.

M: You don't have to remind me; it's my favorite class, even. But I earn good money from my evening job; I can't leave it just like that. It's not like I'm missing my morning class on purpose. The job is just important to me, too.

W: You know what? I just remembered ... that same course is being offered in the afternoon, but it's with a different professor. I can get you the class schedule to be sure. You won't have to let go of your current job then.

M: Seems fair enough ... but this is a big step for me. I need to think about what I'll do very carefully. Whatever decision I make here will greatly affect me ...

W: Let's hope you make the best one!

| Script 해석 |

여자: 안녕, 마이크. 오, 무슨 일 있어? 걱정스러워 보인다.

남자: 응, 계속 괴롭히는 문제가 하나 있어서. 이 현대 역사라는 과목, 이번 학기 수강하는 과목 중에 제일 좋아하는 건데 말이야.

여자: 오, 그런데 그 수업에 무슨 문제가 있는 거야?

남자: 흠, 뭐냐 하면, 내가 저녁마다 바에서 일하는 거 알지? 급료도 높거든. 문제는 밤 늦게까지 일하고 나면 피곤해서 아침에 일찍 못 일어나기 때문에 아침 수업을 계속 빠지게 된다는 것이야.

여자: 그랬구나. 그렇지만 지금은 공부가 다른 어떤 것보다 중요한 시기잖아, 안 그래? 아침 수업을 계속 빠진다면 네 성적에 큰 문제가 생길 거야. 좀더 일찍 할 수 있는 일을 찾아봐. 이렇게 하다가는 좋은 성적을 얻을 수 없을 거야.

남자: 그렇게 말하지 않아도 알아. 그리고 그건 내가 제일 좋아하는 수업이야. 그런데 밤에 일하면 돈을 많이 받는단 말이야, 이렇게 그만 둘 수는 없어. 내가 일부러 오전 수업을 안가는 것도 아니고, 나한테는 일자리도 중요해.

여자: 그거 알아? 방금 기억이 났는데, 오후에도 같은 수업이 있어. 하지만 교수님은 다른 사람일거야. 내가 확실히 시간을 알아봐 줄게. 오후 수업을 듣는다면 일자리를 그만 두지 않아도 될 거야.

남자: 좋은 생각인 것 같아. 그렇지만 중요한 결정이니까, 어떻게 해야 할지 곰곰이 생각해 볼게. 어떤 결정을 내려도 큰 영향을 받을 테니까.

여자: 가장 좋은 선택을 하길 바래!

Listening Note

Problem I can't get up early after working at night

Solutions

1) Get a job with an earlier schedule
   • avoid getting bad grades

2) Attend the same course offered in the afternoon
   • Different professor
   • No need to change your job

Reasons

① Going to class and studying should be a student's first priority.

② If he does poorly in his classes, there is no point in working to earn money for school.

Sample Response

The man's problem is that he keeps missing his early morning class because he works late at night. The woman suggests that he should either get a job where he doesn't have to work until late night or change his morning class to an afternoon class. I think he should try to find a job where he doesn't have to work so late. Going to class and studying should be the student's first priority. The man can always find another way to make money, or he can take out a loan if he really needs to. If he does poorly in his classes because he is working late, that kind of defeats the point of working to earn money for school anyway.

Vocabulary

contemporary history course 현대(근대) 역사 과목   priority 우선순위   defeat 패배시키다

2

| Script |

M: Oh. Hi there! How's it going?
W: Oh ... Hi ...
M: You seem to lack energy today. Are there any problems?
W: Don't mind me ... It's just that I haven't eaten yet. The new people in the cafeteria have been serving an all-meat course. I learned that they will be doing that for the whole week because of some problems with vegetable delivery ... and you know I'm a vegetarian ...
M: I'm so sorry. Can I help? Can I buy you something?
W: Oh, no, thanks ... I have already drunk some coffee ...
M: Well, maybe you can just eat out starting tomorrow ... try the restaurants around ... I heard they serve good vegetable dishes.
W: Yes, I may try doing that ... are you sure it doesn't cost a lot?
M: Well, you could also try preparing your lunch at home. I mean, you could pass by the supermarket before you go home, and then buy vegetables, fruit, and stuff you can eat ... I'm sure you could do that in your spare time at night.
W: I don't know ... that sounds kind of inconvenient. I don't know what to do yet, but I think I should decide before tomorrow comes.
M: Yeah, think about it.

| Script 해석 |

남자: 오, 안녕! 잘 지내니?
여자: 오, 안녕.
남자: 기운이 없어 보인다. 무슨 문제 있니?
여자: 신경 쓰지마. 아직 아무것도 못 먹어서 그래. 식당 사람들이 고기로 된 음식만 팔아. 야채 공급에 문제가 생겨서 일주일 내내 그렇게 할 거라고 들었어. 너도 알다시피 난 채식주의자이잖니.
남자: 안됐다, 좀 도와줄까? 뭐라도 사다 줄까?
여자: 오, 아니야. 고마워. 커피 좀 마셨어.
남자: 내일부터 학교 밖에 있는 식당에 가서 밥을 먹는 게 어때? 야채 요리 잘하는 데가 있다고 들었는데.
여자: 응, 아마 그렇게 해야 될지도. 많이 비싸지는 않을까?
남자: 흠, 그럼 집에서 점심을 싸오는 건 어때? 내 말은 집에 가기 전에 슈퍼에 들러서 야채와 과일이랑 먹을 만한 것을 좀 사는 거야. 밤에 장 볼 시간은 있을 것 같은데.
여자: 잘 모르겠어. 좀 불편할 것 같은데. 어떻게 해야 할지 모르겠지만, 내일이 되기 전에 결정해야겠다.
남자: 그래, 잘 생각해봐.

Listening Note

Solutions

1) Eat out
   - expensive

   ↳ **Reasons**
   ① It's more convenient
   ② It's just a week. Doesn't cost too much!

2) Prepare lunch at home
   - buy food and prepare lunch at home
   - inconvenient

Sample Respone | The woman is having problems with the all-meat courses being served in the cafeteria because she is a vegetarian. It will be like that for a week since there are problems with the vegetable delivery. The man advises her to eat in nearby restaurants, or prepare her lunch at home. In my opinion the woman should eat out, since it's more convenient. Going to the market and cooking at home take so much time, and she'll still be spending much money. Besides, the all-meat menu will only be for a week, so it shouldn't be too much of a strain on her budget.

Vocabulary

all-meat course 고기로만 만든 음식 코스   vegetable delivery 야채공급   inconvenient 불편한   nearby 가까이, 인접한   strain 압력

TASK 06 Summary

Sample Question

| 지문해석 | 약 삼 십에서 오 십만 년 전쯤 초기 선사 인류가 제일 처음으로 불을 사용하기 시작하면서 현대 인류 발전에 기여한 일련의 발전들이 시작되었습니다. 불의 발견은 모든 선사 시대와 문화 발전에 있어서 가장 위대한 일입니다. 우리 대부분은 불이 우리의 선조에게 제공한 여러 이점에 대해 이미 알고 있습니다. 물론, 불을 가지고 추운 날씨에도 보온을 할 수 있고 동물이나 해충을 쫓아내거나 무기를 강하게 하고 또 조리를 통해 음식을 부드럽게 만들 수 있습니다. 그러나 대부분 우리가 모르고 있는 사실은 바로 초기 불의 사용이 불러온 사회적 결과입니다. 사회적 효과 중 하나는 이 피조물들 사이에 더 좋은 조직 관계가 생긴 것 입니다. 여러분이 그들 중 한 사람이라고 상상해 보십시오, 그리고 당신의 무리나 부족이 밤에 휴식을 취하는데 불이 당신의 동굴 안에 지펴져 있다고 생각해 봅시다. 여러분은 물론 불 가까이로 가려 할 것이고 다른 사람들도 그렇게 할 것입니다. 이제 무리의 모든 사람은 얼굴을 맞대고 있습니다. 조만간 이런 밤의 활동은 정기적인 휴식 시간이 될 것이며, 사람들이 다른 사람들과 더 친밀하게 대화를 나누려고 노력함으로써 언어가 더욱 다듬어지고 서로를 더 잘 이해하고 의사 소통하는 결과를 낳게 될 것입니다. 불의 등장으로 인해 이 원시적인 조직 안에 사회적인 질서 또한 형성되었습니다. 불은 불 전문가의 출현으로 이어졌습니다. 알다시피 불을 만들고 이 중요한 도구를 간수하는 비밀을 아는 이 사람들이 바로 전문가들입니다. 이들은 조직에서 존경을 받고, 이 지식을 이용해 다른 이들로부터 존경을 얻어내었을 것입니다. 불 사용법을 배움으로써 그 집단에서 더 중요한 사람으로 인정받기 시작합니다.

Pre-Speaking
p99

STEP 1 • Basic Outlining

1

| Script | Unlike normal goods that can stand alone, related products are dependent on or affect one another, in terms of function. As pricing depends on the need for one or both products, they can either balance one another ... or replace one another. If a product undergoes a price increase, like the price of butter, for example ... people, as a natural tendency, may opt to buy an alternative product that basically serves the same use as butter and is much cheaper. They may start buying margarine instead, and if this happens, it will be the latter product that will be more in demand. As demand for butter decreases, its price will drop, and people may switch back to buying butter. Products that are involved in this kind of cyclical relationship are what we call substitute products. On the other hand, there are complementary products, where a product out in the market serves a particular purpose in relation to another product. For example a CD is only useful to the consumer if he or she goes out and buys a CD player. Uh ... therefore, CDs can't perform well in the market unless CD players also sell well. So, to arrange this, retailers may reduce the price of the player in order to encourage higher sales of CDs. The relationship is reciprocal ... if CDs were priced too highly, then consumers would not have much motivation to buy CD players.

| Script 해석 | 독자적인 일반 상품과는 달리 연관된 상품은 기능면에서 서로 의존적이며 또 영향을 줍니다. 가격을 정하는 것이 한 상품이나 양쪽 상품 모두의 수요에 달려있기 대문에, 그 둘은 균형을 이룰 수도 있고 상대방을 대체할 수도 있습니다. 예를 들어 버터 같은 상품의 가격이 오르면 사람들은 자연스럽게 버터와 같은 기능을 하지만 가격은 더 저렴한 대체품을 사게 될 수 있습니다. 사람들은 버터 대신 마가린을 살 것이고, 수요가 더 많아 지는 것은 마가린이겠죠. 버터의 수요가 줄어 들면 가격도 떨어지고 사람들은 다시 버터를 구매하게 됩니다. 이렇게 순환적인 관계로 연관되어있는 상품이 우리가 대체 상품이라고 부르는 것입니다. 반면에 보완의 기능을 하는 상품들도 있습니다. 즉, 시장의 한 상품의 목적이 다른 상품과 연관되어 있는 것이죠. 예를 들어, CD는 나가서 CD 플레이어를 산 사람에게만 필요한 물건입니다. 그렇기 때문에 CD 플레이어가 잘 팔리지 않으면 CD의 구매도 줄어듭니다. 그래서 소매업자들은 CD의 판매량을 늘리기 위해 CD 플레이어의 가격을 낮춥니다. 이 둘의 관계는 상호적이죠. CD의 가격이 너무 비싸면 CD 플레이어를 사려는 동기도 저하됩니다.

Vocabulary
cultiminate in 결국 ~이 되다.   prehistoric 선사시대의   consequence 결과   creature 창조물   hierarchy 위계, 계층   primitive 원시시대의
emergence 출현   admiration 칭찬, 감탄   related product 관련 상품   natural tendency 자연스러운 경향   alternative product 대체 상품
substitute product 대체 상품   complementary product 보완 상품   reciprocal 상호적인   motivation 동기, 자극, 유인

2

| Script | Our cognition, made up of our perceptions and philosophies, affects our behavior and everyday decisions. There is cognitive dissonance whenever a situation arises wherein there is an apparent conflict between our beliefs and our actions. When such a situation arises, our highest psychological priority is to relieve that dissonance. Let's say you have a family that is planning a vacation, but the only money available to take the vacation is money that they have set aside for their son's education. Um, in this situation, cognitive dissonance will arise because the family's wish to take a vacation conflicts with their belief in providing a good education for their son. This conflict must be resolved in some way. Most likely the family will decide that their son's education is more important and decide not to take the vacation. Uh, in another situation, let's say you have a man who is starving but has no money. He can steal food to feed himself, but he has always been taught that stealing is wrong. Again, the conflict results in cognitive dissonance. This time, however, the man resolves this by altering his beliefs. He reasons that it isn't really wrong to steal food to feed himself. By altering his previously held beliefs, he is able to resolve the dissonance.

| Script 해석 | 지각과 철학으로 이루어진 인간의 인지는 행동과 일상적인 결정에 영향을 미칩니다. 신념과 행동 사이에 명백한 갈등이 있는 상황이 생기면 인지적 불협화가 생겨납니다. 이런 상황이 발생하면 최고의 심리적 우선순위는 불협화를 경감시키는 것입니다. 휴가를 계획하고 있는 가족을 예로 들어보죠. 휴가를 위해 사용할 수 있는 예산은 아들의 교육을 위해서 저축해 둔 것이 전부입니다. 이런 상황에서 휴가를 가고 싶어하는 가족의 소망과 아들에게 좋은 교육을 주고 싶은 신념이 갈등을 일으켜서 인지적 불협화가 생깁니다. 이 마찰은 어떤 식으로든 해결 되어야 합니다. 대부분의 가정은 아들의 교육이 휴가를 가지 못하는 것보다 더 중요하다고 결정을 내리게 됩니다. 굶고 있는데 돈은 없는 한 남자가 있다고 가정해 보죠. 그는 음식을 훔쳐 배를 채울 수도 있지만 도둑질은 나쁜 것이라고 늘 배워왔습니다. 다시 말해 갈등이 인지적 불협화를 만들어냅니다. 그러나 이 경우에 이 남자는 신념을 변화시킴으로써 이 불협화를 감소시킵니다. 그는 배고픔을 해결하기 위해 음식을 훔치는 것이 그렇게 나쁜 것은 아니라고 변명을 합니다. 예전에 믿었던 신념을 바꿈으로써 이런 불협화를 해결합니다.

Listening Note

Problem Cognitive Dissonance - a conflict between our beliefs and our actions

Example 1
Desire vs. obligation

Main Idea 1
- Desire two different things, but has money for one thing

Details
family's money
Vacation vs. son's education
→ prioritize to resolve conflict

Example 2
Need vs. moral beliefs

Main Idea 2
- Is in dire need of something, but getting it may go against morals

Details
a starving man with no money for food
→ believes stealing is wrong
→ what is more important –physical need or mental belief

Vocabulary
perception 인지, 지각   cognitive 인지적인   psychological priority 심리적 우선순위   dissonance 부조화음
set aside (토지, 이윤 따위를) 유보해 놓은 것   obligation 의무, 구속, 책임   belief 신념

3

| Script | Slash-and-burn farming is a type of farming that is commonly used in tropical regions, especially in rainforests. In slash-and-burn farming, all the large trees are cut down and then intentionally set on fire. The resulting fire burns away the stumps of the trees and the remaining vegetation, leaving a clear field that may then be planted with crops. But as you'll see in a few minutes, slash-and-burn farming is heavily destructive to the environment. OK, first of all, uh, slash-and-burn farming destroys large areas of forest. Not only does a farmer have to cut down a section of forest to create a field for farming, but that field also will only be productive for maybe three or four years. Slash-and-burn farming quickly exhausts the nutrients in the soil, and so farmers constantly have to move to a new field. Obviously that means they have to cut down more trees. Thus, slash-and-burn farming represents a significant source of deforestation, which is helping to cause global warming. Another way that slash-and-burn farming destroys the environment is that, uh, well, as I said ... it destroys all the large trees. Those trees have large root structures that go deep into the soil and help hold the soil together. The crops that farmers plant in place of those large trees have very shallow root structures and don't do nearly as good a job at holding the soil together. It becomes loose and easily blown or washed away. So slash-and-burn farming also contributes to soil erosion.

| Script 해석 | 화전 농업은 열대 지역, 특히 열대 우림에서 자주 사용되는 농업 형태입니다. 화전 농업에선, 나무를 다 베어낸 뒤 고의로 불을 냅니다. 불을 내어 나무 그루터기와 남은 초목을 다 없애고 작물을 심을 수 있는 넓은 들판을 만듭니다. 그러나 곧 아시게 되겠지만 이런 농업은 아주 환경 파괴적입니다. 자, 우선, 화전 농업은 넓은 면적의 숲을 파괴합니다. 밭을 만들기 위해서 숲의 나무를 다 잘라내야 하는 것뿐 아니라, 그렇게 해서 생긴 밭은 3-4년 정도만 곡물을 생산해 낼 수 있습니다. 화전 농업은 토양내의 영양분을 빨리 고갈시키기에, 농민들은 계속해서 새로운 토지를 찾아 떠납니다. 이 말은 더 많은 나무를 베어내야 한다는 뜻이죠. 그렇기 때문에 화전 농업은 산림 벌채의 큰 요인이며 이는 지구 온난화의 원인이 됩니다. 화전 농업이 환경을 파괴하는 또 다른 방법은 제가 말했듯이, 이것이 큰 나무를 다 파괴한다는 것입니다. 큰 나무는 큰 뿌리를 가지고 있어 토양 속으로 깊이 들어가서 토양을 지탱해줍니다. 큰 나무가 심겨져 있던 땅에 농민들이 심는 곡식은 뿌리가 얕아서 큰 나무처럼 토양을 잘 지탱해주지 못합니다. 그렇기 때문에 물에 잘 쓸려가거나 바람에 날려갑니다. 그렇기 때문에 화전 농업은 토양 침식의 원인이 됩니다.

Listening Note

Problem Slash-and-burn farming - destructive to the environment

Example 1	Example 2
Contributes to deforestation	Causes soil erosion
Main Idea 1	**Main Idea 2**
• Large areas of forest destroyed	• It destroys all large trees.
Details	**Details**
• nutrients in soil weakened → field is only good for 3-4 years.	• trees' roots hold soil together • new vegetation has smaller, weaker root structure • soil becomes loose and easily blown or washed away

---

Vocabulary
slash-and-burn farming 화전 농업   rainforest 열대 우림   stump 그루터기, 밑동   destructive 파괴적인
deforestation 살림 벌채   global warming 지구 온난화   shallow 얕은   contribute 원조하다, 제공하다   soil erosion 토양 침식

4

| Script | When people aspire to climb the social ladder, material goods generally take on a greater importance in their lives than they had before. The acquisition of luxury goods and other high dollar items serves as a visual symbol, not only to others, but also to oneself, of one's rising status in society. Such an emphasis on the confirmation of one's status through material possessions feeds into the culture of consumerism. You see, class, in a culture of consumerism, it's not only your own needs that determine your purchases; societal expectations play a large role as well. It doesn't matter if what you have is enough to sustain you; if your lifestyle doesn't meet the expectations of society, you will see it as inadequate. Like, say you earn decent money, have a car and a house ... this would seem to be enough, right? But then you look around you, and it seems that everyone has a nicer car ... or a bigger house. Since these material possessions are symbols of our social status, you will be driven to purchase a bigger car or a bigger house, simply to gain the same social stature as those around you ... even though you may not really need the bigger car or the bigger house. Thus consumerism leads to a lifestyle of excess, because you are constantly under pressure to match or, even better, surpass the possessions of those around you. Uh, in addition to creating a culture of excess, uh, consumerism also worsens the effects of poverty. Not everyone has the money for the big car or the big house ... but everyone in society feels the same pressure to buy those things. Thus the poor are often pressured to buy items they really can't afford. Think about the young teenager in a poor family who just has to have a $150 pair of tennis shoes. Given his family's financial situation, this isn't a logical purchase, but societal pressure to prove his social status by purchasing the shoes drives that teenager to buy them anyway.

| Script 해석 | 사람들이 사회적 출세를 열망하게 되면, 물질이 전보다 인생에서 차지하는 중요성이 더 커지게 됩니다. 고급 상품과 비싼 물건을 소유하는 것은 타인에게뿐만 아니라 자신에게도 사회에서 높아지는 지위의 상징이 됩니다. 물질 소유를 통해 사람의 지위를 확인하는 일에 대한 강조는 소비문화 안으로 들어가게 됩니다. 여러분도 알다시피, 소비 문화에서 구매 결정에는 스스로의 필요뿐 아니라 사회적인 기대가 큰 몫을 합니다. 생활을 유지하는데 충분히 가지고 있느냐가 문제가 아닙니다. 자신의 생활 양식이 만약 사회의 기대에 부응하지 못한다면, 적당하지 않다고 생각하게 됩니다. 남부럽지 않게 돈을 벌고 차도 집도 있다고 해봅시다. 이 정도면 충분하다고 생각할까요? 그러나 여러분이 주위를 본다면 모든 사람이 당신보다 더 좋은 차와 더 큰 집을 가지고 있는 것처럼 보입니다. 이런 물질적인 소유는 사회 지위의 상징이기 때문에 더 큰 차와 더 큰 집을 사야 한다는 생각을 하게 됩니다. 비록 더 큰 차와 더 큰집이 실제로는 필요하지 않아도 여러분 주위의 사람들과 같은 사회적인 위상을 얻기 위해서 그렇게 합니다. 여러분은 끊임없이 주변 사람들이 소유한 수준과 비슷하거나 혹은 더 능가 해야 한다고 생각하기 때문에 소비 문화는 과도한 생활 양식을 낳게 합니다. 소비주의는 이런 무절제한 문화를 만들어내는 것 뿐 아니라 가난의 영향에 악화시킵니다. 모두가 다 큰 차와 큰 집을 살 수 있는 돈을 가진 것은 아니지만, 사회에서 모두가 이런 것들을 사야 한다는 압박을 느낍니다. 그래서 가난한 사람들도 자기 능력 밖의 물건을 구매해야 한다는 생각을 하게 됩니다. 어느 가난한 집의 십대가 한 켤레에 150불 하는 테니스화를 가져야 한다고 생각해 봅시다. 이 가정의 경제적인 상황을 보면 이건 이성적인 구매가 아닙니다. 그렇지만 신발 구매를 통해 사회적인 지위를 증명하게 하는 사회적 압박으로 이 십대가 어떻게든 신발을 사게 됩니다.

Listening Note

Problem Effects of consumerism - Social expectations affect your decision to purchase goods

Example 1 Creates a culture of excess

Main Idea 1
- Outside pressure to continually upgrade material goods
- Everyone else has more or better possessions

Details
trying to keep up with ppl. who have better houses or cars.

Example 2 Worsens effects of poverty

Main Idea 2
- Not everyone is rich, but pressure to buy things is the same for everyone
- People buy luxury goods regardless of their financial ability

Details
a teenager from a poor family wants the same expensive athletic shoes as his peers.

Vocabulary

social ladder 사회적 계층   acquisition 습득, 취득   luxury goods 사치품   confirmation 입증, 확인, 승인   consumerism 소비주의
surpass ~을 능가하다   societal pressure 사회적 압력   keep up 계속하다, 유지하다

STEP 2 • Speaking

Topic — p104

2 made up of our perceptions and philosophies
→ The professor discusses cognitive dissonance.

3 commonly used in tropical regions / the stumps of the trees and the remaining vegetation
→ According to the professor, slash-and-burn farming damages the environment.

4 material goods generally take on a greater importance / Such an emphasis on the confirmation of one's status
→ The topic of the lecture is the culture of consumerism and its effects.

Classification — p107

2 cognitive dissonance will arise / conflict must be resolved in some way / the conflict results in cognitive dissonance
→ The professor gives two types of cognitive dissonance. One example is a family that wants to go on a vacation, but can't do so unless they use money intended for the education of their son. The other example is a man who is starving and needs to steal food to feed himself.

3 but that field also will only be productive for maybe three or four years / a significant source of deforestation / Those trees have large root structures that go deep into the soil and help hold the soil together.
→ The professor describes the problems of slash-and-burn farming by giving two examples. The first example shows that slash-and-burn farming destroys the forest. The professor also argues that slash-and-burn farming leads to soil erosion.

4 societal expectations play a large role as well / Since these material possessions are symbols of our social status / the same pressure to buy those things / societal pressure to prove his social status by purchasing the shoes drives that teenager
→ According to the professor, a culture of consumerism is one in which a person's status is determined by material wealth. The professor also says that a culture of consumerism makes problems with poverty worse because the poor are also pressured to buy things that they can't afford.

Detail — p110

2 cognitive dissonance will arise because the family's wish to take a vacation
→ According to the professor, cognitive dissonance occurs mainly because of the family's competing desires, and the family will most likely resolve that dissonance by not going on the vacation.

3 a section of forest to create a field for farming / exhausts the nutrients in the soil
→ According to the professor, cutting down part of the forest was an unavoidable act to make room for farming.

4 in a culture of consumerism / your lifestyle doesn't meet the expectations of society / these material possessions are symbols of our social status
→ Thus consumerism leads to excess because there is constant pressure to buy more in order to gain more status. The culture of consumerism paves the way for people to buy things they don't need or that they can't afford in order to gain status in society.

Practice Questions

p112

1

| Script | Writers have different styles to convey meaning to their readers. It takes creativity to describe or emphasize a situation in a manner that will differentiate it from the straightforward news that we read in the papers. Authors of fiction have a wide array of literary techniques at their disposal to spice up their writing. Well, one of the more common writing techniques is hyperbole, a form of, uh, intentional exaggeration. When we use hyperbole, what we are doing is magnifying a situation to express a feeling or mood, rather than the true facts. If the writer wants to give the reader a rather vivid mental picture of a character's state, instead of merely saying, "I'm tired," the writer will up it a notch or two and may say something like, "I can't take another step!" Obviously this probably isn't true in a strictly factual sense, but it certainly conveys a lot more feeling than simply saying "I'm tired." Metaphor is, um, another technique that is commonly used to add color to an author's writing. In metaphor, the author equates one thing with something that is quite different in order to stress a certain characteristic. For example, let's say an author describes a character as a "ticking time bomb." Again, this is obviously not factually true, but the author uses the comparison to a bomb to stress the character's unstable or violent nature.

| Script 해석 | 작가는 다양한 문체를 사용해서 독자에게 의미를 전달합니다. 우리가 신문에서 읽는 기사의 직접적인 문체와 다른 방식으로 상황을 묘사하거나 강조하기 위해서는 창의력이 필요합니다. 소설작가들은 글에 맛을 맛깔스럽게 쓰기 위해서 다양한 범위의 문학적 기교들을 자유롭게 사용합니다. 흠, 글쓰기 기교 중 비교적 일반적인 것 중 하나는 과장이라 하는 고의적으로 부풀려서 말하는 것입니다. 과장법을 사용할 때에는 사실보다는 감정이나 분위기를 표현하기 위해서 상황을 확대시킵니다. 작가가 독자에게 인물의 상태에 대해서 생생한 심리적 묘사를 주고 싶을 때 단순히 "피곤하다"라고 말하지 않고, 한두 단계 높여서 "한발자국도 더 못 걷겠어!"라고 말합니다. 엄격하게 사실이라는 관점에서는 사실은 아닐 수 있지만, "피곤하다"라고 말하는 것보다는 확실히 더 강한 느낌을 전달합니다. 은유는 작가의 글에 색을 더하기 위해 종종 사용되는 또 하나의 기교입니다. 은유를 이용해서 작가는 어떤 사물의 특징을 강조하기 위해 그것과 꽤 다른 사물을 동일하게 놓습니다. 예를 들어, 작가가 한 인물을 시한 폭탄으로 묘사한다고 해봅시다. 분명히 이것은 사실은 아니지만, 그 인물의 불안정하고 폭력적인 성격을 강조하기 위해 폭탄이라는 비교를 사용한 것입니다.

Listening Note

Literary technique - Writers use it to convey their ideas

1) Hyperbole
   - an author deliberately exaggerates in order to convey a deeper sense of feeling
   - an exaggeration used to convey how tired the character feels.

2) Metaphor
   - one thing is compared to something else
   ex) a character called a time bomb to stress the dangerous nature of the character.

| Sample Respone | In his lecture, the professor gives two examples of literary techniques that writers use to convey their ideas. The first technique is called hyperbole, in which an author deliberately exaggerates in order to convey a deeper sense of feeling. The professor gives an example of an author who writes that a character says that he can't take another step. The statement is not meant to be taken literally; it is just an exaggeration used to convey how tired the character feels. The other literary technique the author discusses is metaphor. In metaphor one thing is compared to something else to stress an important characteristic. Here, the professor mentions an example in which a character is called a time bomb in order to stress the unpredictable and dangerous nature of the character.

Vocabulary

convey 나르다, 운반하다, 전달하다   creativity 창의성   emphasize 강조하다   differentiate 차별화하다   straightforward 직접적인, 솔직한
literary techniques 문학적 기교   at one's disposal 마음대로   hyperbole 과장법   intentional exaggeration magnify 고의적인 과장
vivid mental picture 생생한 심리적 묘사   notch 단계 정도   metaphor 은유   characteristic 특유한, 독특한   unpredictable 예측할 수 없는

2

| Script |

Organisms that live in extreme environments usually become highly specialized for living in that environment through the process of evolution. Most importantly, their anatomy often changes in highly unusual ways to allow them to cope with the pressures placed on them by their environment. Take the angler fish, for example. This is a, uh, fish that lives deep in the oceans. So deep, in fact, that there is no light. So in order to attract its prey, the angler fish has an appendage, uh, kind of like an antenna that hangs in front of its face. This appendage is bioluminescent... it glows in the dark. Basically, it acts as a lure for other fish. When other fish swim up to investigate the light, they are, well, actually swimming right up to the mouth of the angler fish, where they are quickly devoured. This is how the angler fish has evolved to find food. But how about finding a mate? As I said, there's no light in the deep ocean, so how do angler fish find each other in order to reproduce? The answer is pretty amazing. Male angler fish have actually evolved so that they cannot survive on their own. If they don't find a female within a few days of hatching, they die. So the only mission of a male angler fish is to find a female, which they do using a very refined sense of smell. Once they find a female, they actually attach themselves to her and get absorbed into her body ... the male actually becomes part of the female. Thus, the male survives, and the female never has to search out a male when she is ready to mate.

| Script 해석 |

극한의 환경에서 사는 생물체들은 진화의 과정을 통해서 그 환경에 살아남는 데 적합하도록 분화합니다. 가장 중요한 것은 환경에 의해 주어지는 압력을 다룰 수 있도록 해부학적으로는 드문 방식으로 변화를 한다는 것입니다. 심해 아귀를 예로 들어 보겠습니다. 심해 아귀는 심해 층에 사는 물고기입니다. 그곳은 너무 깊어서 빛도 없습니다. 먹이를 유인 하기 위해서 아귀에겐 하나의 촉수가 있는데, 일종의 안테나라고 생각하시면 됩니다. 이것은 얼굴에 달려 있죠. 이 촉수는 어둠 속에서 스스로 빛을 냅니다. 대개는 다른 물고기를 유혹하는 데 사용됩니다. 물고기가 빛을 찾아 헤엄쳐 오는데 실은 아귀의 입으로 헤엄쳐 오는 셈이죠. 그리고 온 물고기는 곧 게걸스럽게 먹힙니다. 이것이 먹이를 얻기 위해 아귀가 진화한 방식입니다. 짝짓기는 어떨까요? 말했듯이, 심해에는 빛이 없는데 번식을 위한 짝짓기는 어떻게 할까요? 그 답은 무척 놀랍습니다. 수컷 아귀는 혼자는 살아 남지 못하도록 진화했습니다. 그래서 부화한 지 며칠 내로 암컷을 찾지 못하면 죽고 맙니다. 그렇기 때문에 수컷 아귀의 유일한 목표는 암컷을 찾는 것이고, 이 과정에서 굉장히 발달된 후각을 사용합니다. 암컷을 발견하면 수컷 아귀는 암컷의 몸에 달라 붙어 암컷의 일부가 됩니다. 그래서 수컷이 이런 방식으로 살아남으면, 짝짓기 준비가 된 암컷은 수컷을 찾아 다닐 필요가 없습니다.

Listening Note

Organisms living in extreme environments become highly specialized

1) Glowing antenna
   - They live in areas where there is not any light. So, they use antenna to lure prey

2) The mating practices of angler fish
   - angler fish have evolved to attach themselves to female angler fish within the first few days of their life.
   - Use smell to find a female

| Sample Respone |

According to the professor, two aspects of the angler fish represent adaptations to extreme environments. The first is the glowing antenna that hangs in front of the mouth of the angler fish. Since angler fish live in areas where there is not any light, this glowing antenna acts as a lure for prey. The other example is about the mating practices of angler fish. The professor says that male angler fish have evolved to attach themselves to female angler fish within the first few days of their life. They use a special sense of smell to find females and attach themselves permanently to them. This allows them to overcome the difficulty of trying to find their mates when it is the time to reproduce.

Vocabulary

specialize 특수화(분화)하다　evolution 진화　anatomy 해부학　cope with 극복하다, 대항하다, 처리하다　angler fish 아귀
appendage 첨가물, 부속물　bioluminescent 생물학적으로 빛을 내는　investigate 연구하다, 수사하다　devour 게걸스럽게 먹다
hatch 부화하다, 꾸미다, 기획하다

PART II Practice Test

Task 01 — Personal Preference

p118~131

2

Sample Outlining

Topic	Townhouse

Reason 1	Reason 2
Spacious	Practical

Details	Details
Difficult to find a house of adequate size Offers more space (multilevel floors)	No worries about maintaining a backyard Security (neighbors are around)

Sample Response

I would say the type of house I want to live in is a townhouse. One of reasons why I'd love a townhouse is because it's practical as well as spacious. Coming from the suburbs, I find it difficult to find a place that has a decent amount of space, just like our family home. With townhouses you can have more space because of the multilevel floors offered by such a design. Townhouses also offer practicality in the sense that you won't have to worry about maintaining a big backyard, or security in the area, since neighbors are literally just a wall away.

3

Sample Outlining

Topic	Chemistry

Reason 1	Reason 2
Gives me a chance to experiment	Have interaction with other classmates

Details	Details
Lead to discoveries that can help improve and save lives	Join group projects Improve my relationship with others

Sample Response

Without a doubt, my favorite subject was chemistry among all my high school subjects. It gave me a chance to experiment with different elements and materials that I could mix to form new ones. These can lead to discoveries that can one day help improve and save lives. I also got to interact with many other classmates, helping me better my relationship with them when we did various experiments in class, especially when paired or grouped together.

4

Sample Outlining

Topic	The Alps in Switzerland	
Reason 1 Calm atmosphere		**Reason 2** Rich history
Details No worry about noise or air pollution Good scenery		**Details** Napoleon Bonaparte and Charlemagne

Sample Response

I believe my dream vacation would be in the Alps in Switzerland due to their calm atmosphere and rich history. Staying in a place that's way up in the mountains gives one a sense of peace. I don't have to worry about noise or air pollution, and the scenic views are breathtaking. Also, I love the fact that famous people in history, those I've only read about in books, such as Napoleon Bonaparte and Charlemagne, have been there.

5

Sample Outlining

Topic	Popular Music	
Reason 1 Many different kinds		**Reason 2** Can relate to lyrics
Details Music to suit any mood Always something new		**Details** Song topics are relevant to my life Songs are about things I've gone through.

Sample Response

In my opinion, pop music is the best. There are several reasons why I like pop music. The first is that even within one genre, there are various different styles to suit any taste or mood. Each singer or band has its own unique sound and look. Also, there is always something new to catch my attention. Another reason I like pop music is that I can relate to the lyrics. The subject matter often reflects things that are happening in my own life.

6

Sample Outlining

Topic	My dog	
Reason 1 Friendly		**Reason 2** He is there for me always
Details Even when I am angry, he greets me with a smile		**Details** When I am sad - he becomes a great conversation partner.

Sample Response

As far as I'm concerned, the dog I have is my favorite pet in the world. One reason why I like this dog is because he is always friendly. Even when I am extremely angry, in particular, he doesn't hesitate to come to you. He is always excited to see me, greeting me with a friendly and innocent smile to cheer me up. I like this dog also because he is always there for me. When I am sad and lonely, I need to have someone to talk to. At that time he becomes a great conversation partner, quietly listening to all my stories of private matters.

7

Sample Outlining

Topic	Thanksgiving	
Reason 1 Get to see relatives		**Reason 2** Delicious food
Details A chance to talk about each other's lives		**Details** Try all different kinds of great dishes.

Sample Response

It seems to me that Thanksgiving is my favorite holiday of the year. What I like about it is that I get to see a lot of my relatives whom I haven't seen in a long while. It gives us a chance to talk and allows us to catch up with each other, which brings happiness to all of us. Another reason is that we can have delicious food. At this time, all family members gather together and prepare delicious dishes. This is a great opportunity to try all different kinds of great dishes.

8

Sample Outlining

Topic	Indian food	
Reason 1 Flavorful		**Reason 2** Many regional variations in its cuisine
Details Many exotic spices are used		**Details** Staples are cooked at in dozens of different ways Endless variety of dishes

Sample Response

In my case, my favorite cuisine is Indian. When I burn the midnight oil to study for my exams, I always have Indian food at night. There are a couple of reasons why I prefer it to any other kind of cooking. First, Indian food is very flavorful. Many exotic spices are used in each dish, so nothing ever tastes bland. Second, India is such a big country that there are many regional variations in its cuisine. Although the same staple foods are used, they are prepared in dozens of different ways. This ensures an endless variety of dishes to choose from. For these reasons, my favorite cuisine is always Indian food.

Vocabulary

townhouse 연립주택　backyard 뒤뜰　literally 과장 없이, 실제로, 정말로　interact with 서로 작용(영향)하다　atmosphere 분위기
scenic view 풍경　breathtaking 대단한, 깜짝 놀랄 만한　relative 친척

Task 02 — Paired Choice

p134~147

2

Sample Outlining

Topic	Seeing a doctor	
Reason 1	**Reason 2**	
Feel safer when seeking professional help	Conscious of my daily health	
Details	**Details**	
My health is important. I will get better soon with a correct diagnosis	Doctors give advice on preventive measures and good health habits	

Sample Response

I prefer to go see a doctor and take my prescription as instructed rather than self-medicating. I feel safer about my health when seeking professional help from people who have spent considerable time and effort curing health conditions. My health is too important for me to be stubborn or lazy about going to see doctors. Since they know what's making me ill, I can get well faster with a correct diagnosis. Furthermore, going to the doctor will help me be more conscious of my daily health. The doctor can give me advice on preventive measures and good health habits so that I can avoid getting sick.

3

Sample Outlining

Topic	Living in a city	
Reason 1	**Reason 2**	
To get good education. Almost all prominent colleges in Korea are located in Seoul.	To get a better chance to get a job	
Details	**Details**	
Good schools are located in cities	Support family and myself by having a decent income	

Sample Response

As far as I'm concerned, living in a city is much more beneficial than living in a small town. One reason why I prefer a city to a small town is because I can get a good education in a city. For example, almost all prominent colleges that are famous in Korea are located in Seoul. To live in Seoul is the best way to receive a quality education in Korea. Also, I can get a better chance to get a job after graduating from a college in a big city because there is much information about how to get jobs in big cities. If I have a job in a city, I will be able to support my family and myself with a decent income.

4

Sample Outlining

Topic	No smoking on campus

Reason 1	Reason 2
Endanger not only their health but also others.	High school students come to tour the campus

Details	Details
Illnesses caused by second-hand smoking Not fair	Set a bad example for them They should smoke off-campus

Sample Response

In my opinion, smoking on campus should not be allowed. Smokers not only endanger their lives but also everyone around them. There are several respiratory problems caused by second-hand smoking, and it's not fair that non-smokers have to breathe in this contaminated air. Furthermore, high school students often come to tour the campus. I think it sets a bad example for them to see college students hanging around smoking everywhere. Smoking on campus should never be allowed.

5

Sample Outlining

Topic	Honest friends

Reason 1	Reason 2
Honest friends	Want to have a long lasting friendship

Details	Details
I can't open my mind if they are not honest	Honesty → continue my relationship Lost friend because of my friend's lies.

Sample Response

Personally, I prefer honest friends over intelligent friends. I can have profound conversations with my friends only if they are honest with me. I can't open my mind and share all that I want to say if they are not honest. Another reason why I want to have honest friends is because I want to have a long lasting friendship with my friends. If they are honest, I can continue my relationship with them. When I was a child, I lost a friend because of her lies. She was a good person, but she sometimes lied to me, and it led to a big problem in our relationship. For these reasons, I'd rather have honest friends than intelligent friends.

6

Sample Outlining

Topic	Watching movies at home

Reason 1	Reason 2
Convenient	Less expensive

Details	Details
Watch any time Don't have to leave house	Low rental fees Cheap snacks No transit costs.

Sample Response

I would say that watching movies at home is more desirable than going to the theater. One reason is that it's very convenient to watch movies at home. In fact, you don't need to leave your house. You can just watch movies at home at anytime. The other reason is that you don't need to pay much. I mean rental fees are low and you can buy cheap snacks at a supermarket nearby. Besides, there is no worry about transit costs. For these reasons, I think it's definitely better to watch movies at home.

7

Sample Outlining

Topic: It doesn't make people closer.

Reason 1	Reason 2
No physical contact	This leaves us open to deception.

Details	Details
Can't have proximity through chatting or emails.	No body language Can't resolve problems easily

Sample Response

The way I see it, online communication puts more strain on relationships rather than making them stronger. One reason is that there's no physical contact. I feel that proximity is a big factor in close relationships. I mean, you can't have that with online chatting or emails. Moreover, communicating this way leaves us open to deception. Sincerity is uncertain because you can't see the other person or their body language. They can just tell you what you want to read or hear, and if there's a problem, you can choose not to resolve it, since there's nothing either one of you can do to force the issue.

8

Sample Outlining

Topic: Buying my own CDs

Reason 1	Reason 2
Teach me responsibility	Practical

Details	Details
I take extra care of the things	No need to ask for permission Uncomfortable feelings

Sample Response

As I see it, buying my own CDs is better than borrowing them from friends. Although borrowing doesn't cost money, buying my own stuff teaches me responsibility, since in that way I take extra care of the things I buy so that they will not get broken or lost. Another reason is that buying CDs is more practical in the long run, because you will have the stuff when you need it, and you won't have to rely or ask permission from other people to use them. I feel a little uncomfortable borrowing CDs from a friend because there is a possibility that I might lose or break them.

Vocabulary

stubborn 완고한, 확고한, 고집이 센   diagnosis 진단, 판단, 진찰   preventive measure 예방책   tax revenue 세수(입)   investment 투자
aesthetic value 미적 가치   beautify 미화하다, 아름다움을 더하다   respiratory 호흡의, 호흡기관의   second-hand smoking 간접흡연
contaminated air 오염된 공기   transit cost 교통비   proximity 근접

Task 03 Fit & Explain

1
p148

|지문해석| **컴퓨터실 조교 선발 정책 변경**: 학생들의 고용 기회의 부족과 학내 컴퓨터 전공 인원으로 적음으로 인해, 컴퓨터실의 일자리를 전공자뿐만 아니라 학교 내에서 일자리를 구하는 모든 학생들에게 개방하기로 했다. 이는 다음 주 월요일부터 시행될 예정이다. 학생지원 처 사무실과 컴퓨터실에 지원서 양식이 비치되어 있다.

|Script|
W: Can you believe this? They're opening employment at the labs to all students ... I don't get it ...
M: What are you talking about? You mean the new hiring policy in the labs? Well, what's not to get? It says in the new policy it's to give students more opportunities ...
W: Yeah, I understand that, but that really isn't a valid argument. Students who want to work aren't limited to finding jobs at the computer labs. The local stores employ a lot of university students, so I don't think it's such a big deal to find a job.
M: Okay, how about the fact that there are indeed only a few computer majors on campus? Not everyone's interested in working for the labs ...
W: True ... but, if you employ students who aren't really computer majors, or have similar courses, they won't be much help to the students using the computer labs. They might not be able to assist them with their questions ... or do troubleshooting if a computer breaks or something, debugging a virus ... something like that. I mean, what's the point of having a computer lab if the people in it don't know anything about computers?

|Script 해석|
여자: 믿을 수 있어? 컴퓨터실 일자리에 모든 학생들이 지원할 수 있대. 이해가 안 간다.
남자: 무슨 얘기하는 거야? 컴퓨터실의 새로운 고용 정책 말이야? 뭐가 이해가 안 가는데? 학생에게 더 많은 기회를 제공하기 위한 것이라고 나와 있잖아.
여자: 응, 그건 알겠는데 설득력이 있는 주장이 아니잖아. 일하고 싶어하는 학생들이 컴퓨터실에서만 일해야 되는 것이 아니라고. 주변 가게에서도 많은 대학생을 고용하고, 나는 일자리를 찾는 것이 큰 문제가 될 것 같지는 않아.
남자: 그럼, 학교 내에 컴퓨터를 전공한 사람이 실제로 얼마 되지 않는다는 사실에 대해서는 어떻게 생각해? 모든 사람이 컴퓨터실에서 일하는데 관심이 있는 건 아니라고.
여자: 그 말도 맞아. 하지만 컴퓨터나 그와 비슷한 전공이 아닌 학생을 고용하는 건 컴퓨터실을 이용하는 학생들에게 큰 도움이 되지 않을 거야. 아마 질문에 대답도 제대로 못할 거고, 컴퓨터가 고장 나거나 바이러스에 걸리는 등의 일이 있을 때 제대로 고치지도 못할 거야. 내 말은 컴퓨터실에 있는 사람들이 컴퓨터에 대해서 아무것도 모른다면 컴퓨터실이 무슨 소용이냐는 거야.

Vocabulary
- shortage 부족, 결핍   demographic 집단, 그룹   employment 고용
- valid argument 설득력(타당한) 주장   troubleshooting 고장의 수리, 분쟁의 조정   debug 결함을 없애다, 해충을 없애다

2

|지문해석| **독자 의견 - 대학 신문:** 학교 내에 더 많은 나무와 식물을 심겠다는 내용의 학교의 미화계획에 대한 지지를 보냅니다. 저는 늘 학교가 너무 황량하게 보인다고 생각했습니다. 대부분 지역이 시멘트나 아스팔트로 덮여 있어, 학교의 환경이 보통보다 더 더웠습니다. 학교의 이런 계획은 많은 유익함을 안겨 줄 것 입니다. 즉, 학생들이 공부할 수 있는 공간이 더 생겨나고 학교 환경이 더 푸르러져서 학교에 대한 인식이 더욱 개선될 것입니다.

관심 있는 학생

|Script|
W: Good morning, Andy! Do you know a place where we can review for our exams?
M: No, none right now ... The library is kind of full today ...
W: Oh, no! We'll be forced to sit in the lobby again ... but it seems we will soon be able to get out of that. I've read this letter to our school paper and found out about the school's plan to put more trees on campus. This letter hits the nail right on the head ... I think the call for more trees in the campus is great ... If there are trees here and there, we can sit on the grass, even under the sun ...
M: Yeah, that will be nice ...
W: Besides providing us with a place to study, a green university is a good thing in itself, well, as the letter says ... it would mean that our school would be better appreciated by people ...
M: But putting up trees may cost a lot ...
W: Not necessarily ... There are many foundations that help put up trees for free. The school will spend some money, of course, but not that much.

|Script 해석|
여자: 좋은 아침이야, 앤디! 시험 공부할 만한 곳을 알고 있니?
남자: 아니. 지금은 아무데도 없어. 오늘 도서관은 꽉 차고.
여자: 아, 이럴 수가! 또 로비에 앉아야 할거야. 그런데 조만간 이 문제가 해결될 것 같기도 해. 학교 신문에서 한 편지를 읽었는데 학교 당국이 교내에 더 많은 나무를 심을 거래. 이 편지는 문제점을 딱 알아 맞췄어. 학교에 더 많은 나무를 요구한 건 아주 잘 된 일이야. 여기 저기 나무가 있다면 풀밭에 앉아 태양 아래에서도 쉴 수 있고.
남자: 그래, 그러면 좋겠다.
여자: 게다가 거기서 공부할 수도 있고, 푸른 교정은 그 자체로도 정말 좋은 것 같아. 편지에도 그렇게 말했듯이, 아마 학교에 대한 평가도 좋아질 거라고.
남자: 그렇지만 나무를 심는 건 돈이 많이 들텐데.
여자: 꼭 그렇지는 않아. 무료로 나무 심는 것을 도와주는 단체들이 많거든. 물론 학교 차원에서도 돈이 들겠지만 그렇게 많이 드는 것은 아니야.

Reading Note
Policy The beautification of the school
Letter ((Agree) or Disagree)
Reason 1
Add study places for students
Reason 2
A greener university environment
Promote better appreciation of our university

Listening Note
Opinion
Agree
Reason 1
Give them an alternative to the library
Reason 2
Foundations will help plant trees.

|Sample Response| The woman agrees with the idea raised in the letter appealing for more trees in the university. She says that planting trees on campus would give them an alternative to the library when studying, since it's usually full of other students. The trees would also beautify the campus environment and, in turn, attract other people to the university. She means that the school will be better appreciated by people. In response to the man's remark that it will cost a lot of money, the woman points out that spending wouldn't be much of a problem, since there are foundations that are on hand to help plant trees.

Vocabulary
reiterate 되풀이 하다, 반복하다   appeal 호소하다, 간청하다   beautification 미화, 장식   barren 황량한   appreciation 평가, 비평, 감상
lobby 복도, 휴게실   foundation 협회, 재단

3

| 지문해석 | **사무처에서 알림**: 캠퍼스 생활의 질을 개선시키기 위한 부단한 노력의 일환으로, 수요일 저녁 학생 식당에서 세계 요리의 밤 행사를 열게 된 것을 발표하게 되어 기쁘게 생각합니다. 매주 수요일 밤 학생들은 세계 각국의 요리들을 맛보게 될 것입니다. 이 행사의 목적은 학생들에게 각 지역의 진정한 요리들을 소개하는 것입니다. 학교는 이미 유명한 전통 민속 음식점의 주방장들에게 문의하여 요리법을 전수 받았습니다. 저희는 여러분이 이 변화와 음식을 통해 타 문화를 경험하는 기회를 즐기기 원합니다.

| Script |
M: Oh! This sounds cool! They're going to start serving ethnic food on Wednesdays in the cafeterias.
W: Great, I can't wait.
M: What? You don't like any foreign food?
W: No, I'll eat foreign food. They can bring me a hamburger from anywhere in the world, and I'll be perfectly happy. Know what I'm saying?
M: Jane, that's just like you. You have to try new things.
W: No, I don't. Look, seriously, if they want to make Wednesday "World Cuisine Night," fine with me ... as long as they serve some normal food, too. There might be times when I want to try something new, but I definitely don't want to eat something weird every Wednesday just because the university thinks it will broaden my horizons.
M: Well, I think it's a great idea. It'll be fun.
W: I'm not saying it won't be. I just want the choice, that's all. We got three cafeterias on campus, right? I think they should do this in maybe two of them, and just serve normal stuff in the other one.

| Script 해석 |
남자: 오! 멋진데! 식당에서 수요일마다 민족 음식을 제공한대.
여자: 대단한데, 기다려지는 걸.
남자: 뭐? 너 외국음식 안 좋아한다는 거야?
여자: 별로, 외국 음식을 먹기는 해. 세계 어딘가에는 햄버거도 있겠지, 그러면 만족이야. 무슨 말인지 알겠니?
남자: 제인, 정말 너답다. 새로운 것을 좀 시도해 봐.
여자: 싫어. 이것 봐. 만약 수요일을 '세계 요리의 밤'으로 만들 거라면, 뭐 난 괜찮아. 일상적인 음식도 같이 제공한다면 말이야. 가끔 새로운 것을 시도해보고 싶을 때도 있겠지만 대학이 내 시야를 넓혀준다는 이유만으로 매주 수요일에 이상한걸 먹어야 한다는 건 정말 싫어.
남자: 음, 난 좋은 생각인 것 같은데. 재미있을 거야.
여자: 내 말은 재미가 없을 거 라는 게 아니고. 내가 선택을 하게 해달라는 거지. 그게 다야. 학교에 3개의 식당이 있잖아? 그 중 두 곳에서만 하고, 나머지 한 곳에서는 원래 먹던걸 제공하면 되잖아.

Reading Note

Policy
Starting the world food night at campus dining halls.

Reason 1
Try different kinds of food

Reason 2
Experience different cultures

Listening Note

Opinion
Doesn't agree

Reason 1
She wants to have normal food

Reason 2
Wants to try foreign food occasionally but not always

| Sample Response | The woman has a different opinion from the director of campus affairs. She doesn't really seem to like foreign food and doesn't seem very eager to try different kinds of food. She says that she doesn't care if the dining hall serves foreign food as long as that is not her only choice. She also says that she may want to try foreign food occasionally, but she doesn't want to be forced to do so. She says that the university should only have the world food night at some of the dining halls so that students who don't want to try foreign food would have the choice not to.

Vocabulary
- ongoing attempts 진행되는(계속되는) 시도
- designated 지적된, 임명된, 지명된
- cafeteria 학교식당
- cuisine 요리, 조리법
- consulted chef 유명한(권위 있는) 주방장
- recipe 요리법
- broaden one's horizon 안목을 넓히다
- stuff 물건
- dining hall 대식당

4

p154

| 지문해석 |

음악과에서 알립니다: 더 많은 수업 공간이 요구됨에 따라, 공연예술 건물 1층에 있던 악기 보관실이 겨울 방학 동안 교실로 개조됩니다. 이 조치로 많은 음악 전공자들이 학교 내에 악기를 보관할 수 없게 되어 많은 어려움을 겪으시리라 예상됩니다. 그러나 교실 공간은 수업에 등록하는 증가된 신입생 인원을 모두 수용하기 위해서는 반드시 필요합니다. 첼로나 튜바와 같이 매우 큰 악기를 위한 보관 공간은 3층에 마련하도록 하겠습니다.

| Script |

M: Well, I have to say, Hillary, this may be the one time when I envy you for playing the cello.

W: Yeah, no joke. When I first read that announcement, I almost had a heart attack, until I got to the bottom. Can you imagine having to ride the bus and lug my cello around? I sure got lucky there.

M: It's pretty annoying for the rest of us, though. I mean a bass guitar isn't exactly light, but I doubt they'll let me keep it on the third floor. Plus, even if I had a smaller instrument like a flute or something, it would still be a pain. I mean you have to carry it around to each class, constantly watching it to make sure it doesn't get stolen ...

W: I see what you mean, but the department does need the space. Right now, we're packed into classrooms like sardines.

M: That's my other point. It's like that all over campus. What we really need is to expand the campus. They need to just cough up the money and put up some more buildings on campus.

| Script 해석 |

남자: 음, 힐러리. 처음으로 네가 첼로를 연주한다는 사실이 부럽다고 말해야 할 것 같다.

여자: 그래, 맞아. 처음 발표를 듣고 사실을 알 때까지는 심장마비로 죽는 줄 알았어. 버스를 타고 첼로를 질질 끌고와야 한다는 사실을 상상 할 수 있겠니? 난 운이 좋은 것 같아.

남자: 그렇지만 나머지 사람들에겐 정말 화나게 하는 정책이야. 내 말은 내 베이스 기타는 가볍지도 않은데 3층에 보관장소를 마련해 줄지 의심스러워. 게다가 플룻 같은 가벼운 악기였다고 해도 역시 문제야. 도둑맞지 않나 계속 확인 하면서 여기 저기 수업을 들으러 가야 하잖아.

여자: 무슨 말인지 알아, 그래도 학부 차원의 공간이 필요하긴 해. 지금만해도 콩나물 시루같은 교실에서 수업을 듣잖아.

남자: 그것도 내가 하고 싶은 말이야. 학교 전체가 그렇잖아. 우리에게 필요한 건 캠퍼스 확장이야. 예산을 세워서 더 많은 건물을 세워야 한다구.

Reading Note

Policy
The instrument storage rooms will be converted to classrooms

Reason 1
Due to the need for greater classroom space

Reason 2
The rising numbers of freshmen in the program

Listening Note

Opinion
Doesn't agree

Reason 1
His bass guitar is heavy
- inconvenient

Reason 2
Bad for students who have small instruments, too.
- they need to worry about their instruments being stolen.

| Sample Respone |

The man is opposed to the university's new policy. He says that his bass guitar is heavy, but he probably won't be able to keep it in the one remaining storage area. Instead, he will have to carry his bass guitar around with him, and he says this will be inconvenient. He also says that it will be annoying even for students with small instruments because they will have to constantly worry about their instruments being stolen. He is also unhappy because the university has a chronic lack of space. He believes that what they really need to do is to spend money on putting up more buildings.

Vocabulary

storage 저장, 보관   convert 바꾸다, 전환하다   hardship 고난, 고생   enroll 등록하다, 기재하다   extremely 극도로
lug 끌고 가다, 억지로 끌어넣다   sardine 꽉 들어차게 하다

5
p156

| 지문해석 | 공고: 증가하는 재정 지출을 억제하기 위해 해외 연수 프로그램에 학교가 제공했던 보조금을 다음 두 학기 동안 중단합니다. 대학은 최상의 교육을 위해 헌신하는 것은 여전히 가장 우선 순위라는 것을 확실히 해두는 바입니다. 이 방침은 학교 예산에서 불필요한 지출을 가려내려는 목적의 일부일 뿐입니다. 언급된 프로그램에 참여하려고 했던 학생들은 각각의 단과 대학을 방문하셔서 세부 사항을 알아가시기 바랍니다.

| Script |
M: This is unbelievable ... I wonder who came up with this great idea this time.
W: Yeah, well it does sound rash ...
M: It's stupid, that's what it is. How can they even think that the foreign study program is a waste of the academic budget? We do study, you know. Just because we're in a different country, it doesn't mean we're on vacation. It even gives us a chance to learn new things ... it gives us a different perspective. If the school really wants to be a first-class university, they shouldn't take this program away.
W: The school's just trying to be on the safe side with the finances ... and they have had a lot of expenses lately ...
M: Shouldn't they be looking at how they're managing the budget first? And why don't they start looking at their spending for non-academic programs, like that constant remodeling of the faculty lounges? How come student programs always get cut, but the spending on the faculty never does? The school's supposed to be here for the students, not the professors.

| Script 해석 |
남자: 믿을 수가 없어. 이번엔 누가 이렇게 대단한 아이디어를 냈는지 궁금하군.
여자: 그러게. 좀 경솔해 보인다.
남자: 이건 멍청한 거야. 어떻게 해외 연수 프로그램이 교육 예산의 낭비라고 생각할 수가 있어? 우리는 정말 열심히 공부하잖아. 우리가 외국에 간다고 해서 휴가를 가는 건 아니란 말야. 해외 연수를 통해 새로운 것도 배우고 새로운 시각도 갖게 되는 것도 사실인데. 학교가 정말 일류대학이 되고 싶으면 이런 프로그램을 없애면 안 되지.
여자: 학교도 재정적인 부분을 안정시키려고 하는 거야. 그리고 최근에 지출이 많았잖아.
남자: 자기들이 예산을 어떻게 사용하고 있는지를 먼저 봐야 하는 것 아냐? 도대체 교직원 휴게실을 계속 리모델링하는 것 같이 교육과 관련 없는 곳에 사용하는 예산은 왜 생각해보지 않느냐구? 학생을 위한 예산은 계속 줄이면서 직원을 위한 예산은 왜 줄이지 않지? 학교는 학생을 위해 존재하는 것이지 교수를 위한 곳이 아니잖아.

Reading Note

Policy
Suspending grants for foreign study programs
• for next 2 semesters

Reason 1
To identify unnecessary costs in the academic budget.

Listening Note

Opinion
Against

Reason 1
Foreign study program
• Not a vacation / students study
• a chance to learn new things

Reason 2
Finances
• Uni. Should reduce spending in other ways
  Ex) non-academic programs, the faculty lounges

Sample Response

The school has decided to suspend grants for the foreign study program in order to avoid spending unnecessary money from the academic budget. The man, however, is against suspending grants for the foreign study program. He gives two reasons for holding his opinion. First, he points out that students attending the foreign study program don't play but study and try to learn new things. Second, he mentions that the university should reduce spending in non-academic programs such as renovating the faculty lounges and support academic programs that are beneficial for students.

Vocabulary
- curb 억제하다   unnecessary costs 불필요한 예산
- remodel 개조 하다   faculty lounges 교직원 휴게실   renovate 수선하다, 수리하다

6

| 지문해석 | 편집장님께: 여름에 모든 4학년 학생이 적어도 1개의 공립 학교에서 의무적으로 자발 학습 지도하도록 하겠다는 학교의 생각에 대한 제 의견을 나누고 싶습니다. 많은 학생들이 이 제안에 반대하는 것을 알고 있습니다만, 저는 개인적으로 학교의 결정을 환영합니다. 이 새 정책은 공부로 어려움을 겪는 많은 아이들에게 교육적인 도움을 줄 것이라고 믿습니다. 또한 사회적 양심이 되겠다는 학교의 공약을 사회에 더 잘 보여줄 수 있으며, 이는 학교 이미지 개선이라는 결과를 낳을 것입니다.

케이크 윌슨 (2학년)

| Script |
M: Have you planned your summer yet?
W: The school's actually done that for me with their latest news. And this guy in the newspaper is saying that the policy is fantastic.
M: Why do I get the feeling you're not up to being charitable with your time?
W: I'm concentrating on my studies, that's why. I mean, if I had the time, I wouldn't mind helping out, especially with children. But, I also need time for my own education ... I was supposed to enroll for summer classes to lighten my load for senior year. I won't be able to get anything out of this, academic-wise.
M: Hmm ... well, but it can be beneficial to all of us. It is good for the school's image within the community.
W: The school just wants to maintain its good public image at the seniors' expense. They're just using social awareness as an excuse. The school won't even cut us some slack and give any credit for our time. A very unfair arrangement, if ever I saw one ... I mean, why do they even say it's "volunteer" work when you're being forced to do it?

| Script 해석 |
남자: 여름 계획 짰니?
여자: 최근 뉴스를 보니 학교가 대신 해준 것 같은데. 그리고 이 신문 안의 이 편지는 그 정책이 정말 좋다고 하던데.
남자: 왜 난 네가 시간적 여유가 없다는 것처럼 들리지?
여자: 내가 공부에 집중해서 그래. 그러니까, 나도 시간이 있다면 돕고 싶지, 특히 애들 일은. 그렇지만 나도 내 공부할 시간이 필요해. 4학년 때 부담을 줄이려고 여름 계절학기에 등록을 하려고 했거든. 학업 면에서 봤을 때 내가 이 프로그램으로부터 얻을 수 있는 것은 없을 거야.
남자: 글쎄, 이 프로그램이 우리 모두에게 유익할 수도 있어. 사회에서 학교 이미지에 도움도 되고.
여자: 학교는 4학년생들을 희생시켜서라도 단지 좋은 사회적 이미지를 유지하고 싶은 거야. 사회 의식이라는 것을 구실로 삼는 거라구. 학교는 우리를 좀 더 여유롭게 해주거나 우리 시간에 대한 학점을 주지도 않을 거라고. 이거 하나만 봐도 굉장히 불공평하잖아. 내 말은 우리가 하라고 강요 받을 거라면 왜 "자발적 활동"이라고 말하는 거야?

Reading Note

Policy
Requiring seniors to do volunteer mentoring in public schools.

Letter ((Agree) or Disagree)

Reason 1
Help children w / their studies

Reason 2
Enhance the public image of the uni.

Listening Note

Opinion
Disagree

Reason 1
Don't have time
• Plans to enroll for summer classes

Reason 2
School is using seniors to create a good image
• students get nothing, not even credit

| Sample Response | The student who wrote the letter agrees with the idea of the university that requires all seniors to do volunteer mentoring with at least one public school in the community. The woman, however, disagrees with the university's policy. Her reasons for holding that opinion are twofold. Firstly, she already planned to attend summer classes so that she won't have as many classes during senior year. Secondly, she believes that students don't get any benefits from participating in the mentoring program. She believes, however, that the university is using seniors to matain a its good public image.

Vocabulary
- mandatory 의무적인
- volunteer mentoring 자발적인 학습지도
- social consciousness 사회적 양심
- fantastic 훌륭한
- enroll 출석하다, 등록하다
- academic-wise 학업 면에서
- beneficial 유익한

---

7 p160

|지문해석| 재학기간 축소: 대학 당국은 학생의 최대 재학 기간을 줄이기로 결정했다. 이번 학년부터 시작해서 학생들은 4년의 학위 과정을 6년이 아닌 5년 안에 마쳐야 한다. 당국에 의하면 이 정책은 더 나은 학습 분위기를 증진하기 위한 결정이다. 지난 10년 간 졸업을 유예하며 학교에 남아있는 학생의 수가 증가하면서, 교수당 학생의 비율을 증가시키고 기숙사와 주차 공간의 부족을 야기시키고 대학이 제공하는 교육의 질에 심각하게 영향을 끼쳤다. 현재 1,2학년은 모두 이 새 정책에 적용을 받게 된다.

|Script| W: Charlie, what's up? Got time for lunch?

M: Ah, okay, but let's make it real quick ... I got to rush to my other classes. My schedule has been crazy ever since I heard about that stupid policy.

W: Ah ... The new policy that limits our stay to five years?

M: Yeah. It's kind of unfair, you know ... especially for a working student like me. I've been taking just a few subjects per semester so that I can work and support myself ... and my plan to graduate in six years was all mapped out. Now that I only got five years, I have to take a full load ... and that means giving up my job.

W: Well, you know ... they say they're doing it because the quality of education is going down.

M: OK, but what about me? What if I fail in some subjects? What if I don't complete the requirements in five years? And I'll bet I'm not the only one who's upset about this. Not everyone is a genius ... I'm sure that with this new policy, many of us won't be able to finish our courses on time ...

Script 해석

여자: 찰리, 무슨 일이야? 점심 식사 안 할래?
남자: 아, 그래. 그런데 빨리 먹고 와야 해. 다른 수업 시간에 맞춰 가야 하거든. 그 이상한 정책 때문에 내 시간표가 엉망이 되어버렸어.
여자: 아, 5년 안에 졸업해야 한다는 그 정책 말이야?
남자: 응. 특히 나같이 일을 해야 하는 학생에게는 불공평한 정책이야. 일하고 돈을 벌기 위해서는 한 학기에 과목 몇 개만 들어왔거든. 그래서 6년 안에 졸업하려는 계획도 이미 다 세워두었고. 그런데 이제 5년 안에 졸업을 해야 하니 꽉 채워서 수업을 들어야지. 일도 하지 못하는 거고.
여자: 글쎄, 교육의 질이 자꾸 떨어져서 이런 정책을 실행하는 거라던데.
남자: 알아. 하지만 나는 어떻게 해? 몇 과목에서 낙제를 하게 되면? 5년 안에 모든 필수 과목을 다 마치지 못하면? 나만 이렇게 기분이 상한 것은 아닐 거야. 모두가 다 천재는 아니니까. 이 정책으로 인해서 많은 사람이 제 시간 안에 학교를 마치지 못하게 될 거야.

Reading Note

Policy
Reducing the maximum residency period from six to five years.

Reason 1
Many students have maximized their stay at college
- Extend student-teacher ratios / create shortages in dormitory and parking spaces

Listening Note

Opinion
Disagree

Reason 1
Unfair for working students.

Reason 2
Impossible to complete the requirements in five years / there would be many other students in the same situation.

Sample Response

The university has decided to reduce the maximum residency period for students to five years due to the high student-teacher ratios and shortages in dormitory and parking spaces. The man, however, is opposed to the university's policy. He provides two reasons for holding his opinions. First, it's unfair for students who should manage to work and study at the same time. Second, it would be almost impossible to complete the requirements in five years. And he believes that there would be many other students who wouldn't be able to graduate within five years.

Vocabulary

the maximum residency period 최대 재학 기간　promote 증진시키다　maximize 극대화하다　student-teacher ratio 교사당 학생의 비율　dormitory 기숙사　severely 엄하게　sophomore 2학년

a full load 꽉 찬 양, 채워진 분량

8　p162

지문해석

학생들의 목소리가 사라진 깨끗한 캠퍼스?: 최근에 저는 학교 안에 현수막이나 깃발 또는 다른 문서 자료를 금지한다는 학교의 정책에 대해서 알게 되었습니다. 이 말은 앞으로는 건물 외벽이나 가로등의 기둥 그리고 다른 학교 시설에 붙어있는 어떠한 게시물도 볼 수 없다는 뜻입니다. 학교 당국은 청결과 학교 내의 안전을 유지하기 위해서라고 했지만, 학교 청결이요? 그건 좋습니다. 그러나 현수막이나 깃발이 학교 안전과 정말 관련이 있습니까? 전 어떻게 연관되었는지 잘 모르겠습니다. 게다가 우리의 의견을 붙여 놓을 수 있는 공간을 몇 개의 게시판으로 축소한다는 것은 우리가 의견을 표현하는 기회를 심히 감소시킬 것입니다.

이사벨 존슨 (3학년)

Script

W: What are you reading, Mark?
M: Hey. I'm reading this student's letter to the editor ... Wanna have a look?
W: Oh, that one. I've read it too. Do you agree with the student?
M: Well, no ... actually, I agree with the university policy. I'm sick and tired of looking at building windows littered with banners and flags ... blocking the light whenever we have classes. I've always thought something should be done about campus cleanliness anyway ...

W: Wow ... I didn't realize you felt this strongly about the signs ... As for me, I kinda agree with the letter. I think we should be able to put up posters on campus.

M: You do? You know, in addition to making the campus look kind of messy, all those posters and flyers are kind of a fire hazard. They might suddenly get caught up on electric wires ... and that to me, is a bigger problem than students not getting their posters seen by everyone.

W: Well, but how about student rights? Don't you think this kind of prohibition limits our rights as students?

M: I don't think so. The school does have places where you can post things without being obtrusive. I don't see any reason why the signs should be posted everywhere.

| Script 해석 |

여자: 무엇을 읽고 있는 거야, 마크?

남자: 어서 와. 한 학생이 편집자에게 보낸 편지를 읽고 있었어. 한번 볼래?

여자: 아 이거 말이구나. 나도 읽었어. 이 학생의 의견에 동의하니?

남자: 흠. 아니 … 사실 난 학교의 정책에 찬성해. 나도 건물 창문에 걸린 현수막과 깃발 때문에 짜증이 났거든. 그것 때문에 수업할 때 빛도 안 들어오고. 나도 늘 깨끗한 학교 환경을 위해 어떤 결단이 내려져야 한다고 생각했어.

여자: 와 … 게시물에 대해서 그렇게 생각하는 줄 몰랐어. 난 이 편지를 쓴 학생의 의견에 동의하는 편이야. 우리에게 캠퍼스에 포스터를 걸 권리가 있다는 생각하거든.

남자: 정말 그렇게 생각해? 캠퍼스를 지저분하게 만드는 것 이외에도, 이런 종류의 포스터와 전단은 화재를 일으킬 수 있는 위험성을 가지고 있잖아. 전선에 감길 수도 있고. 나한테는 이런 위험이 모든 사람이 포스터를 보지 못하게 된다는 점보다 더 큰 문제로 보이는걸.

여자: 음 그렇지만 학생들의 권리에 대해서는 어떻게 생각하니? 넌 이런 제재가 학생으로서의 권리를 침해한다고 생각하지 않니?

남자: 난 그렇게 생각하지 않아. 학교는 이미 눈에 거슬리지 않고도 포스터를 걸 수 있는 장소를 마련해 두었어. 모든 곳에 게시물을 게시해야 할만한 이유는 못 찾겠는걸.

Reading Note

Policy
Forbidding banners, flags, etc. In campus buildings
• for cleanliness & safety

Letter (Agree or (Disagree))

Reason 1
Banners & flags have nothing to do with safety

Reason 2
Violation of student rights

Listening Note

Opinion
Disagree

Reason 1
Campus cleanliness
• tired of banners and flags on windows (blocking the light)

Reason 2
Safety
• may cause fire (if caught up on electric wires)

Reason 3
Policy doesn't violate student rights
• there are places for posting signs

| Sample Response |

The man doesn't share the view of the student who wrote the letter about the school policy to forbid the placing of banners in campus buildings. He gives three reasons for holding this opinion. The first is that the ban will make the campus clean and neat. He says that he is tired of banners and flags on windows, blocking the light. Another reason is safety. While the letter says that there is no connection between banners and safety, the man thinks there is a connection because banners may cause fire if they're caught up on electric wires. Finally, he points out that this policy doesn't violate student rights, because there are places for posting signs.

Vocabulary

bulletin board 게시판

 be sick and tired of it 그것에 진절머리가 난다   cleanliness 청결   prohibition 금지

Task 04 — General / Specific

1

| 지문해석 | **위험 보상**: 위험 보상이란, 위험 속에서 자신의 행동을 인지한 변화에 적응시키려는 효과를 의미하는 동물 행동학 용어이다. 이 이론은 겉으로는 이해하기 어려운 상황을 설명해준다. 상식적으로 위험 가능성이 감소하면 사고 발생율 또한 감소할 것이라고 예상한다. 그러나 대부분의 경우, 이 예상이 빗나가는데 왜냐하면 사람들이 위험을 덜 느끼게 되어 더 부주의하게 되는 경향이 있기 때문이다. 이는 당신이 어떤 상황의 한 부분에서 안전함을 느끼게 되면 다른 부분에서 더 많은 위험을 무릅쓰게 된다는 것을 보여준다.

| Script | SUVs, or sport utility vehicles, are often criticized for putting other drivers at greater risk. According to the theory of risk compensation, however, the size of the car is only part of the problem. In June 2006, researchers watched 41,000 passenger vehicles passing through London over two weeks, and the results showed that drivers of SUVs and 4x4s are more likely to use mobile phones while driving. They were also less likely to wear seatbelts. Their behavior could be attributed to their belief that they are relatively safe because the SUV is large enough to protect them in the event of an accident. Most of you might think wearing a helmet when cycling will protect your brain and therefore reduce the rate of accidents, right? Of course, helmets protect your brain from damage to some extent in the event of an accident. However, studies show that they do not necessarily reduce the accident rate. Here again, risk compensation may be to blame. The thought of wearing a helmet affects the behavior of cyclists in a negative way, i.e., they tend to behave less cautiously than when they are not wearing a helmet, and this leads to offset the protective benefit of helmets in accidents.

| Script 해석 | SUV 즉, 스포츠 범용차는 종종 다른 운전자를 큰 위험에 노출시킨다는 비난의 대상이 되죠. 하지만 위험 보상 이론에 따르면 차량의 크기는 그 문제의 부분일뿐입니다. 2006년 6월, 조사자들은 2주 동안 런던을 지나가는 41,000대의 차를 관찰했습니다. 그 연구의 결과, SUV와 4륜 구동차의 운전자들이 운전 중 더 많이 핸드폰을 사용하는 경향이 있다는 점이 나타났습니다. 또한 안전벨트 착용률도 다른 운전자에 비해 낮았습니다. 이런 행동은 사고가 났을 경우 SUV의 크기가 충분히 커서 자신을 보호해 주기 때문에 비교적 더 안전하다고 믿는 믿음 때문입니다. 여러분 다수는 자전거를 탈 때 헬멧이 머리를 보호해주기 때문에 사고율이 감소할 것이라고 생각할 수 있어요. 그렇죠? 물론 헬멧은 사고가 날 경우 어느 정도까지는 머리를 보호해 줍니다. 그러나 조사에 따르면 사고율을 감소시켜주지는 않아요. 이 역시 위험 보상을 탓해야 할 것입니다. 헬멧을 착용하고 있다는 생각은 운전자의 행동에 부정적인 방향으로 영향을 미칩니다. 다시 말해 운전자는 헬멧을 착용하지 않았을 때보다 더 부주의하게 행동하게 되고 이 점이 사고가 났을 때 헬멧이 보호해주는 이점을 상쇄해 버리죠

Vocabulary
- compensation 보상 ethological 동물 행동학적인 describe 묘사하다 seemingly 외면상으로, 겉으로 incomprehensible 이해할 수 없는, 무한한 possibility 가능성, 실현성
- vehicle 자동차 criticize 비평하다 seatbelt 안전벨트 attribute 기인한다고 생각하다, ~탓이라 생각하다 protective benefit 보호해주는 이점

2

|지문해석| **집단 사고:** 사람들이 집단이나 조직에 순응하기 위해 다른 사람의 신념이나 인식에 맞춰가기 시작하면 집단 사고가 일어난다. 이는 개인적으로는 반대해도, 조직적인 일치에 따르려고 하는 천성적인 경향 때문에 일어나는 사고 방식의 일종이다. 이 경향은 다른 신념이나 의견을 가지고 있다는 이유로 쫓겨날까 걱정하는 두려움에 의해 정당화된다. 그 결과, 집단 사고가 적용되면 개인이 집단에 순응하기 위해서 자신의 반대 의사를 표현하지 않음에 따라, 건전하지 못한 의사 결정 과정이 생기는 결과를 낳게 된다.

|Script| Do you think I could get you to agree with a statement that you felt was false? Chances are I probably could. To demonstrate why, I'd like to tell you about a psychology experiment that was done some years ago. Uh, in the experiment, a group of students was placed in a room together and shown two cards with lines drawn on them. They were then asked which line was longer. The first three students to answer were actually cooperating in the experiment, and they deliberately gave the wrong answer. Amazingly, most of the other students went along with their opinion, even though it was clearly incorrect. In a follow-up experiment, those same students were brought in one by one and shown the same two cards. When they were alone, and had not heard any previous answers, each student was able to correctly pick the card with the longer line. That tells you quite a bit about man's wish to fit in, doesn't it?

|Script 해석| 여러분이 틀렸다고 생각 한 진술에 대해 제가 동의하도록 할 수 있다고 생각하십니까? 그럴 수 있을 것입니다. 왜 그런지 설명해 드리기 위해서 몇 년 전에 있던 심리학 실험을 말씀 드리겠습니다. 그 실험에서 한 무리의 학생들은 방 한 가운데 앉아서 선이 그어진 두 장의 카드를 보았습니다. 그리고 어느 선이 더 긴지에 대한 질문을 받았습니다. 처음 세 명의 학생은 실은 원래 그 실험을 돕기로 된 사람들이었고 고의로 틀린 답을 말했습니다. 놀랍게도 다른 학생들 중 대부분이 그 세 명의 의견에 동조했습니다. 비록 확실히 틀렸지만 말이에요. 그 다음 실험에서, 학생들을 한 명씩 불러다가 동일한 카드 두 장을 보여주었습니다. 혼자 있게 되고 다른 대답을 듣지 않은 상태에서 학생들은 더 긴 금이 그어진 카드를 골라내었습니다. 이 실험은 다른 이들과 조화를 이루고 싶어하는 인간의 소망에 대해서 많이 설명해줍니다, 그렇죠?

Reading Note

Topic
Groupthink

Main Idea
People tend to adapt their beliefs to other people's thinking

Supporting Ideas
1) This happens due to man's inherent tendency to follow the group consensus
2) This is justified by one's fear to be singled out due to his different belief.

Listening Note

Example 1
The first three subjects chose the wrong line
• occurs influenced by the group

Example 2
The same subjects were able to select the correct line
• occurs in private

|Sample Response| Groupthink is defined as people's tendency to adapt their beliefs to other people's thinking. In the lecture, the professor describes a psychology experiment in which subjects were asked to pick the longer of two lines. In the experiment, the first three subjects deliberately gave the wrong answer, and most of the subjects after them were influenced by those incorrect answers and chose the wrong line as well. Later, the same test subjects were shown the same lines, but they did not hear the answers of the other test subjects. In this situation, most subjects were able to select the correct line. This experiment clearly demonstrates the concept of groupthink. The subjects gave the wrong answers so that they could conform to the group.

Vocabulary

 **perception** 지각, 이해   **conform** (규칙, 관습 등)에 순응하다   **inherent tendency** 선천적으로 타고난 경향   **consensus** 일치, 조화
single out 선출하다, 선발하다
psychology experiment 심리학 실험   **deliberately** 고의로, 신중히, 심사숙고 하여   **demonstrate** 논증하다, 입증하다

3

p168

|지문해석| 플로우: 사람이 한 가지 활동에 완전히 집중하게 되는 정신적인 상태에 있게 되는 것은 정상적인 일이다. 어떤 활동에 완전히 몰입되어 그 일을 하면서 일종의 성취감을 느끼면서, 지금 하고 있는 일에 강력한 집중을 느끼는 순간이 존재한다. 이런 요소들이 명확하게 나타날 때 이 사람은 플로우라고 하는 심리적 상태에 있는 것이다. 그러나 성취해야 하는 명확한 목표와 그 활동에 대해서 엄청난 집중력을 갖는 것이 필수적이다. 또한, 플로우 상태로 들어가기 위해서는 방해 받지 않는 환경이 필요하다. 왜냐하면 아주 조금만 정신이 흩어져도 집중력은 방해 받기 때문이다.

|Script| So we've been discussing a mental state called flow. Here is an example. A friend of mine is a professor of mathematics. Once she didn't sleep the whole night just to solve this one math puzzle that came up in one of her lectures. She missed dinner trying to solve it ... the blackboard was filled to the brim with notes ... eventually, she was able to solve it the following morning ... and amazingly, she didn't feel tired. She felt more happiness than exhaustion after finally getting her answer. Another friend of mine was also a professor. Recently he retired from university teaching. Still, he wants to continue his studies on his own. But the problem is, he isn't good at concentrating on something long enough to carry out or follow through on his activities. He's been having trouble sleeping; he's been having nightmares, too. He cannot focus his attention on a problem, no matter how hard he tries to keep his attention on what he is doing. He says that he keeps getting distracted by little noises and movements. Can you guess why he can't concentrate unlike the other professor? It is because he doesn't have any clear goals, since he's retired from teaching. This lack of motivation causes him to be easily distracted even by a small noise.

|Script 해석| 자, 우리는 플로우라고 부르는 정신적 상태에 대해서 논의했습니다. 여기 예를 한번 들어 보죠. 제 친구 한 명은 수학 교수입니다. 언젠가 그 친구는 강의 때 나온 수학 문제 하나를 풀기 위해서 밤새 잠을 자지 않았던 적이 있습니다. 그 문제를 풀기 위해 저녁도 걸렀죠. 칠판은 메모로 가득 찼습니다. 마침내 다음날 아침 그 문제를 풀수 있었고 놀랍게도 그 친구는 전혀 피곤하지 않았습니다. 답을 찾아내고 난 뒤에 피곤함 보다는 더 많은 행복감을 느꼈습니다. 또 다른 제 친구도 역시 교수였는데 최근 강단에서 물러났습니다. 그래도 그 친구는 계속해서 자신의 연구를 하고 싶어합니다. 그런데 문제는 그가 무엇인가를 이루거나 하던 일을 다 마칠 수 있을 정도의 오랜 시간 동안 집중을 하지 못한다는 것입니다. 그 친구는 악몽을 꾸는 등의 수면 장애를 가지고 있습니다. 그는 하고 있는 일에 아무리 집중을 하려고 해도 잘 안됩니다. 그 친구는 작은 소리나 동작에서 늘 방해를 받는다고 말합니다. 그 친구가 다른 교수들과는 달리 왜 집중을 못하는지 아십니까? 그 이유는 그 친구가 이미 은퇴를 해서 뚜렷한 목표가 없기 때문입니다. 동기가 부족하기 때문에 작은 소리에도 쉽게 주의가 산만해지게 됩니다.

Reading Note

Topic
Flow

Main Idea
A mental state of high focus on one activity

Supporting Ideas
1) Clear goals
2) Concentration
3) Non-disturbing environment

Listening Note

Example 1
A prof. of math
- didn't sleep while solving a problem
- not tired but happy

Example 2
Another prof. retired
- cannot concentrate
- gets easily distracted
- lacking goals & motivation

|Sample Respone| According to the reading, flow is a term that describes a mental state of high focus on one activity. In order to engage in the state of flow, one should have clear goals, concentrate on a single activity, and avoid a disturbing environment. The professor gives two examples to describe the state of flow. The first example is the professor of mathematics trying to solve a math question by spending the whole night on it. She didn't feel fatigue, but happiness. The other example was another professor retired from college teaching. He couldn't concentrate and was easily distracted because he didn't have goals and motivation to work after retirement.

Vocabulary

- intense concentration 극도의 집중
- psychological 정신적인, 심리학적인
- distraction 혼란, 산만함
- exhaustion 극도의 피로, 소진
- nightmare 악몽
- motivation 동기
- fatigue 피로
- retirement 퇴직

4 p170

|지문해석| 창조적 파괴: 혁신은 언제나 산업과 경제에 혁신을 불러 오는데 필요한 활력을 제공한다. 혁신의 결과물 중 하나는 바로 창조적 파괴이다. 이 과정은 새 제품의 창조가 유사한 상품을 생산하는 회사의 시장 내에서의 위치나 일하는 방식을 파괴하는 것을 의미한다. 창조적 파괴는 경제학자인 조제프 슘페터에 의해 도입된 개념으로, 혁신이 오래된 목록, 생각, 기술, 기교, 장비들을 어떻게 쓸모 없게 하는지를 설명한다. 오래된 상품이나 사업 방식이 새로운 상품에 의해 사용되지 않거나 쓸모 없는 상태로 남겨지게 되면, 그것이 창조적 파괴로 알려져 있다.

|Script| As you all know, when computers came into homes and offices, they replaced much of the equipment people had used previously. Uh, computers replaced bulky typewriters for making documents ... they displaced the slower counting machines. Computers also became the main tool for long distance communication. Through the use of e-mail and the Internet, computers came to perform many of the functions that the reaular postal mail had served. In fact, this transition has been so complete that typewriters and counting machines can only be found in dusty old storage rooms or antique shops, while postal mail is often used only as a last resort. You know ... if you think about it, a similar thing happened with automobiles. In the space of about 30 years, cars completely replaced horse-drawn carriages, wagons, and other slower modes of land transportation. Automobiles evolved into all sorts of sizes and shapes – trucks, jeeps, vans – to accommodate friends, family, and freight ... Of course, rapid technological advances have accelerated the rate of creative destruction. So there's no telling when the computer and the automobile might also become the victims of creative destruction.

|Script 해석| 모두 아시다시피 컴퓨터가 가정과 사무실에 등장하면서 예전에 사용하던 많은 장비들을 대체했습니다. 어, 컴퓨터는 서류 작성을 하는 부피 큰 타자기를 대체했고 느린 계산기들을 몰아냈습니다. 컴퓨터는 또한 장거리 통신의 주요한 도구입니다. 이메일과 인터넷을 통해 컴퓨터는 일반적인 우편제도가 했던 여러 역할들을 수행하게 되었습니다. 사실 이 변환은 너무 완벽하게 이루어져, 타자기와 계산기는 먼지 나는 창고나 골동품 점에서나 찾아볼 수 있고 우편제도는 대개 최후의 수단으로서만 사용이 됩니다. 모두 알겠지만 생각해 보면, 자동차 분야에도 비슷한 현상이 생겼습니다. 30년이라는 시간 안에 자동차는 말이 끄는 마차나 4륜 마차 그리고 그 밖의 속도가 느린 운송 수단들을 대체했습니다. 자동차는 친구, 가족, 화물을 나르기 위해 트럭, 지프, 밴 등 다양한 크기와 모양으로 진화해왔습니다. 물론 급속한 기술 발전이 이 창조적 파괴를 가속화해 왔습니다. 그렇기 때문에 컴퓨터와 자동차가 또한 언제 이 창조적 파괴의 희생물이 될지는 알 수 없습니다.

Reading Note

Topic
Creative destruction

Main Idea
Creation of new products → Destruction of existing similar products or business

Supporting Ideas
Innovations → old technologies, etc.
Become obsolete
- Old things → give way to new products

Listening Note

Example 1
Computers
- replaced equipment that was used before
  Ex) typewriters, counting machines
- became the main tool for long distance comm.
  (replaced regular postal mail)

Example 2
Automobiles
- replaced slower modes of land transportation
  Ex) horse-drawn carriages, wagons

Sample Response

Creative destruction is a term that explains how new products replace existing similar products. This concept can be seen with the dawning of computers which replaced dated equipment, such as typewriters and counting machines. Computers also have enabled e-mail and the Internet to take the place of regular postal service. Another example that shows creative destruction is the development of the automobile. The development of cars has made the old ways of transportation like wagon and carriage dispensable. However, as discussed by the professor, both the computer and the automobile themselves might be someday victims of creative destruction by giving way to more innovative products or machines.

Vocabulary

innovation 혁신   revolutionize 혁명을 일으키다   creative destruction 창조적 파괴
whereby 그것에 따라   equipment 장비   bulky 부피가 큰   freight 화물

5

| 지문해석 |

수렴진화: 수렴진화는 서로 다른 종들이 유사한 신체적 특징이나 능력들을 발전시켜 가는 과정이다. 수렴진화의 경우에서, 다양한 종들은 서로가 밀접하게 관련된 것이 아니다. 하지만 그들은 유사한 환경적 조건들에서 생존하기 위해, 개별적으로 유사한 신체적 특성들이나 능력들을 발전시켰다. 이러한 특징들을 진화시킨 동물들은 결국, 그들 개개의 종의 번식을 지배하곤 했고, 따라서 이러한 특징들은 그 종의 다른 구성원들에게도 퍼져 나갔다.

| Script |

Today we are going to discuss how certain mammals use echolocation to survive in different environments. Echolocation is a way of detecting one's surroundings through the emission and detection of sound waves, much like radar. Mammals use echolocation for navigation, finding prey, and finding potential mates. Now, you may ask, "Why can't they use their vision, like other mammals?" Well, this is because they live in conditions that are devoid of sunlight, so ocular vision is useless. To compensate for their lack of vision, these mammals have developed echolocation as their primary means of navigation. For instance, most bats are active at night. Being able to move at night gives them advantages in hunting, because it allows them to hunt while other animals are sleeping. Also, the night provides them with cover from the vision of the animals that hunt them. However, they don't have enough light to see properly. As a result, most species of bats have developed echolocation in order to maneuver in total darkness. Another mammal that benefits from echolocation is the dolphin. While dolphins are active during both the day and the night, many dolphins dwell at deep sea levels where sunlight barely penetrates. To adapt to this, all dolphins have developed echolocation. Echolocation works well in the ocean because of good acoustics, whereas oceanic organisms that rely on vision can be hindered by the water's texture.

| Script 해석 |

오늘 우리는 특정 포유류들이 다양한 환경에서 살아남기 위해 어떠한 방식으로 '반향정위'를 사용하는가에 대해 논의할 것입니다. '반향정위' 란 레이더와 같이 음파를 방출하고 탐지하는 것을 통해 누군가의 주변을 탐색하는 방식입니다. 포유류들은 탐색을 위해, 먹잇감을 찾기 위해, 그리고 장래의 배우자를 찾기 위해 반향정위를 사용합니다. 그러면 여러분들은 "왜 그들은 다른 포유류들처럼 시력을 사용할 수 없나요?" 하고 물을 수 있겠죠. 글쎄요, 이는 그들이 일광이 부족한 환경에 살기 때문에, 눈의 시력은 불필요하기 때문입니다. 부족한 시력을 보완하기 위해, 이러한 포유류들은 자신들의 탐색에 있어서 주요한 수단으로 '반향정위'를 진화 시켜 왔습니다.

예를 들면, 대부분의 박쥐는 야간에 활동적입니다. 밤에 활동이 가능하다는 것은 그들이 사냥하는 데 있어 이점들을 제공하는데요, 이는 그들이 수면 중인 동물들을 사냥할 수 있게 하기 때문입니다. 또한 밤은 그들을 사냥하는 동물들의 시야로부터 보호막을 제공해 주기도 하죠. 하지만 그들에겐 제대로 볼 수 있는 빛이 충분하지 못합니다. 그 결과, 대부분의 박쥐 종들은 완전한 암흑 속에서도 교묘히 활동할 수 있도록 '반향정위'를 발달시켜 온 것입니다. '반향정위'의 이점을 갖는 또 다른 포유류는 돌고래입니다. 돌고래들은 밤낮 활동적으로 움직이는 한편, 많은 돌고래들이 일광이 거의 투과하지 못하는 심해층에 살고 있습니다. 이에 적응하기 위해 모든 돌고래들은 '반향정위'를 발달시켜 왔습니다. '반향정위'는 음향 상태가 좋은 해양에서 잘 작용하는데, 그곳에서 시력에 의존하는 해양 생물들은 물결에 의해 저지를 받습니다.

Reading Note

Topic
Convergent Evolution

Main Idea
The process by which different species develop similar physical characteristics or abilities

Listening Note

Example 1
Bats have developed echolocation to maneuver in total darkness being able to move at night gives them advantages in hunting

Example 2
All dolphins have developed echolocation but oceanic organisms rely on vision which can be hindered by the water's texture.

| Sample Response | Convergent evolution occurs when a certain animal tries to adapt to a new environment. The professor's discussion about how bats and dolphins use echolocation is an example of convergent evolution. First, the professor mentions that echolocation is necessary for animals that live where normal vision is useless. Because bats are active at night and dolphins live in ocean depths where sunlight can't penetrate, both species developed echolocation. These animals aren't closely related, but evolved the same behavior to adapt to similar environments, and that is convergent evolution. Second, the professor mentions that bats have an advantage hunting prey at night, and dolphins have an advantage over animals that must rely on vision in murky water. Thus, both animals have advantages that allowed them to survive, dominate breeding, and pass echolocation on to their whole species. |

Vocabulary
convergent evolution 수렴진화   breeding 번식
mammal 포유류   echolocation 반향정위   devoid 부족한, 없는   maneuver 움직이다, 이동하다   penetrate 투과하다, 침투하다
the water's texture 물결

6
p174

| 지문해석 | **해프닝 예술**: 예술은 상대적인 것이므로 다양한 해석이 존재할 수 있다. 이런 점에서 어떤 사람들은 예술이란 예술가와 청중 모두가 경험하고 있는, 실시간 일어나고 있는 사건이나 상황이라고 생각한다. 예술은 정지해 있는 것이 아니라 상호 작용하는 것이 된다. 이렇게 만들어지는 예술을 '해프닝'이라고 부른다. 이 방식은 청중의 참여를 필요로 한다는 점에서 조직적이라고 할 수 있다. 또한 해프닝에 동참하게 된 사람들이 계획되지 않은 반응을 보여준다는 점에서 즉흥적이다. |

| Script | As we discuss how art affects the world, the audience and the artists who make art, um ... one of the more amusing art forms, I think is ... it's called happening. Wouldn't you want to be able to experience art as it happens, knowing that interacting with an artist at that particular time is considered art? Let's say that you had a painter who set up his easel in a park for the day to do a painting ... nothing too new about that, right? But let's say the artist began engaging other people in the park, uh, asking for suggestions and then working those suggestions into his painting. Well, then, the complete work of art would be a product of not just the painter, but also the other people who gave suggestions ... it would be the result of their interaction. The artist may intentionally solicit suggestions from the crowd ... but he can't control the suggestions they make, uh, injecting some spontaneity into his painting. Or let's say you have a play in which the actors converse directly with the audience. The comments made or the questions asked by the actors may be pre-scripted, but the responses of the audience members certainly aren't. In this way, the audience becomes an integral part of the artistic performance. |

Script 해석 | 예술이 어떻게 세계와 관중, 그리고 작품을 만드는 작가에게 영향을 미치는지에 대해 이야기할 때, 재미있는 예술형태 중 하나에 해프닝이라고 불리는 것이 있습니다. 당신과 예술가가 특정한 순간에 이루어지는 상호작용이 예술이 된다는 것을 아신다면, 예술이 일어나는 그 순간을 경험해보고 싶지 않으시겠습니까? 화가 한 명이 그림을 그리기 위해서 공원에 이젤을 세워두었다고 해봅시다. 별로 새로운 것은 없죠? 그런데 이 화가가 공원 안의 사람들을 끌어들이기 시작하면요? 의견을 부탁하고 그 의견을 자신의 그림에 반영하기 시작 했다면? 그렇다면 완성된 작품은 화가 혼자서 만들어낸 것이 아니라 그에게 의견을 준 사람들의 것이기도 합니다. 즉, 상호작용의 결과물이라는 것이죠. 화가는 고의적으로 군중에게 의견을 구했을 수도 있습니다. 그러나 청중이 낸 의견을 통제하지 못해서 무의식 중에 그림 속에 들어갈 수도 있죠. 혹은 배우가 관객들과 직접 대화를 하는 연극이 있다고 해봅시다. 배우가 하는 대사나 질문은 미리 쓰여진 것일 수 도 있지만 관객의 반응은 절대로 그렇지 않습니다. 이런 식으로 관객이 예술 행위의 한 구성 요소가 됩니다.

Reading Note

Topic
The art of happening

Main Idea
The art of happening requires the participation of audience

Listening Note

Example 1
An artist painting while taking suggestions from the audience
- artist has no control over his work / spontaneous work b/w artist and audience

Example 2
An actor asks questions of the audience in a play.
- the audience becomes part of the performance

Sample Respone | The art of happening refers to a kind of art that requires the spontaneous participation of the audience. The professor gives two examples of this kind of art. The first example is if an artist painted a painting while taking suggestions from the audience. Since the artist would have no control over what kind of suggestions the audience gave, the art created would be both spontaneous and a collaboration between the artist and the audience. The professor also gives an example in which the actors in a play ask questions directly to the audience. While the actors might be able to plan their questions, they would not be able to plan the responses of the audience, and the audience would become part of the performance.

Vocabulary
- interpretation 해석
- interactive 상호 작용하는
- simultaneously 동시에
- spontaneous 자연 발생적인
- solicit 바라다, 유인하다
- integral 필수의, 불가결한
- performance 행위, 공연

7

지문해석 | 불신의 유예: 사람들이 불신의 유예 기간을 갖는 것은 드물지 않은 방법이다. 불신의 유예란 실제 현실성을 놓고 볼 때, 논리적인지 분별 있는지 판단하는 것을 잠시 유보하는 것을 수반하는 현상이다. 어떤 상황은 우리 주위에서 일어난 사건을 인식하거나 받아들이는데 있어서 유연성을 요구한다. 사실일 수 없을 것 같은 것은 기존의 믿음에 도전하지만, 그것을 사실로 받아들이려는 의지나 반의식적 결정은 그로부터 지속성과 오락성을 발견하기만 하면 더 이상 그것의 진실성을 의심하지 않는다.

Script | In general, people are highly willing to indulge in fantasy for the sake of entertainment. Take for example, video games ... those role-playing games or RPGs. With RPGs, the willingness to accept ludicrous or impossible situations is an essential element of the game experience. Obviously, from a purely logical standpoint, we all know that the situations presented in these games are impossible. You're never going to encounter a dinosaur rampaging through your neighborhood, for example. And obviously, if you die in real life, you don't really get to start over again. But during the game experience, we are willing to put reality aside and just enjoy the game, despite its lack of realism. The same can be said of watching professional wrestling. You know that it's a kind of sports theatrics ... you see these guys hitting each other with chairs or dropping each other on their heads ... nobody in real life could actually take that sort of punishment. Um, basically we all know it's fake ... just stunts and play acting, but many viewers get highly involved in professional wrestling. Again, basically they are willing to put logic aside for thirty minutes and enjoy the spectacle.

| Script 해석 | 일반적으로 사람들은 재미를 위해 허구에 깊게 빠지게 되기 쉽습니다. RPG라고 불리는 비디오 게임인 롤플레잉 게임을 예로 들어봅시다. RPG를 할 때 우스운 상황이나 불가능한 상황을 받아들이려는 태도가 게임 경험의 필수적인 요소입니다. 확실히 순수한 이성으로 보면, 우리는 모두 게임에서 제시한 상황이 불가능한 것임을 알고 있습니다. 예를 들면, 공룡이 집 주위에서 날뛰는 일을 겪게 될 일은 절대 없죠. 그리고 현실 세계에서는 당연히 한번 죽었다고 해서 다음 기회가 오는 것도 아니죠. 그러나 게임을 할 때, 현실성이 부족하더라도 우리는 현실은 젖혀두고 게임을 즐깁니다. 프로 레슬링 경기를 보는 것도 동일하다고 할 수 있습니다. 그것이 연출이라는 것을 알고 있을 것입니다. 의자로 사람을 치거나 서로를 던져서 머리가 땅바닥으로 떨어지게 하는 그런 난폭함을 실생활에서 보는 경우는 없습니다. 우리는 대부분 그것이 눈속임임을 알고 있습니다. 일종의 묘기이자 연기라는 것을 알죠. 그러나 많은 사람들이 프로 레슬링에 열광합니다. 다시 말해 사람들은 경기가 진행되는 30분 동안 이성을 뒤로하고 그 광경을 즐깁니다.

Reading Note

Topic
Suspension of Disbelief

Main Idea
A willingness to accept improbabilities cancels any doubts about their verity.

Listening Note

Example 1
When playing video games, people accept impossible situations so that they can enjoy the games.

Example 2
When watching prowrestling, they suspend their disbelief to be entertained.

| Sample Respone | Suspension of disbelief is seen where there is a willingness to accept improbabilities. The professor says that people willingly accept what they know are impossible situations when they play video games. Everyone knows that situations in video games can't happen, but the professor says that people are willing to accept these situations so that they can enjoy the video game. Likewise, the professor says that people who watch professional wrestling know that it is not a real sport, because if it was, the wrestlers would get seriously hurt. But, again people suspend their disbelief so that they can be entertained. These two examples clearly demonstrate the concept of the suspension of disbelief according to the professor.

Vocabulary
- suspension 유예, 금지   disbelief 불신   phenomenon 현상   flexibility 유연성, 융통성   perception 지각, 이해
- improbability 일어날것 같지 않음   consistency 지속성   demonstrate 증명하다
- rampage (사납게) 날뛰다

8

| 지문해석 | 시너지 관계: 시너지란 두 가지 물체나 사건이 상대의 여세나 진행 과정에 힘을 주는 과정이다. 시너지 관계는 두 개체가 혼자일 때 얻을 수 있는 것보다 더 높은 수준의 힘을 얻기 위해서 함께 일하는 것이다. 사업적인 시너지 관계는 관련된 기술 상품 간에 두드러지게 나타난다. 그런 경우 한 제품의 기술적인 발전은 다른 제품의 기술적인 발전 또한 돕는다. 시너지 관계는 기술적인 발전을 가져올 뿐만 아니라 상품에 대한 소비자의 수요도 증가시킨다.

| Script |

OK, uh, today we are going to talk about the development of two technologies: digital cameras and flash memory cards. These two technologies are related because, uh, well, obviously digital cameras require flash memory ... and, uh, because ... to begin with at least, digital cameras were the primary use for flash memory. OK, now, I don't know if you all remember ... but digital cameras originally had very small pixel resolutions ... uh, the first cameras were generally well below 2 megapixels. That was at least in part due to the fact that flash memory cards didn't have a great deal of memory storage. However, as flash cards began to hold more memory, it was possible to make cameras with high megapixel resolutions. That, in turn, forced flash card manufacturers to develop cards with more memory.

Anyway, these two phenomena kept feeding off each other, and today flash memory cards average around 2 gigabytes, and digital cameras often have resolutions of at least 6 megapixels. Uh, another point is that the markets for these products have grown drastically. Digital cameras have largely replaced film cameras, and flash memory cards are the primary storage device for computers. You could argue that without each other, neither of these technologies would have been nearly as successful.

| Script 해석 |

네, 오늘은 디지털 카메라와 플래시 메모리 카드라는 두 기술의 발전에 대해서 이야기해 보겠습니다. 디지털 카메라는 플래시 메모리가 꼭 필요하기 때문에 이 두 기술은 관련되어 있습니다. 그리고, 적어도 처음에는 플래시 메모리가 디지털 카메라 용으로 사용되기 시작했습니다. 네, 자, 여러분들이 모두 기억할지는 모르겠지만 디지털 카메라는 원래 작은 해상도를 가지고 있었습니다. 최초의 카메라는 원래 2메가 픽셀 이하였죠. 그 원인 중에는 플래시 메모리 카드가 많은 양을 저장하지 못했다는 사실도 있습니다. 어쨌든, 플래시 카드가 더 많은 메모리를 저장할 수 있기 시작하면서 카메라도 더 높은 해상도를 가질 수 있게 되었습니다. 그리고 그 결과 메모리 카드가 더 많은 양을 저장할 수 있도록 카드 제조사에게 영향을 주게 되었죠. 어쨌든 이 두 현상은 서로에게 계속 영향을 주었고, 요즘 플래시 메모리는 평균 2기가의 용량을 담을 수 있고 디지털 카메라는 적어도 6메가 픽셀의 해상도를 보유하게 되었습니다. 또 하나의 포인트는 바로 이 두 상품시장이 급격하게 성장해 왔다는 것입니다. 디지털 카메라는 필름 카메라를 대체했고, 플래시 메모리 카드는 컴퓨터에 쓰이는 주요한 저장 장치가 되었습니다. 이 두 제품 모두가 서로 덕분에 큰 성공을 거두었다는 점은 의심할 여지가 없습니다.

Reading Note

Topic
Synergistic Relationships

Main Idea
One product helps to drive technological advances in the other as well.

Listening Note

Example 1
The capacity of flash memory cards allowed digital camera manufacturers to produce cameras with higher resolutions.

Example 2
The higher resolutions in digital cameras promoted flash memory manufacturers to produce cards with ever greater capacities.

| Sample Respone |

In the lecture the professor illustrates how the advances in flash memory cards and digital cameras were mutually beneficial to both industries. According to the professor, advances in the capacity of flash memory cards allowed digital camera manufacturers to produce cameras with higher resolutions. In turn, the higher resolutions in digital cameras prompted flash memory manufacturers to produce cards with ever greater capacities. Thus advances in one industry drove further advances in the other. This is a perfect example of a synergistic relationship because both products achieved greater success because of the advances made by the other product.

Vocabulary

- synergy 공동작용
- momentum 여세, 힘, 기세
- coordination 공동작용
- manufacturer 제조업자
- mutually 상호간에
- capacity 능력
- synergistic relationship 공동 작용의 관계

Task 05   Problem / Solution

1

|Script|

M: Tanya, I heard the university's doing a major renovation on the free student parking areas. Is that true?

W: Hey, Nick. Yeah, that's true. They say it's gonna take at least a whole semester before they can be fully operational again.

M: So, how'd you get to school today?

W: My dad dropped me off this morning. It's such a hassle for him to take me to school, though. I really have to bring my own car every day, but right now, I'm not sure where I'll be parking my car come next week.

M: Didn't campus management provide alternative parking spaces? You could check those out. I heard the spaces are located across from the main school gates. They're kind of a long walk from the main buildings but parking there is free.

W: Hmmm ... I'm not too sure that'll work for me ...

M: Well, why not get a slot at those paid parking lots? I know there are some that are located near the main buildings. That way, you won't have to worry about being late for your classes. It'll cost you, but you'll save time ...

W: That's another possibility ... I'll have to think about this over the weekend. I'm glad I bumped into you, Nick. Thanks!

M: No problem. Glad to help.

|Script 해석|

남자: 타냐, 학생 무료 주차구역을 크게 수리한다는 소식을 들었는데, 그게 사실이야?

여자: 안녕, 닉. 그래 사실이야. 다시 정비 되려면 적어도 한 학기가 걸린다는데.

남자: 그래서 넌 오늘 어떻게 등교했어?

여자: 아버지가 태워다 주셨어. 하지만 아버지한테는 나를 학교에 태워다 주는 것이 정말 귀찮은 일이지. 이젠 정말 매일 내 차로 등교해야 하는데, 당장 다음주부터는 어디에다 주차해야 할지 모르겠어.

남자: 학교 관리과에서 대체 주차 공간을 마련해주지 않을까? 한번 확인해봐. 학교 정문 건너편에 있을 거라고 들었는데. 학교 건물에서 좀 많이 걸어야 하긴 하지만 주차는 무료래.

여자: 글쎄, 그게 나한테 좋은 방법인지는 잘 모르겠다.

남자: 음, 유료 주차장에서 자리를 찾아보면 어때? 본관 건물 근처에 몇 군데 있는 걸로 아는데. 그렇게 하면 지각할 걱정은 없을 거야. 돈은 들겠지만 시간은 아낄 수 있어.

여자: 그것도 한 방법이구나. 주말 동안 생각 해봐야겠어. 널 만나게 돼서 다행이다, 닉 고마워!

남자: 괜찮아. 도움이 돼서 기쁘다.

Vocabulary

renovation 수리, 수선   **operational** 사용 가능한   **drop off** 하차하다, 하차시키다   **management** 경영, 관리   **alternative** 대안의, 대체의   **possibility** 가능성   **bump** 마주치다, 부딪치다

2

| Script |

M: Hey! Lisa, I finally caught up with you ... I've been looking for you everywhere.

W: I just got back from vacation. Why were you looking for me? Anything wrong?

M: I was wondering if you could point me in the right direction ... I know you organized last year's alumni ball. I'm doing it this year ... and I had it all figured out, but then the dean told me the date's been moved up a week. The caterers I've hired said they'll have to charge me an extra 50% of the original contract ... our current budget can't afford that right now. So, any good ideas?

W: You do have your hands full there ... Ever thought of hiring another caterer for the event? You could shop around for other services that might be able to accommodate you on short notice. Tell them when, where and for how much — and they'll let you know if they can manage it.

M: I might have trouble finding a good one, though ... hmm ...

W: Or, talk to the dean about having your budget increased. This way, you won't have to worry about making any changes. I'm sure he'll hear you out ... I mean he is the one who changed the schedule. But you'll have to take care of the paperwork requesting approval from the finance board as soon as possible, though. It's not just the dean that needs to sign off on the approval. So if you go that route, you need to get moving quickly.

| Script 해석 |

남자: 안녕, 리사. 겨우 따라왔다. 너 찾아서 한참 헤맸어.

여자: 휴가 마치고 막 돌아왔어. 근데 날 왜 찾아 다녔어? 무슨 문제 있어?

남자: 내가 어떻게 해야 하는지 알려줄 수 있을까 싶어서. 네가 작년에 동창회 파티 운영을 맡았잖아. 올해는 내가 하거든. 이미 계획을 다 짰는데 학장님이 날짜를 일주일 앞당겨야 한다고 하셨거든. 그랬더니 내가 고용한 연회 담당자는 원래 금액에다가 50%을 더 내야 한다고 하는데, 지금 예산으로 그만큼을 내기는 어려워. 좋은 생각 있어?

여자: 정말 정신 없겠구나. 다른 연회 담당자를 찾아볼 생각은 해봤어? 짧은 시간에 맞춰서 도와줄 수 있는 회사를 찾을 수 있을 거야. 언제 어디서 얼마에 할 것인지를 알려줘서 그 조건으로 할 수 있는지를 알아봐.

남자: 좋은 데를 찾을 수 있을지 걱정이다.

여자: 아니면 학장님께 늘어난 예산에 대해서 말씀 드려. 그러면 다른 변화가 생기는 것에 대해서 걱정하지 않아도 되잖아. 학장님이 들어주실 거야. 내 말은, 스케줄을 바꾼 건 그 학장님이잖아. 그렇지만 재무 이사회에 허가 요청할 서류를 가능한 빨리 제출하도록 신경 써야 할 거야. 학장님만 승인을 해서 되는 것이 아니니까. 그러니까 어떤 방법을 쓸지 결정하게 되면 빨리 움직여야 해.

Listening Note

Problem The caterer is going to charge him more money, but he doesn't have enough money in his budget.

Solutions

1) Find a different caterer
   - shop around for other services
     - accomodate you on short notice.
     - negotiate with them

2) Ask the school to increase his budget
   - no worry about making any changes
   - paperwork

Reasons
① A lot less work than trying to find a new caterer.
② It is not his fault that the date of the ball was moved, so it is not really his problem.

| Sample Respone |

The man is trying to organize a ball for his university, but he has a problem with the caterer who plans to charge him more money due to the date change. His problem is that he doesn't have enough money in his budget. The woman suggests that he either find a different caterer or ask the school to increase his budget. I think he should ask the school to increase his budget. This will be a lot less work than trying to find a new caterer. Also, I don't think it is his fault that the date of the ball was moved, so it is not really his problem; the university should fix that problem by increasing the budget for the ball.

Vocabulary

alumni 동창생　　figure out 생각해내다, 이해하다　　caterer 요리 조달자, 연회업자　　accommodate 편의를 도모하다　　on short notic 갑작스럽게
paperwork 서류　　approval 승인, 허가

3
p184

| Script |

W: My ankle's really starting to be a nuisance. Ever since I broke it in that soccer game, I've been having problems getting to and from town for my weekly mentoring at the high school. Getting there usually takes about 20 minutes when I drive ...

M: So, what's the problem?

W: The problem is that I can't drive for at least a month with my cast on. And there aren't any buses servicing the area. I thought of taking a cab just to get there without constantly stopping, but I'm pretty low on cash lately ...

M: Oh, okay ... what if you ask a friend to give you a ride, then? Your friends probably won't mind helping you out for a month ...

W: And wait for me while I'm teaching the kids? Oh, I'm not exactly comfortable doing that. Don't you think it's too much to ask a friend on a weekly basis?

M: Well it's either that or pay that cash for the cab, I think.

W: Maybe. Hey, thanks for the input ... I just need to seriously weigh my options before I do anything ...

M: No problem. I know what you mean.

| Script 해석 |

여자: 발목 때문에 정말 성가셔. 축구 하다가 다친 이후로 고등학교로 매주 학습 지도하러 다녀오기가 정말 불편해. 보통 운전하면 20분 정도 걸리거든 …

남자: 뭐가 문제라는 거야?

여자: 깁스를 한 채로 적어도 한 달은 운전을 못한다는 거야. 그 동네로 가는 버스도 없고. 정지하지 않고 그냥 계속 가게 택시를 타는 것도 생각해봤는데, 요즘 재정적으로 좀 어려워서.

남자: 아, 친구한테 태워다 달라고 하면 어때? 한 달 정도는 태워다 줄 수 있지 않을까?

여자: 그리고 내가 애들 가르치는 동안 기다리고? 오, 내 마음이 편하지 않을 것 같아. 매주 그렇게 친구에게 부탁하는 것은 너무 하지 않겠니?

남자: 그렇게 하던지 아니면 택시비를 내던지 해야겠지.

여자: 아마도 의견 고마워. 잘 생각해보고 결정해야겠다.

남자: 괜찮아. 무슨 뜻인지 알아.

Listening Note

Problem　Can't drive for a month at least
Solutions

1) Ask a friend to give you a ride
   - Won't mind helping you out

2) Pay the cash for a cab

> Reasons
　① Taking a cab is expensive, and she is short in cash
　② She can return the favor later.

Sample Response

The woman is in trouble because she broke her ankle and can't drive her car. Yet, she needs to get to the high school where she is doing mentoring. The man suggests two solutions to her problem. First, he suggests that she could ask one of her friends to give her a ride. He also suggests that she could just pay for a cab. I think she should ask her friends, even though it may be inconvenient for them. Taking a cab each week will probably be really expensive, and the woman mentions that she really doesn't have cash for that. It may be inconvenient for her friends to drive her, but she can always do something nice for them later to return the favor.

Vocabulary

nuisance 귀찮은 존재, 성가신 사람   **constantly** 끊임 없이   **a weekly basis** 매 주당

4

Script

W: Hi, Chris! Nice to see you. I really need to talk to you about the class ...

M: Oh, hello ... Yeah ... What is it, Professor Rogers?

W: I'm sorry ... but you failed the second periodic exam in our Theater Arts course.

M: Oh, gosh ... I'm sorry, but it was really quite hard ...

W: Well, if it was just that one test, it would not be a huge deal ... but the thing is, you also failed the first periodic exam, and I'm afraid that it's going to be difficult for you to pass the course ...

M: Oh, my ... What shall I do now ... You know I'm all set to graduate this term.

W: Well, you could try getting an excellent mark in the final exams ... I'm sure you can do your best in that ... and if you get a very high grade, then it may be enough to make up for your two failing marks, and you may still be able to pass the course.

M: Yeah, maybe I can prepare for it ...

W: Or you could try joining the Theater Arts Club. It's like a performing varsity group ... I heard that you are a good ballet dancer. If you are accepted, then you automatically pass my class ... It'll take up a lot of your time, though, as the auditions run for about a month ...

M: Oh, my ... I need to think about this. Thanks a lot, Professor.

Script 해석

여자: 안녕, 크리스! 만나서 반갑다. 마침 수업에 관해서 너와 이야기를 나누고 싶었거든 …

남자: 오, 안녕하세요. 예, 무슨 일이세요, 로저스 교수님?

여자: 유감이지만, 네가 연극 예술 과목 두 번째 정기 시험에서 낙제를 했어.

남자: 오, 이런, 죄송해요. 그런데 정말 시험이 어려웠어요.

여자: 흠, 만약 한 번만 그랬으면 큰일은 아니었을 텐데. 문제는 첫 번째 정기 시험에서도 낙제점을 받았다는 사실이야. 이 수업을 통과할 수 있을지 걱정이 돼.

남자: 오, 이런, 이제 어쩌죠? 이번 학기에 졸업을 하기로 되어있다는 거 아시죠.

여자: 흠, 마지막 시험에서는 높은 점수를 얻도록 노력을 해야겠지. 잘 할 수 있을 거라 생각하는데. 그리고 높은 점수를 얻는다면, 처음 두 번의 시험 점수를 만회할 수 있을 거야. 그렇게 되면 통과할 수 있겠지.

남자: 네, 준비를 해야겠어요.

여자: 아니면 공연 예술 동아리에 들어오는 방법도 있어. 대학 내의 공연 동아리인데, 네가 훌륭한 발레리노라고 들었는데. 만약 그 동아리에 들어간다면, 자동적으로 수업을 통과하게 돼. 오디션이 한달 동안 진행될 예정이니 시간이 좀 걸리긴 할 테지만 말이야.

남자: 오, 생각을 좀 해봐야겠네요. 감사합니다, 교수님.

> **Listening Note**
>
> Problem   Failed the second periodic exam and find it hard to pass the course, even though he is graduating
>
> Solutions
>
> 1) Get a high grade in the final exam
>
> 2) Join a Theater Arts Club to pass the course
>
> Reasons
> ① He is a good dancer. No trouble getting into the club
> ② He might not pass the final exam.

Sample Response

The man is having a hard time passing Theater Arts course. The problem is that he failed the second periodic exam in Theater Arts, and thus may find it difficult to pass the course, even though he is graduating. The professor tells him to either get a very high grade in the final exam, or to join the Theater Arts Club to be able to pass the course. I think that it is better to just join the club, because he is a good dancer, and he will have no trouble being accepted into the club. He also might not pass the final exam, as shown by his previous test records.

Vocabulary

periodic exam 정기 시험   varsity 대표 팀   automatically 자동적으로   audition 채용심사, 오디션   previous 이전의

5

Script

W: Derek, do you know a good coffee shop in the area that has fast Internet access ... and closes late?
M: Yeah, there's one two blocks from the main avenue. Why, what's up?
W: I have to look for another place to work on my papers this weekend. The school decided to close the library to do inventory. Of all the weeks, why'd they have to do it the weekend before my research papers are due? And I don't have a fast Net connection in my room.
M: That is quite a problem. So you're going to a coffee shop instead?
W: I don't really know. That was my initial plan ... I mean, it seems logical to me. It's a good place to stay, comfortable couches and all ... and the connection's as good as in the library; but then again, I can't really tell other people to keep quiet in a coffee shop, so that I can concentrate ...
M: Hmmm, you got a point there. Why not stay in your room and just borrow the books you need before the weekend? I know it's not as comfortable, with limited space and all, but at least you'll have the place all to yourself. You'll just have to do research a bit more slowly, though.
W: That is something to consider. Glad I ran into you today. Thanks!

Script 해석

여자: 데렉, 근처에 고속 인터넷이 깔려있고 늦게 문을 닫는 좋은 커피숍 아는 데 있니?
남자: 응, 큰길에서 두 블록가면 한 곳 있어. 왜, 무슨 일이야?
여자: 주말에 리포트 쓸 곳을 찾아야 하거든. 학교 도서관이 재고 조사 때문에 휴관한대. 하고 많은 날 중에 하필 내 리포트 마감 전주에 재고 조사를 할게 뭐람? 내 방 인터넷 연결 속도는 느리거든.
남자: 정말 문제다. 그래서 대신 커피숍에서 하려고?
여자: 그게 잘 모르겠어. 그게 처음 내 계획이었거든, 그러니까 처음엔 괜찮은 생각 같았어. 앉아있기도 좋고 푹신푹신한 소파도 있고 도서관만큼 인터넷 속도가 빠르니까 말이야. 그런데 다른 사람들한테 내가 집중할 수 있도록 조용히 좀 해달라고 말할 수는 없잖아.
남자: 그 말이 맞아. 주말이 되기 전 필요한 책을 빌려서 방에서 하는 게 어때? 공간이나 모든 것이 제한되어 있어서 그리 편하지는 않겠지만 적어도 너 자신만의 장소를 가질 수 있잖아. 조금 느린 속도지만 조사만 하면 되는 거지.
여자: 그것도 생각해봐야겠다. 널 만나게 돼서 다행이야. 고마워!

> **Listening Note**
>
> **Problem** Needs a place to study for her papers -the library is closed
>
> **Solutions**
>
> 1) Going to a coffee shop
>   - fast Internet access
>   - comfortable
>   - other people's talk
>
> 2) Studying at home with borrowed books
>   - not as comfortable & spacious as a café
>   - quiet
>   - takes longer to research
>
> → Reasons
>
> ① More convenient
>   - may need to look for sth. on the Net
>   - typing on the computer is faster
>
> ② Better for concentrating
>   - can stay up late (can resist an urge to sleep b/c there's no bed)

Sample Respone

The problem they discuss is that she won't be able to use the library to do research for her papers. There are two solutions presented. The first option is to study at a coffee shop. And the other option is to study at home with borrowed books. Between the two options, I prefer going to a coffee shop. First, she has access to the fast Internet, and it offers a great environment for studying. If she studies at home, she has to fight hard to resist an urge to sleep because there is a comfortable bed at home. For these reasons, I think it's much better to study at a café.

Vocabulary

internet access 인터넷 접근성   couch 소파   urge 무의식적인 혹은 본능적인 충동

6

Script

M: You look pretty bothered lately ... what's on your mind?

W: Oh ... hey ... sorry, I'm just at a loss right now. I have to live in Spain for about a year. I'm not relocating permanently; my dad just needs a family member to stay with him after a major operation. But I don't want to quit school ... next year being my junior year and all ...

M: mmm ... I see your point there. It's hard to get your momentum back once you stop school, even for a short while.

W: Exactly. I'm thinking of a way to do both, take care of my dad and still continue my studies ...

M: Don't we have a cross-registration program? I know the university has a campus over there. Ask academic affairs if you can take some of your subjects overseas ... then you won't have to worry about choosing between your dad and school. A new school setting isn't bad either, making new friends and all ...

W: Quite tempting, but ... I don't know ...

M: Or you could take online courses for the time being. Get classes that can be credited to your degree. You'll be killing two birds with one stone ... you get to stay in school and be at home at the same time. You can even be there for your dad all day. You know what I mean?

W: I'll definitely think about what you said. Thanks!

| Script 해석 | 남자: 요즘 너무 힘들어 보인다. 무슨 고민 있어?

여자: 오, 안녕. 미안, 지금 어떻게 해야 할 지를 몰라서. 일 년 정도 스페인에서 살아야 하거든. 완전히 이사 가는 건 아니야. 아버지가 큰 수술을 후에 가족과 함께 있기를 바라셔. 그런데 학교를 그만 두고 싶지는 않아, 내년이면 3학년이고.

남자: 흠. 무슨 말인지 알겠다. 잠깐이라도 학교를 쉬면 원래의 감을 회복하기 어려운 거지.

여자: 바로 그거야. 두 가지 다 할 수 있는 방법을 생각 중이야. 아버지도 돌봐드리고 공부도 계속 할 수 있는

남자: 교환 학생 프로그램이 없을까? 그쪽에도 캠퍼스가 있는 대학이 있다고 알고 있는데. 학부 사무실에 물어봐, 네가 해외에서 수업을 들을 수 있는지 말이야. 그렇게 되면 둘 다 포기 안 해도 되니까. 새로운 학교에서 공부하는 것도 그렇게 나쁘지는 않을 거야, 새로운 친구들도 사귀고.

여자: 괜찮을 것 같다. 그런데 잘 모르겠어.

남자: 아니면 그 동안 온라인 수업을 들을 수도 있어. 너의 학년에 해당하는 수업을 들어. 일석이조잖아. 집에 있으면서도 수업을 들을 수도 있고. 아버지와 하루 종일 함께 있어 드릴 수도 있어, 무슨 말인지 알겠어?

여자: 네가 해준 얘기 생각해 봐야겠다. 고마워!

Listening Note

Problem   Needs to take care of her dad who is in Spain and sick, but she has to study in college.

Solutions

1) Get into the cross-registration program of the university
   • no decision to make: dad vs. school

2) Enroll online courses
   • earn credits
   • in school and be at home

Reasons
① It's convenient
② She needs more time with her dad.

| Sample Response | The woman has difficulty making a decision. She needs to take care of her dad, who is in Spain and sick, but she also wants to continue her studies, since she's not relocating permanently. The man suggests that she either get into the cross-registration program of the university or just enroll for online courses. I think the best way is to take online courses because it is better and more convenient. She will have more time for her dad than if she actually takes courses on campus. Since online courses can be credited to her degree program, she will have no problem taking much time for her dad.

Vocabulary

harass 괴롭히다, 시달리게 하다   relocate 재배치하다, 이전시키다   permanently 영구적인, 불변의   momentum 기세, 여세
cross-registration program 교환학생프로그램   academic affairs 학부 사무실

7

| Script | W: Hey, George, what's wrong? You look worried ... anything I can do to help?

M: Well, every now and then, I volunteer to help out elementary students. Thing is, I'm taking them to the zoo tomorrow, but the rental shop has no available van that I can use. I can't let the kids down on this one. So, do you know a way I can make this trip happen tomorrow?

W: Let me see ... um, why not ask a fellow volunteer who has a car to help you out? I'm sure that person won't mind, knowing it's for the children and all ...

M: Hmm ... but my fellows' cars are not as big as a van ... If I do that, I'm going to need at least three cars to take all the kids to the zoo. I'm not sure if that's such a good idea

W: Well, there is public transportation. Why don't you just commute to the zoo? This way you'll all be together during the ride. You just need to keep an eye on them all ... know what I mean?

M: Yeah, I get it, but ... keeping tabs on all of them is going to be a handful, though. Supervising is going to be difficult ... But thanks for the help! I'll mull it over before I decide.

| Script 해석 |

여자: 안녕 조지, 무슨 일 있어? 걱정이 있어 보인다. 내가 도와줄 일이 있니?

남자: 음, 가끔 초등학생들을 돕는 자원 봉사를 하거든. 문제는 내일 그 애들을 데리고 동물원을 가야 하는데 필요한 밴이 렌트카 업체에 없다. 아이들을 실망시킬 수는 없는데. 내일 놀러 갈 수 있는 방법이 없을까?

여자: 어디 보자. 음, 차를 가지고 있는 동료 봉사자에게 도와달라고 하면 어때? 애들을 위해서 하는걸 알면 싫어할 것 같지 않은데.

남자: 음. 내 동료들 차는 밴보다 작아. 애들을 모두 데리고 가려면 적어도 차 세 대가 더 필요해. 좋은 생각인지 모르겠다.

여자: 대중 교통도 있어. 버스를 타고 동물원에 가는 건 어때? 그렇게 하면 한번에 갈 수 있을 거야. 아이들을 잘 살펴보기만 하면 되는 거야. 내 말 알겠니?

남자: 응, 알겠어, 그래도 일일이 신경을 써야하는 건 벅찰거야. 감독하는 일이 어려워 질거야. 그래도 도와줘서 고마워! 잘 생각해보고 결정 할게.

Listening Note

Problem   Taking children to the zoo
- no available van

Solutions

1) Ask a fellow volunteer who has a car for help
 • a car is small → will need two more cars

 Reasons
 ① Safer
  • kids are hard to control
  • some of them might get lost if he takes them by bus

2) Use public transportation
 • can take all the kids on one ride
 • watching them will be difficult

| Sample Respone |

The man is facing a dilemma. He needs to take children to the zoo, but there is no available van that he can use. The woman recommends that he ask a fellow volunteer who has a car for help or to use public transportation. I believe the best way is to ask his fellow volunteer for help. Though he may not be able to take all the kids on one ride, it will be a safer way to take kids to the zoo. Besides, he can control the kids effectively and doesn't have to worry about losing any kid.

Vocabulary

handful (손에) 가득찬, 벅찬   mull over ~에 관해서 생각하다

8

| Script |

M: Hey, why the long face?

W: I just got my grade from my Art Studies class ... and it's way below my expectations. Normally, I would just let this pass, but I need a high grade to raise my average to maintain my scholarship.

M: Hmm ... So, why don't you see your teacher? Maybe something got mixed up ...

W: I'm actually thinking of doing that. I mean, I have the results of my exams and other stuff ... there was no way I was gonna get a grade this low, unless my teacher made some mistakes, or created a new grading system that I wasn't aware of. I don't know

M: Well, you really gotta talk to your teacher. He may consider changing your grade if you explain your problem. Show him why you think he gave you a grade you don't deserve, you know?

W: Hmm ... yeah, I'll probably do that. I mean ... it might have been an honest mistake on his part.

M: Or you can go directly to the Appeals Committee. That way, you'll be discussing your problem in the presence of a third party and avoid possible confrontations. It's always better to have someone around so it won't be his word against yours later on.

W: Uh-huh. I'll think about it. Thanks, Al.

| Script 해석 |

남자: 이봐, 왜 그렇게 시무룩한 거야?

여자: 예술학 수업 성적이 나왔거든. 생각했던 것보다 훨씬 낮아서. 원래는 이런 거 신경 안 쓰는데, 장학금을 계속 받을 수 있게 평균을 높이려면 더 높은 점수가 필요해.

남자: 흠, 교수님을 찾아가 보는 게 어때? 뭔가 잘못 됐을 수도 있잖아?

여자: 안그래도 그래 볼까 생각 중이야. 내 말은 시험 성적이랑 다른 서류들을 가지고 있는데, 만약 교수님이 실수한 게 아니거나, 혹은 내가 모르는 새로운 시스템으로 성적을 매긴게 아니라면 이렇게 성적이 낮게 나왔을 리가 없어. 잘 모르겠어.

남자: 흠, 정말 교수님을 찾아가봐야겠다. 너의 상황을 말씀 드리면 성적을 다시 주실지도 몰라. 네가 받은 성적이 왜 이상 하다고 생각하는지 말씀 드려, 알겠어?

여자: 흠, 그래. 그렇게 해야겠다. 솔직히 교수님이 실수하신 것 일수도 있으니까.

남자: 아니면 탄원 위원회를 바로 찾아가던지. 그렇게 하면 삼자 앞에서 너의 문제를 토론해 볼 수도 있고 대립을 피할 수 있으니까. 나중에 다른 말이 나오지 않게 하려면 누군가가 있는 것이 항상 나으니까.

여자: 어, 생각해 볼게. 고마워 알.

Listening Note

Problem
Needs to get a high grade to maintain her scholarship but received a low grade from her Art Studies class.

Solutions

1) See the teacher

Reasons
① Can find out what the exact problem is.
② Can go to the Appeals Committee anytime even after meeting her teacher

2) Go directly to the Appeals Committee
- discuss your problem in the presence of a third party and avoid possible confrontations.

| Sample Response |

The woman wants to maintain her scholarship, but she isn't able to receive her scholarship anymore because she got a low grade from her Art Studies class. The man advises that she could talk to the teacher or go directly to the appeals committee. I consider talking to the teacher to be the most reasonable solution because she can find out what the exact problem is as soon as she talks to her professor. In addition, she can go to the Appeals Committee anytime she wants even after meeting her professor.

Vocabulary

the Appeals Committee 탄원 위원회   confrontation 대면

Task 06 Summary

1

| Script | All organisms have the ability to build up a resistance to various toxins. If any organism is exposed to a toxin at non-lethal levels for a long enough period, it will become resistant to that toxin. Consider a drug addict who has to take ever greater amounts of a drug to get the same effect, for example. Anyway, this natural ability of organisms poses serious problems when one is trying to deal with pests and health threats, and I'll show you how that works through two examples. OK, now since the advent of modern chemistry, farmers have been using pesticides to control any number of insect and animal pests. But no pesticide kills 100% effectively. Uh, so some pests survive, build up a resistance, and pass that resistance on to their offspring. Eventually, the species as a whole becomes more resistant to the pesticide. So farmers are forced to use ever more powerful pesticides in order to control harmful insects and animals. Um, another example would be the use of antibiotics, the medicines that we commonly use to fight infections. Infections are caused by bacteria. And here it's the same thing that we talked about earlier. As antibiotics are used more frequently, bacteria become more resistant, and doctors have to prescribe more powerful antibiotics to fight even basic infections. The danger here is that, eventually, some bacteria may become resistant to even our most powerful antibiotics, and then how will we fight disease?

| Script 해석 | 모든 유기체는 독소에 대해 저항력을 기를 수 있는 능력을 가지고 있습니다. 어떤 유기체라도 충분히 오랜 기간 동안 치명적인 수준이 아닌 독소에 노출이 된다면 그 독소에 대해서 저항력을 갖게 됩니다. 예를 들어, 같은 효과를 얻기 위해 계속 더 많은 양의 약을 복용해야 하는 중독자를 생각해 보십시오. 어쨌든 유기체의 이런 능력은 해충이나 건강 문제를 다룰 때 큰 문제가 됩니다. 두 가지의 예를 통해 보여드리겠습니다. 현대 화학의 출현이래로 농부들은 곤충이나 동물 해충을 견제하기 위하여 살충제를 사용해 왔습니다. 그러나 어떤 살충제도 100% 다 죽일 수는 없습니다. 그래서 일부의 해충은 살아 남아 저항력을 기르고 그 저항력은 후손에게 유전이 됩니다. 결국 그 종은 전체적으로 해충제에 대한 저항력을 갖게 됩니다. 그래서 농부는 해충과 해로운 동물을 조절하기 위해 더 강력한 해충제를 사용할 수 밖에 없게 됩니다. 또 한 예는 감염과 싸우기 위해 사용하는 항생제입니다. 박테리아가 감염을 시키게 되는데요. 앞에서 이야기한 동일한 현상이 일어납니다. 항생제를 자주 사용하면 박테리아는 더욱 저항력을 가지게 되고 의사는 간단한 감염에도 더 강력한 항생제를 처방해야 합니다. 결과적으로 위험한 것은 어떠한 박테리아는 가장 강력한 항생제에도 저항력을 가질 수 있다는데 있습니다. 그러면 우리는 질병과 어떻게 싸워야 할까요?

Vocabulary
resistance 저항, 반대   toxin 독소   nonlethal level 치명적이지 않은 수준   addict 중독자   pest 해충   pesticide 살충제
antibiotic 항생물질   infection 전염, 감염, 전염물질   prescribe 처방하다

2

| Script |

As we go about our daily lives, we engage in imitation … uh, a necessary action that is both involuntary and instinctive. We learn to walk, talk and do other physical activities through imitation. And as we grow older and become aware of different social situations, the things we copy turn toward the artistic. We also start to imitate or portray people. Artistic imitation is done with skill and talent, and our orientation toward this kind of imitation is fueled by humor and criticism. One example of artistic imitation is the caricature. Caricatures are found in news editorials and other literary publications. These drawings are usually accompanied by critical or social articles. The image presented comes from the perspective of the artist or writer. They illustrate the subject by exaggerating his or her physical features. Uh, some artists add animal-like qualities. Others incorporate critical remarks to complete the cartoonish image and convey something about the subject's personality. People who do caricatures play with a lot of imagery and present it as a single unit. Another form of imitation that has enjoyed mass patronage throughout history is impersonation. We often see on television, or in clubs and theaters: comedic actors giving their impersonation of other famous actors, political personages and other famous celebrities. Hours of practice and preparation are invested to come up with the best performance to render this artistic imitation. The impersonator assumes the role of the subject in an exaggerated manner, complete with physical and vocal features like those of the original person. This presents the subjects in a completely different manner exaggerating something humorous or critical they said or did.

| Script 해석 |

일상 생활에서 우리는 모방을 하게 됩니다. 이는 무의식적이고 본능적인 꼭 필요한 행동이죠. 우리는 모방을 통해서 걷고 말하고 다른 신체적인 활동을 배워갑니다. 나이가 들고 다양한 사회적 상황들을 인식하게 되면서 바로 우리가 모방하는 것이 예술이 되어갑니다. 우리는 또한 다른 사람을 모방하거나 묘사하기 시작합니다. 예술적인 모방은 기술과 재능이 필요합니다. 그리고 이런 종류의 모방은 유머와 비판 정신에 의해 가속화됩니다. 예술적 모방의 한 종류는 캐리커처입니다. 캐리커처는 신문 논설이나 다른 문학 발간지에서 볼 수 있습니다. 이런 그림은 대개 비판적이거나 사회적인 내용과 함께 나옵니다. 보여지는 이미지는 화가나 작가의 관점을 통해 제시됩니다. 그들은 신체적인 특징을 과장함으로써 주제를 그려냅니다. 어떤 화가들은 동물과 비슷한 특징을 첨가하기도 하고, 다른 사람들은 만화 같은 이미지를 완성하기 위해 비판적인 말을 집어 넣고, 대상의 품성에 대해 무언가를 전달합니다. 캐리커처를 그리는 사람들은 많은 비유를 사용하여 하나의 단일한 작품으로 제시합니다. 역사적으로 대중의 환영을 받았던 모방의 또 다른 형태는 바로 연기입니다. 종종 텔레비전, 혹은 클럽이나 극장에서, 희극 배우들이 유명한 배우나 정치적인 인물 혹은 유명한 배우를 흉내 내는 것을 볼 수 있습니다. 이 예술적 모방을 하기 위해 수 시간의 연습과 준비를 합니다. 배우는 원래 인물의 신체적 특징과 목소리의 특징을 곁들여 이 인물의 역할을 과장된 방식으로 가정합니다. 그들이 말하거나 행동했던 재미있는 말이나 비판적인 말을 과장함으로써 이 인물을 완전히 다른 방식으로 보여줍니다.

Listening Note

Topic
Artistic imitation
- Something that is done with skill and talent

Example 1
Caricatures
- Exaggerated drawings in newspapers
Ex) An artist draws a person highlighting certain characteristics of the person.

Example 2
Impersonation
• Good imitators try to look and act like their subjects
 -Show their personalities in an artistic manner
Ex) Present the subject in a completely different way
 - with exaggeration

| Sample Response | The topic of the lecture is artistic imitation. Artistic imitation is something that is done using skill and talent. One example of artistic imitation may be seen in caricatures, those exaggerated drawings that you see in newspapers, where the physical features of subjects are emphasized. These drawings imitate the subjects, but express their personalities in a rather different way. For example an artist may draw a picture of a person, but give that person animal-like qualities in order to highlight certain characteristics of that person. The other example of artistic imitation is impersonation, wherein really good imitators try to look and act like their subjects, and show their personalities in a rather artistic manner. According to the professor, both of these forms of artistic impersonation are used for both humorous and critical purposes.

Vocabulary

imitation 모방 **involuntary** 무의식의 **portray** 표현하다, 묘사하다 **criticism** 비평 **caricature** 풍자만화 **exaggerate** 과장하다 **incorporate** 섞다, 합체하다 **cartoonish image** 만화에서 그려지는 이미지 **patronage** 단골 **celebrity** 유명인서 **impersonator** 의인화 **humorous** 해학적인

3

| Script | One of the most important concepts that the nation's founding fathers built into the Constitution was the concept of checks and balances. This is the system in which each branch of government, the legislative, the executive, and the judiciary, has the ability to limit the power of the other branches to some extent. I'm going to give you two examples of the system of checks and balances in action so that you can see how important this is. The president is the leader of the nation, right? And as such he has great power. He can veto the laws that Congress makes, uh, he can send our nation to war, etc. But the power of the president is limited. If the legislature feels that the president is seriously abusing his power or acting in an illegal manner, then it can vote to impeach him and remove him from office. As you all probably know, this is actually what happened to President Nixon in 1974. When it became apparent that he had used his power as president in an illegal manner against his political opponents, Congress decided to impeach him. So, he resigned from office to avoid impeachment. My other example is ... uh, a bit more modern. After the September 11th attacks, President Bush started a program to secretly listen to the telephone conversations of suspected terrorists. Now, normally, before the government can listen to telephone conversations, it has to get permission from the courts, but Bush said that this was not necessary. Last year, the courts decided that Bush's wiretapping program was illegal and ordered him to stop it.

| Script 해석 | 헌법을 통해 표현된 국가 창시자들의 가장 중요한 개념 중 한 가지는 견제와 균형입니다. 이는 정부의 부서인 입법부, 행정부, 사법부가 어느 정도까지는 다른 부서를 견제할 수 있도록 하는 시스템입니다. 견제와 균형이 나타난 실제 두 가지 예를 들어 이 개념이 얼마나 중요한지 설명 드리겠습니다. 대통령은 한 나라의 지도자입니다, 그렇죠? 그렇기 때문에 대단한 권력을 가지고 있습니다. 의회가 만든 법을 거부할 수도 있고, 국민을 참전시킬 수도 있습니다. 그러나 대통령의 권력은 제한되어 있습니다. 만약 입법 기관이 대통령이 불법적인 방식으로 권력을 남용한다고 느끼면, 대통령을 탄핵해서 자리에서 물러나도록 투표를 할 수 있습니다. 아마도 모두 알겠지만, 이것이 바로 1974년 닉슨 대통령에게 일어난 일입니다. 그가 불법적인 방식으로 정치적 맞수에게 대통령의 권력을 사용한 것이 명백해지자, 의회는 탄핵 투표로 그를 대통령 자리로부터 사임시키려 했습니다. 그래서 그는 탄핵을 피하기 위해 사임을 했습니다. 다른 한가지 예는 비교적 최근 것인데요. 9.11 공격 이후에 부시 대통령은 테러리스트로 의심되는 사람들의 전화 통화를 도청하는 프로그램을 시작했습니다. 지금은 정부가 전화 통화를 들으려면 법원의 동의를 얻어야 하는데, 부시는 이 절차가 필요 없다고 했습니다. 지난 해, 법원은 부시의 전화 도청 프로그램이 불법이라고 정하고 그것을 그만둘 것을 명령 했습니다.

Listening Note

Topic
The concept of checks and balances
- Each branch of government has the ability to limit the power of the other branches.

Example 1
President Nixon
- Used his power as president illegally
Ex) Congress was able to act to limit the power of the president once he started to misuse his power.

Example 2
President Bush
- Listened to people's conversations without permission from the courts
Ex) The courts ordered to him to stop.

| Sample Respone | The professor discusses both President Nixon and President Bush to demonstrate how checks and balances work in American politics. According to the professor, President Nixon used his power as president illegally. In this case, Congress was able to impeach him and force him to resign. Thus Congress was able to act to limit the power of the president once he started to use his power in an abusive manner. The other example is of President Bush. According to the professor, President Bush began to listen to people's conversations without permission from the courts, which is normally not allowed. The courts, however, decided that Bush was not allowed to do this and ordered him to stop. This is another example of how the system of checks and balances can work to limit the power of one branch of government.

Vocabulary

constitution 구조, 구성, 체격   legislative 입법부   executive 행정부   judiciary 사법부   veto 거부권을 행사하다   apparent 명백한
impeach 탄핵하다   wiretapping 도청   illegal 불법적인

4

| Script | Usually we think about the impact of certain musicians when we talk about how new musical styles are created, uh, say, the role of the Beatles in pioneering rock and roll. But technology also played an important role in the directions that music has taken. As new technologies emerge, they create new possibilities for musicians. One excellent example of this would be the electric guitar, which was first developed in the early 1930s. Now, the biggest difference between an electric guitar and an acoustic guitar is that an electric guitar is ... well, louder. If you play an acoustic guitar in a band, it's going to be pretty soft, especially if you are playing single notes instead of strumming chords. That meant that guitars had been primarily rhythm instruments before the invention of the electric guitar. But with the louder sound that they created, electric guitars became lead instruments. This led to the evolution of new musical genres in which the guitar was the focus of attention, such as blues ... and later on, rock and roll, of course. Another technological advance that changed music was the multiple track recorder. Until the 1960s all recording was done on two tracks. What this meant was that you had to record all the instruments at once, and if someone made a mistake ... well, then you just had to record everything again. But multi-track recorders recorded each individual instrument on a separate part of the recording tape. This meant that if a musician made a mistake, you didn't have to re-record the whole band. You could just record that one instrument again. This led to longer, more complex songs because musicians felt less pressure while recording.

Script 해석 | 새로운 음악 스타일이 어떻게 만들어 졌는지 이야기할 때면, 대개 특정한 음악가의 영향에 대해서 생각하게 됩니다. 말하자면, 로큰롤 분야를 개척하는데 있어서 비틀즈의 역할이 그러합니다. 그러나 음악이 새로운 방향을 잡을 때 기술도 중요한 역할을 했습니다. 새로운 기술이 등장하면 음악가들에게 새로운 가능성을 만듭니다. 1930년 초에 처음 개발된 일렉 기타가 그 훌륭한 예입니다. 자, 일렉 기타와 어쿠스틱 기타의 가장 큰 차이점은 일렉 기타의 소리가 크다는 점입니다. 밴드에서 어쿠스틱 기타를 연주한다면 소리가 무척 약할 것입니다. 특히 통기지 않고 한 음만을 연주한다면요. 그 의미는 일렉 기타의 발명 전에 기타는 주로 리듬 악기였다는 뜻입니다. 그러나 일렉 기타가 큰 소리를 낼 수 있게 되면서 선두 악기가 될 수 있었습니다. 이는 예를 들어 블루스나 물론 나중에 로큰롤 같이 기타가 중심이 되는 새로운 음악 형태의 진화를 이끌었습니다. 음악을 변화시킨 또 다른 기술적인 발전은 바로 다중 트랙 녹음기입니다. 1960년대까지 모든 녹음은 두 개 트랙에 되었습니다. 이 말은 모든 악기를 한꺼번에 녹음해야 하며, 누군가 실수하면 전부 다시 녹음 해야 한다는 뜻입니다. 그러나 다중 트랙 녹음기는 각각의 악기를 개별적인 녹음 테이프에 녹음 했습니다. 이것은, 연주자가 실수를 해도 전체 밴드의 녹음을 다시 하지 않아도 된다는 말입니다. 한 악기만 다시 녹음할 수 있습니다. 이 기술 덕분에 음악가들은 녹음하는 동안 부담을 덜 받기 때문에 더 길고 복잡한 노래가 나오게 되었습니다.

Listening Note

Topic
Technology influencing the progress of music

Example 1
The invention of electric guitar
- Guitars were able to take on a more prominent role in music

Ex) This change gave rise to new types of music like blues and rock.

Example 2
The invention of multi-track recorder
- Allowed artists to record one part at a time

Ex) This freed them from the time pressures related to recording and enabled them to produce complex songs.

Sample Respone | The professor talks about the influence of thechnology on the progress of music. According to the professor, the invention of the electric guitar and the invention of the multi-track recorder are two examples of how technology influenced the progress of music. The professor says that electric guitars were louder than acoustic guitars. As a result, guitars were able to take on a more prominent role in music and moved from being a rhythm instrument to a lead instrument. This change gave rise to new types of music like blues and rock. The invention of the multiple track recorder had a similar effect on music. According to the professor, the multi-track recorder allowed artists to record one part at a time. This freed them from the time pressures associated with recording and led to longer, more complex songs.

Vocabulary

pioneer 개척하다   emerge 나타나다, 떠오르다   strumming chords 현악기 화음(코드)   primary 주요한, 최초의, 근본적인   instrument 악기
musical genres 음악 장르   prominent 눈에 띄는, 탁월한

5

p204

| Script |

No matter how careful we are with handling food, food is bound to go stale and spoil, making it unsafe for consumption. Knowing how to properly handle and keep food will help prevent harmful bacteria from getting into our digestive system through our food intake. Since bacteria, just like any other living organism, rely on good levels of temperature and moisture, we can manipulate these two factors to prevent the spoilage of food. A widely used and practical method of protecting food from spoiling, uh, is by lowering the temperature. We don't just put fresh meat or leftover food in the fridge or freezer because we have nowhere else to put it ... it's convenient, but not really the main purpose for doing so. Keeping food at such temperatures, although it doesn't kill the bacteria, greatly slows their growth. Bacteria, just like humans, have an optimal body temperature, and if you move them outside of that temperature, they do not function as well. So, if you take away the warm temperature, bacteria won't easily spread ... Aside from lowering the temperature, uh, we can also lower the humidity so as to prevent spoilage. Bacteria not only rely on heat to survive, they also require water ... so, consumers sometimes prefer to buy dry goods in lieu of fresh or liquid-form products. For example, you can stock up on dry, powdered milk, leaving it in the cupboard for months without having to worry about its expiration date. But, you can't do the same for fresh or liquid-form milk because of its water content.

| Script 해석 |

아무리 조심스럽게 음식을 다룬다고 해도 음식은 신선도가 떨어지며 부패하게 되고 먹기에는 해로운 상태가 됩니다. 올바르게 음식을 다루고 유지하는 법을 안다면 음식 섭취를 통해 해로운 박테리아가 소화기관 안으로 들어오는 것을 막을 수 있습니다. 왜냐하면 다른 생물체처럼 박테리아도 적당한 온도와 습도에 의존하기 때문에, 이 두 요인을 조절함으로써 음식의 부패를 막을 수 있습니다. 음식의 부패를 막는 널리 사용되는 한 가지 실제적인 방법은 온도를 낮추는 것입니다. 신선한 고기나 남은 음식을 냉장고나 냉동고에 넣어 두는 것은 보관할 장소가 없어서 그런 것이 아닙니다. 편리하죠, 그러나 이 점이 그렇게 하는 중요한 이유는 아닙니다. 그 정도의 온도에서 음식을 보관하면 박테리아를 없애지는 못하지만 성장 속도를 훨씬 낮출 수 있습니다. 박테리아도 인간처럼 최적의 온도라는 것이 있기 때문에, 그 온도 범위 밖에서는 제대로 기능을 발휘하지 못합니다. 그렇기 때문에 여러분이 따뜻한 온도를 없앤다면, 박테리아가 쉽게 늘어나지 않습니다. 온도를 낮추는 것 외에 습도를 낮추어서 부패를 막을 수도 있습니다. 박테리아는 생존을 위해 열에만 의존하는 것이 아니라 수분도 필요로 합니다. 그래서 소비자들이 때로 신선하거나 액체 형태의 식품 대신 건조된 식품을 구입하는 것입니다. 예를 들어, 건조된 분말 우유는 유통기한을 걱정하지 않고 찬장에 몇 달이고 놔둘 수 있습니다. 그렇지만 신선하거나 액체 형태의 우유를 그렇게 하지는 못합니다. 왜냐하면 안에 수분이 포함되어 있기 때문입니다.

Listening Note

Topic
Preventing food spoilage in order to avoid bacteria

Example 1	Example 2
Cold storage of food	Lowering humidity
• fresh meat or leftovers kept in fridge	• bacteria need water to survive
• low temperature slows down bacteria growth	• dry goods (e.g. powdered milk)
	• bacteria won't grow b/c there's no water

| Sample Respone |

According to the professor, it's important to know how to prevent harmful bacteria from getting into our digestive system by properly handing and storing food. The professor explains two methods of protecting food from deteriorating. One is to lower the temperature. The other is to reduce the humidity. Food deterioration occurrs mainly because of the high temperature. According to the professor, therefore, one can prevent spoilage by lowering the temperature. Also, bacteria need water to survive. If one lowers the humidity, he can keep food from spoiling. One example the professor gives is powdered milk, which contains no water and thus cannot spoil.

Vocabulary

consumption 소비, 소모   digestive system 소화기관   moisture 습기   manipulative 조절하는   spoilage 손상, 파괴   leftover 남은 음식
fridge 냉장고   humidity 습기   in lieu of ~ 대신에   powdered 분말의

6

| Script |

Probably one of the most influential, if not the most, modern art movements in the early 20th century was Cubism. This movement paved the way for new ways of defining and interpreting art and life as perceived in the real world. Artists influenced by Cubism incorporated geometric shapes and unconventional depictions of nature and life in general, pushing into the background traditional attempts at creating the illusion of space. How this is achieved is where fragmentation and ambiguity, two devices specific to Cubism, come into play. In any artwork, the subject matter is a fundamental element. With the non-traditional perspective applied by cubist painters, such as Pablo Picasso, nature, along with other subjects, are broken into geometric shapes and fragments. So, a depiction of, let's say, a series of trees, instead of having normal features like branches and leaves, might consist of a collection of little cones and triangles. So an image that we would normally view as a whole, is broken into fragments ... like pieces of a puzzle. Other than fragmentation, cubists also employ a sense of ambiguity in their artwork. Uh, not only are geometric forms used for the subject matter, um, but even the background also becomes a series of these simplistic shapes. For example, if you are looking at a painting of the sun setting on the horizon as seen from a beach, you might have to scrutinize the work more closely, because by using ... say, a series of different squares to render the landscape, no clear demarcation where the sea ends or where the sky starts is made in the work.

| Script 해석 |

20세기 초반 가장 영향력 있는 현대 예술 운동 중 하나가 바로 큐비즘 입니다. 이 운동은 예술과 삶을 현실 세계 안에서 인식되는 대로 정의 내리고 해석하는 새로운 방식을 가능하게 했습니다. 큐비즘의 영향을 받은 예술가들은 공간의 환상을 창조해 내려는 전통적인 시도를 밀어내고 기하학적인 모양과 자연과 생활의 비관습적인 묘사를 도입했습니다. 큐비즘의 두 가지 구체적 특징인 분열과 모호함이 활동을 시작하면서 이것이 이루어졌습니다. 어떤 작품에서든 주제가 가장 중요한 요소입니다. 파블로 피카소 같은 큐비즘 화가들이 사용한 비전통적 관점에 의해, 자연은 다른 소재들과 마찬가지로 기하학적인 형태와 분열로 나누어졌습니다. 그래서 나무들이 죽 늘어서있는 장면을 묘사하는 그림은 일반적인 가지나 잎 대신에 작은 원뿔이나 삼각형들로 이루어져 있을 수 있습니다. 이렇게 우리가 대개는 하나로 인식하는 이미지가 마치 퍼즐 조각처럼 조각들로 나뉘어 있습니다. 분열 말고도 입체주의 작가들은 예술 작품에 모호함이라는 개념을 사용했습니다. 주제를 표현하기 위한 기하학적인 형태뿐 아니라, 배경 역시 단순한 형태의 연속으로 바뀌었습니다. 예를 들어, 해변에서 보이는 수평선의 일몰 그림을 보고 있다고 해봅시다. 여러분은 아마도 작품을 더 자세히 관찰해야 할 것입니다 왜냐하면 풍경을 표현하기 위해 다양한 사각형들을 사용했기 때문에, 작품에서 바다가 끝나는 곳과 하늘이 시작하는 곳 사이의 경계가 명확하지 않기 때문입니다.

Listening Note

Topic
Key elements of Cubism

Example 1
Fragmentation
- subjects portrayed using geometric shapes and fragments
- whole image is fragmented, like a puzzle

Example 2
Ambiguity
- background consists of shapes; may be difficult to recognize separate elements of bg.
Ex) sea and sky – no clear demarcation line

| Sample Respone |

According to the lecture, fragmentation and ambiguity are two key elements of Cubism which paved the way for some new ways to define and interpret art and life as perceived in the real world. The professor illustrates fragmentation by describing how Picasso depicts a series of trees, for example, as broken fragments, a collection of little cones and triangles like a puzzle. The professor then talks about the sense of ambiguity being used in the artwork. Not only are geometric forms used in the artwork, but the background also becomes a series of these simplistic shapes. The professor then gives an example of sea and sky having no clear demarcation line to illustrate the use of ambiguity in Cubism.

| Vocabulary | geometric 기하학적인   unconventional depiction 비습관적인 묘사   fragmentation 분열   ambiguity 모호함   demarcation 경계
simplistic shape 단순한 형태 |

7

| Script | Biodiversity is the abundance and variety of life, like plants, animals and micro-organisms ... including their genetic make-up and the ecosystems that they form, okay? Ideally, there has to be a balance in the number of species present and their resources ... But factors like civilization, deforestation, natural calamities and human economic activities constantly pose threats to the balance of ecosystems by, uh, displacing species from their habitats and driving them to extinction. In recent years, though, conservation of biodiversity has become a global concern, and more groups have been working together to protect and restore biodiversity. Now ... one type of conservation option is the in-situ conservation, which is the conservation of species in their natural habitat. Um, this is being done by creating protected areas for endangered species of plants and animals, often in forest or sea areas. The preservation or restoration of biodiversity includes protecting or cleaning up the habitat itself, and protecting the species from their predators. This method is considered the ideal conservation strategy, although it is much harder to do, since species meet many threats in their natural habitat. In some cases, conservation is being done ex-situ, wherein the endangered species are being preserved off-site. Such species are taken out of their natural habitats and brought to ex-situ conservation sites such as zoos, botanical gardens and seed banks, where they are put under the care of humans. There, they are nurtured for breeding and groomed for reintroduction to the wild. Aside from providing housing care for the endangered species, ex-situ conservation also has educational value, since it informs people about the threatened status of some species, and thereby creates interest in reversing the perils to biodiversity.

| Script 해석 | 생물 다양성이란, 식물, 동물, 미생물 등이 유전적인 구성에서든 형성하는 생태계이든, 많아지고 다양해지는 것입니다. 알겠죠? 이상적으로는 현존하는 종의 수와 그 자원이 균형을 이루어야 합니다. 그러나 문명화, 산림 개간, 자연적인 재난과 인류의 경제 활동 등이 끊임 없이 이 종들을 서식지로부터 몰아내고 멸종 위기로 몰아 넣음으로써 생태계의 균형에 위협을 가하고 있습니다. 그러나 최근에 생물 다양성의 보호가 전지구적인 이목을 끌게 되었고, 더 많은 단체가 생물 다양성을 보호하고 회복시키기 위해서 함께 일하기 시작했습니다. 이 방법 중 현지 내 보존이라는 것이 있는데, 이는 자연의 거주지에서 이 종들을 보호하는 것입니다. 이는 흔히 숲이나 해안 지역에서 멸종 위기에 처한 식물과 동물을 위한 보호지역을 만듦으로써 이루어집니다. 거주지 자체를 보호하거나 청소하는 것, 그리고 천적으로부터 보호하는 것도 생물 다양성의 보존 혹은 회복 작업의 일부입니다. 이 방법은 가장 이상적인 보존 전략으로 인정됩니다. 비록 종이 자연의 거주지에서 많은 위협을 만나기 때문에 더 어렵긴 하지만 말입니다. 어떤 경우에는 현지 외 방법으로 보존을 하는데, 위험에 처한 종이 멀리 떨어진 곳으로 격리되는 것입니다. 이종들은 원래 거주지로부터 분리되어 동물원, 식물원, 종자 은행과 같이 인간이 돌볼 수 있는 보호 장소로 보내집니다. 그들은 그곳에서 새끼를 낳고 야생으로 다시 보내질 수 있게 길러집니다. 멸종 위기에 처한 종에게 거주지를 제공하는 것 외에도, 이 현지 외 보존은 사람들에게 이 종이 처한 위험을 알리고 멸종의 위기에서 생물 다양성으로 바뀌는 것에 대한 흥미를 불러일으킬 수 있기 때문에 교육적 가치도 있습니다.

Listening Note

Topic
Conserving various species is important to preserve biodiversity.

Example 1
Conserve species in their natural habitats by having protected areas.
- the best way to conserve many species
- but this is very difficult

Example 2
Undertake conservation measures outside an animal's natural habitat.
- like a zoo
- off-site preservation areas educate people about the nature and value of biodiversity.

Sample Response

The lecture is mainly about preserving biodiversity. The professor argues that conserving various species is important to preserve biodiversity. Many ways have been devised to preserve biodiversity. One of these is to conserve species in their natural habitats by having protected areas in natural environments such as forests or seas. Creating protected natural habitats is the best way to conserve these species, but it is very difficult as well. Another way to preserve biodiversity is to undertake conservation measures outside an animal's natural habitat, such as in a zoo. Aside from protecting species, off-site preservation areas educate people about the nature and value of biodiversity.

Vocabulary

abundance 다량, 다수, 풍부   micro-organism 미생물   genetic 유전적인   ecosystem 생태계   calamity 재난, 불행
displace 퇴거시키다, 추방하다   habitat 서식지   biodiversity 생물의 다양성   in-situ conservation 현지 내 보존   endanger 위험에 빠뜨리다
restoration 회복   ex-situ 현지 외   off-site 떨어진, 부지 밖의   botanical garden 식물원   seed bank 종자은행   reintroduction 재도입, 재투입
threaten 위협하다   undertake 맡다, 의무를 지다

8

| Script |

Alright ... even though we have many different senses to take in various stimuli, we can only focus our full attention on one kind of stimulus at one particular moment. This is known as selective attention. It has been proven in scientific studies that we don't pay attention to everything around us, and that we selectively attend to some forms of information at the expense of others. When you are in front of a computer, for example, you focus your awareness on the computer screen most of the time. While looking at the monitor, you probably don't see your nose, but it's in your line of sight. Uh, you probably don't feel your elbow pressing hard on the table. You may also be unaware of many other types of stimuli present, such as the rustling of leaves outside, or the conversation of office workers around you. This clearly shows selective attention, where at any point, we only focus on a selected aspect of all that we experience – so we can concentrate on what is most important to us at the moment. OK, another example of selective attention is the cocktail party effect ... uh, the ability to focus attention on one voice among many. I'm sure you can remember a situation in which you've been in a noisy room talking to a friend, and all of a sudden you hear your name called out from across the room, right? OK, now up until that point, while you were talking to your friend, your ears were taking in all the sounds in the room, but your brain was filtering them out and focusing on listening to your friend in front of you. But all of a sudden, the sound of your name grabbed your attention because your brain recognizes it instantly as an important sound.

| Script 해석 |

자, 비록 우리가 다른 감각기로 다양한 자극을 받아들일 수 있지만, 한 순간에는 한 가지 자극에만 집중할 수 있습니다. 이는 선택적 주의 집중이라고 알려져 있습니다. 주위의 모든 것에 집중을 하지 않고, 선택적으로 어떤 정보에만 집중을 한다는 사실은 과학적으로 증명이 되었습니다. 예를 들어, 컴퓨터 앞에 앉아 있을 때 대부분은 컴퓨터 화면에 집중을 하게 됩니다. 모니터를 보는 동안은 코를 보게 되지 않을 것입니다. 시야 안에 코가 있어도 말이죠. 아마 팔꿈치로 책상을 세게 누르고 있다는 것도 못 느낄 겁니다. 근처에 있는 다른 자극도 역시 인식하지 못할 수도 있는데, 예를 들어 바깥의 낙엽이 굴러가는 것이나, 여러분 주위 동료들의 대화 소리 같은 것 말입니다. 이는 선택적 주의 집중의 특징을 명확하게 보여줍니다. 어느 순간이든 우리가 경험하고 있는 모든 것 중 선택된 한 단면에만 집중합니다. 다시 말해서 그 순간 가장 중요한 것에 집중할 수 있다는 것이죠. 선택적 주의 집중의 또 다른 예는 칵테일 파티 효과입니다. 즉, 많은 사람 중에 한 사람의 목소리에만 집중하는 능력이죠. 시끄러운 장소에서 친구와 이야기를 하다가 갑자기 반대편에서 누군가 당신의 이름이 갑자기 불리는 것을 듣는 상황을 경험해 봤을 거라고 생각합니다. 네, 그때까지 친구와 이야기하고 있지만 여러분의 귀는 방안의 모든 소리를 듣고 있는 것입니다. 그러나 뇌는 그 소리들을 걸러내고 당신 앞의 친구 목소리만 듣게 하죠. 그러나 갑자기 당신의 이름이 주의를 끕니다. 왜냐하면 뇌가 그것을 중요한 소리로 인식했기 때문 입니다.

> **Listening Note**
>
> Topic
> Selective attention
> - We selectively pay attention to one kind of stimulus at a certain moment
>
> Example 1
> When sitting in front of a computer
> - focus attention on the screen
>   → unaware of your nose or elbow, rustling sound of leaves, conversation of people (concentrate on what is important)
>
> Example 2
> The cocktail party effect
> - focus attention on one voice & ignore others
>   ex) talking to a friend in a crowded space→ brain filters out other voices
> *someone calls your name
>   → you immediately catch the sound
> - b/c the brain recognizes its importance.

Sample Respone

According to the professor, selective attention refers to a tendency to pay attention to one kind of stimulus at a certain moment. The professor discusses two situations to illustrate the concept of selective attention. Selective attention occurs because of our natural tendency to focus on what is important or familiar to us. The first example describes how a person, sitting in front of his computer monitor, can ignore noise or other physical and visual stimuli present in his surroundings. The person has selective attention because his main focus is centered on what he is looking at on the screen, and nothing else. The other example involves the so-called "cocktail party effect," wherein you are able to distinguish your name out of all the noise at a party when someone calls your name, because your brain recognizes it as an important sound.

Vocabulary

stimuli 자극물   scientific studies 과학적 연구   awareness 인지, 인식   filter 필터   grab ~을 갑자기 꽉 잡다.

PART III Actual Test

Actual Test 01

1
p216

Sample Respone

My most memorable birthday to date would be my most recent birthday. My friends surprised me by coming to my house at daybreak to greet me. It was such a special feeling to wake up to the sound of my friends singing "Happy Birthday," complete with cake, balloons and the works. I think that was really nice and thoughtful of them to do that for me. We ended up having breakfast together, sharing laughs and just basically having fun. Also, I had never had a breakfast party before, so that made it quite memorable, too.

2
p217

Sample Respone

I think evaluating students based on overall performance in class is more reasonable than focusing strictly on term papers and exams. First of all, an exam or term paper is not necessarily an accurate reflection of how well someone knows the material. Maybe they get nervous during exams and can't adequately express themselves. Or maybe the material they know really well doesn't appear on the exam or isn't offered as a term paper topic. Also, we hand in assignments and participate in discussions for the entire semester. These types of contributions are just as important as exams or essays.

3
p218

|지문해석|

교무처에서 알립니다: 일부 교수들이 대학의 출석 정책을 엄격하게 시행하지 않고 있다는 사실이 행정 부서에. 알려졌습니다. 이 정책은 대학 교육정책의 기본으로 모든 교수들은 이 정책을 즉각적으로 지켜야 할 의무가 있음을 알려드립니다. 학생들에게 다시 한번 알립니다. 어떤 강의든 무단으로 세 번 결석하면 낙제될 것입니다. 무단 결석에 해당하는 조항에 대해 더 알고 싶으면 학생 요람을 참고하십시오.

|Script|

M: Lisa ... you are not going to believe this ...

W: What? The attendance policy? Already heard.

M: You think there's any way we can protest this?

W: I doubt it, but why would you want to? We pay to come to class, so it doesn't make much sense to skip them, does it?

M: No ... but I don't pay to have the university fail me automatically either. That's not fair. I know when I need to go to class and when I don't. Sometimes it's better to skip a class so that I can study for a big exam or something like that. But now I can't make that choice because the university will fail me if I do.

W: Well, what do you want the university to do? They can't have a policy that professors don't have to enforce. That just doesn't make any sense.

M: Well, maybe they should take a cue from the professors.

W: Not sure I follow you.

M: The professors haven't been enforcing the policy because they know it's unreasonable. The university should just take the hint and change the policy.

| Script 해석 | 남자: 리사, 넌 이걸 믿지 못할 거야.
여자: 뭔데? 출석 정책 말이야? 벌써 들었어.
남자: 우리가 항의할 수 있는 방법이 있을까?
여자: 글쎄, 그런데 왜 항의하고 싶어? 우리 돈 내고 수업을 듣는데 빼먹는다는 건 말이 안되지 않아?
남자: 그렇지. 하지만 대학이 날 자동적으로 낙제시키라고 돈을 내는 것도 아니잖아. 억울해. 내가 수업을 들어야 할 때와 안 들어도 될 때는 내 자신이 안단 말이야. 어떤 경우에는 수업을 듣지 않고 더 중요한 시험 같은 걸 준비하는 게 더 나을 때도 있다고. 그런데 이젠 그렇게 하면 낙제시킬 테니 그렇게 할 수 없게 됐어.
여자: 글쎄, 학교에 바라는 게 뭐야? 교수가 강요할 필요 없는 정책을 만들 수는 없지. 그건 말이 안되잖아.
남자: 흠, 아마도 교수님들로부터 좀 배워야 하겠구나.
여자: 무슨 말인지 모르겠어.
남자: 교수님들도 그 정책이 말이 안되기 때문에 강요하지 않았던 거라고. 대학도 교수님들로부터 좀 배워서 정책을 바꿔야 해.

| Sample Response | The man is very upset about the university's decision to start requiring professors to enforce the attendance policy. The man says that it is not a fair policy and that he knows when he needs to go to class and when he can skip a class. He says that sometimes it is necessary to skip a class so that he has time to study, but now he can't make that choice because he will fail his class if he skips it. He also says that the professors don't enforce the policy because they know the policy is unreasonable, and that the university should follow the example of the professors.

4

| 지문해석 | 생산 공정에 대한 환경 영향 분석: 생산 공정에 대한 환경 영향 분석은 특정한 상품을 생산이 환경에 끼치는 영향을 측정하는 방법이다. 이를 측정하기 위해서 환경 엔지니어들은 그 상품을 생산하는데 필요한 에너지의 총량과 생산 과정에서 배출되는 쓰레기를 계산해야 한다. 생산 공정에 대한 환경 영향 분석의 목표는 더 적은 에너지를 사용하거나 더 적은 쓰레기를 배출할 수 있도록 생산 과정의 어떤 영역이 개선 될 수 있는지 측정하는 것이다.

| Script | What do you think is the environmental cost of a bottle of wine? This is the question that one Italian winemaker, uh, with help from an Italian university, set out to answer. The university sent a team of specialists to observe the wine making process from start to finish. What they found was that the wine making process in this winery, uh, it was a rather small winery, by the way, was incredibly wasteful. The winery was consuming more than 4 liters of water for every bottle of wine it produced, and it was creating tons of paper and plastic waste. The owner of the winery was shocked, uh, because he had always considered his business to be ecologically friendly. Anyway, based on the findings of the university experts, the winery changed its production methods and is now far less wasteful. Now, this winery is not unique. Uh, many small businesses are not aware of how wasteful their production methods actually are. In fact, you might be surprised to learn that small businesses account for 60% of all industrial pollution. Fortunately, however, we are now developing the tools to help these businesses identify and modify wasteful practices.

| Script 해석 | 와인 한 병에 담긴 환경적인 가치가 얼마라고 생각하세요? 이 질문은 한 이탈리아인 와인 제작자가 한 이탈리아 대학의 도움을 받아 대답하고자 했던 질문입니다. 대학은 전문가들을 보내 와인 생산을 처음부터 끝까지 관찰했습니다. 그들이 알아낸 것은, 좀 규모가 작은 양조장이었지만 하여튼, 이 양조장에서 와인을 만드는 것이 굉장히 낭비적인 과정이었다는 것입니다. 양조장에서는 한 병의 와인을 생산하는데 4리터의 물을 사용하고, 수 톤의 종이와 플라스틱 폐기물을 배출합니다. 양조장의 주인은 항상 자신의 사업이 환경친화적이었다고 생각해 왔기 때문에 충격을 받았습니다. 어쨌든 대학 전문가의 연구에 기초해서 이 양조장은 제조 방법을 바꾸었고 낭비가 훨씬 줄어들었습니다. 자, 이런 양조장이 유일한 것이 아닙니다. 많은 영세 기업들은 자신의 제조 과정에 얼마나 낭비가 많은지 잘 모르고 있습니다. 사실, 이들이 산업 오염의 60%를 차지하는 원인을 제공한다는 것을 알면 아마 놀랄지도 모릅니다. 그러나 다행히 우리는 지금 이런 사업체들이 낭비적 생산 과정을 인식하고 개선하도록 도와줄 장치를 개발하고 있습니다.

| Sample Respone | The professor talks about a study that a university in Italy did at a winery. In the study, the university sent people to watch the wine making process and identify the wasteful parts of the process. The university team found that the winery's process was very wasteful, which greatly surprised the owner. The owner was largely unaware of the environmental problems caused by his winery, and he used the university's findings to improve his wine making process. This is an example of environmental impact analysis of the production process, in which environmental engineers analyze the environmental impact of a production process, in order to help manufacturers improve their production methods and make them more environmentally friendly. |

5
p220

| Scrip |
W: Matt, I haven't seen you in quite a while. What's up? Anything interesting you've been busy with that I should know about?
M: It's my torturous calculus course … I can't seem to grasp the concepts. I'm worried I'm not gonna pass the class. I really need help on this one …
W: Well, why don't you try going to a tutorial center or something? There'll be a lot of graduate students who can help you out with calculus. It's not going to be difficult for them to explain it to you. They charge for the sessions, though … I'm not sure how much.
M: Yeah, that sounds like a good idea, but the lessons will cost me money …
W: Okay then, if you're worried about money, you can always attend a study group. It's free and there'll also be a lot of people who can help you figure out calculus. That's what I did last semester, and it did help me pass my class.
M: A study group … I did that last year with one class and I learned more about the group's personal affairs than my subject.
W: True … but the decision is yours. Think it through; see which one will help you more. OK?

| Script 해석 |
여자: 매트, 오랜만이네. 무슨 일 있어? 내가 알아야 할 무슨 재미있는 일이라도 있는 거야?
남자: 그 고통스러운 미적분학 수업 때문이야. 통 무슨 말인지 모르겠어. 낙제 할까 걱정이야. 정말 도움이 너무 필요해.
여자: 글쎄, 학습 센터 같은 데 가보지 그래? 미적분학을 도와줄 대학원생들이 많을 거야. 그 사람들한테는 설명하기 어렵지 않은 과목이겠지. 비록 얼마인지는 모르겠지만, 수업료를 요구하겠지만 말이야.
남자: 응, 좋은 생각이긴 한데 돈이 들잖아.
여자: 그래 그럼, 돈이 걱정 되면 스터디 모임 찾아봐. 그건 무료고 또 너의 미적분학 공부를 도와줄 사람도 많을 거야. 나도 지난 학기에 그렇게 했는데, 통과하는데 많은 도움이 되었어.
남자: 스터디 모임, 나도 작년에 한번 했었는데, 공부보다는 멤버들의 사생활에 대해 더 많이 알게 된 것 같아.
여자: 그 말도 맞아. 그렇지만 결정은 네 몫이야. 어떤 것이 더 도움이 되는지 잘 보고 생각해. 알겠지?

| Sample Respone | The man is having problems in his calculus class and is worried that he might fail the class. The woman suggests that he either go to the tutorial center, where there are graduate students who can help him, or that he go to a study group, which would be free. I think the man should first go to the study group because it is free. If the study group doesn't help, then he can decide to pay to go to the tutorial center. There is no reason to pay for the tutorial center before he knows if the study group would help him or not. |

6

Script

One of the most important shifts in the process of human evolution was when our earliest hominid ancestors began to eat more meat. Uh, for right now, I'm not going to worry about how or why this happened. The point that I really want to make is that the shift towards a more carnivorous diet allowed these early hominids to develop more complex brains and greatly boosted their intelligence. So how's that possible? Why would eating meat have made them smarter? Well, first, it meant they got more protein. Protein, as you probably know, is high in calories. So by eating more meat, these earlier hominids were able to greatly increase their total intake of calories. That, of course, meant they had more energy to burn, uh, not only for physical activity, but for mental activity as well. You've got to remember that our brains use quite a bit of energy. The other way that this change in diet led to increased levels of intelligence is that it required these early hominids to hunt. I mean, they had to catch an animal before they could eat it, right? Now, hunting actually requires quite a bit of thinking. First, you have to figure out a way to make the weapons you'll use. Then you have to come up with some kind of plan for how you're going to get close enough to the animal to kill it … um, for early hominids that usually meant planning some sort of trap, because they were slower than most of the animals they hunted. So anyway, you get the picture: hunting took a lot of mental activity, and that obviously made our early ancestors smarter as time went by.

Script 해석

인류 진화 과정에서 가장 중요한 변화 중 하나는 초기 원시 인류 조상이 더 많은 고기를 먹기 시작했을 때 일어났습니다. 이번 시간에는 어떻게 혹은 왜 이런 일이 일어났는지 알아보지는 않을 것입니다. 제가 말하고 싶은 것은, 육식성 식단으로의 변화로 인해 원시 인류의 뇌가 더 발달하고 지능이 훨씬 더 높아졌다는 것입니다. 이 일이 어떻게 가능할까요? 고기를 더 먹는 것이 어떻게 그들을 더 똑똑하게 만들었을까요? 음, 우선은, 더 많은 단백질을 섭취하게 됐다는 점입니다. 아마 알겠지만, 단백질은 칼로리가 높습니다. 고기를 더 많이 먹음으로써, 이 원시인류는 더 많은 칼로리를 섭취할 수 있게 되었습니다. 이 말은 인류가 열량을 내는 더 많은 에너지를 가지게 되었다는 뜻인데, 이는 육체적인 활동뿐만 아니라 정신적인 활동에도 해당됩니다. 뇌의 활동을 위해서 꽤 많은 양의 에너지를 쓴다는 사실을 기억할 필요가 있습니다. 식단에서의 이러한 변화가 지능의 발달을 가져온 다른 이유는 원시 인류가 사냥을 해야 했기 때문입니다. 말하자면, 고기를 먹기 위해서는 사냥을 해야만 합니다, 그렇죠? 자, 사냥을 하기 위해선 많은 생각이 필요하죠. 우선 어떻게 무기를 만들 것인가를 결정해야 합니다. 그러고 나서 일종의 계획을 짜야 하죠, 어떻게 동물을 죽일 수 있을 만큼 가까이 접근할 것인가에 대해서요. 초기 원시 인류에게 있어서 계획이란 일종의 덫을 놓는 것이었습니다. 왜냐하면 그들은 사냥하는 동물들보다 느렸기 때문이죠. 아무튼 그러니까, 무슨 뜻인지 아시겠죠. 사냥은 상당한 지능적 활동이며, 명백히 시간이 갈수록 우리의 조상들을 영리하게 해주었습니다.

Sample Respone

According to the professor, eating meat increased the intelligence of early hominids in two ways. First, the higher intake of protein gave the early hominids more total calories to burn. Thus they had more energy for both physical and mental tasks. The professor points out that our brains actually use a lot of energy and that eating meat provided that extra energy. Eating meat also contributed to greater levels of intelligence because it required the early hominids to do more hunting. This meant that they had to engage in complex mental tasks like planning traps and making weapons. Over time, engaging in these complex mental tasks made the early hominids smarter.

Actual Test 02

1
p224

Sample Response

My favorite books are biographies or autobiographies. Most books in this genre detail the life of someone who is very successful in his or her field. I really enjoy reading these books because they provide a fascinating insight into the life of a great person. It's really interesting to find out what shaped these people and drove them to such achievement. Another reason I like these kinds of books is that they usually contain a lot of background information that teaches me a lot about politics, for example, or maybe history. This means I learn quite a lot about other areas as well.

2
p225

Sample Response

I would prefer talking over a cell phone and chatting because it is more convenient, time-saving and cost-efficient. I don't have to disrupt my schedule, or my friend's or family's for that matter, just so I can talk to them. We are already in the 21st century, and we have many technological advances we can use to our advantage, so we might as well make use of them. Also, chatting or text-messaging gives one a chance to phrase and think over the things that one wants to say, eliminating the wrong signals that non-verbal communication may send when one is talking face-to-face with another person.

3
p226

| 지문해석 |

학생처에서 알립니다: 지난 학기 음주와 관련한 사건들이 심상치 않게 증가함에 따라, 당국은 교내에서의 음주 위반에 대해 더 강력한 처벌이 요구된다는 결론을 내렸습니다. 이 정책은 즉시 실행되며, 교내 음주 위반에 의한 규율 가급제 기간이 한 학기에서 최고 1년까지로 늘어납니다. 알다시피 가급제 기간 동안 또 위반한다면 제적 처리까지 당할 수 있습니다. 정책의 수정 조항을 숙지하시고, 학교를 더욱 안전하고 음주가 없는 곳으로 만들도록 협조해 주십시오.

| Script |

M: Susie, did you hear about the new probation period? Wow, that's tough. Guess I won't be going to any more on-campus parties.

W: You took that seriously? You've got to be joking, Craig.

M: What do you mean?

W: That announcement is just window dressing for our parents … if you think anything is really going to change, you're dreaming.

M: But they doubled the length of the probation period for alcohol violations.

W: Oh, yeah, let me show you how scared I am. You know Jason Fridley, don't you?

M: Sure, everyone knows Jason. What's your point?

W: Well, did you know that he got put on probation last semester, and that he got caught with alcohol twice after that? Each time they brought him into the dean's office for a stern talking to, but in the end they didn't do anything to him … they certainly didn't kick him out of school.

M: Really? Twice? I always knew Jason was a bit of a wild man, but wow.

W: The point is, who cares how long the probation period is? Nothing's going to happen. That policy isn't going to change a thing, I'm telling you. It certainly isn't going to affect my social plans.

| Script 해석 | 남자: 수지, 새로운 가급제 기간에 대해서 들었니? 와, 대단하더라. 생각해 봐, 난 이제 학교 파티에는 안 갈 거야.
여자: 정말이야? 크레이크, 농담하는 거지?
남자: 무슨 말이야?
여자: 그 발표는 그냥 부모님들을 위한 눈속임이야. 뭔가 정말 바뀔 거라고 생각한다면 착각하는 거야.
남자: 그렇지만 음주 위반에 대한 가급제 기간이 두 배가 되었잖아.
여자: 아, 그래. 내가 얼마나 겁먹었는지 보여줄게. 너 제이슨 프레들리 알지?
남자: 그럼, 걔 유명하잖아. 그런데 왜?
여자: 흠, 그 애가 작년에 가급제 처벌 받았던 거 알지, 그리고 나서 두 번 더 음주 단속에 걸렸대. 매번 학장실에 가서 엄격한 꾸중을 들었지만, 결국은 아무 일도 없었대. 학교 밖으로 내쫓지 않는 거지.
남자: 정말? 두 번이나? 제이슨이 제멋대로라는 건 알았지만, 우와.
여자: 요는 누가 가급제 기간에 대해서 신경 쓰냐는 거야. 아무 일도 일어나지 않아. 내가 단언하는데, 그 정책은 아무 소용이 없을 거야. 내 사교 계획에 어떤 영향도 주지 못할 거야.

| Sample Respone | The woman says that the university's extension of the probation period for alcohol violations is a big joke and that she isn't worried about it. She says that being put on probation doesn't matter. She says that she has a friend who was on probation last year. She says that he was caught drinking twice while he was on probation, but nothing happened to him. He had to go talk to the dean, but he didn't really get punished. So the woman isn't worried about the extension, because she thinks that being put on probation doesn't really matter anyway and that it won't change anything on campus.

4

| 지문해석 | **약탈적 융자**: 약탈적 융자는 소비자, 특히 경제 시스템에 대해 지식이 부족한 사람들을 이용하기 위해 만들어 졌다. 약탈적 융자는 빠른 현금을 약속하며 소비자를 유혹한다. 그러나 대출의 조건은 소비자에게 우호적이지 않다. 약탈적 융자는 과도하게 높은 이자나 비현실적으로 긴 상환 기간을 제시한다. 약탈적 융자의 진정한 목적은 소비자들이 대출을 갚지 못하는 상황으로 이끌어서, 대출금보다 더 높은 가격을 가지고 있을 소유물을 회수하는 것이다.

| Script | In the last few years we have seen an increase in the number of companies offering mortgage refinancing services. Uh, basically, when you refinance your mortgage, you take out a second loan, using your home as the collateral for the loan. Now sometimes, this is a sensible option. Let's say you need money to open a business. Refinancing your mortgage may be a good way to get that money. But in many cases today, mortgage refinancing companies encourage people to refinance even when they don't really need the money. Let's look at a hypothetical example. OK, we have a homeowner who has a credit card bill of $5,000, and he's a little stressed because it's going to take him a while to pay off that bill. One day that homeowner is approached by a refinancing company. The company suggests that he refinance his mortgage and use the money to pay off his credit card bill. This seems like an easy solution, so the homeowner accepts. Well, the problem with this is that a mortgage has a 30 year term. So now that homeowner is going to be paying off the mortgage for 30 years, when he probably could have paid off his credit card in just a few years with a little hard work. And, if, uh, anything happens and he can't pay back the mortgage, the refinancing company can take his home.

| Script 해석 | 최근 몇 년 동안 담보 대출 서비스를 제공하는 기업의 수가 증가했습니다. 기본적으로, 담보 대출을 받는다는 것은 집을 담보로 해서 재 대출을 받는 것입니다. 자 때때로 이것은 현명한 선택입니다. 사업을 시작하기 위해 자금이 필요하다고 생각해 봅시다. 담보 대출을 받는 것은 돈을 얻는 좋은 방법일 수 있습니다. 그러나 오늘날 많은 경우, 주택 담보회사는 사람들에게 돈이 필요하지 않는데도 대출을 받으라고 부추깁니다. 한 가지 예를 가정해 봅시다. 자, 신용 카드 빚이 5,000불인 한 주택 소유자가 있습니다. 그 사람은 그 돈을 갚는데 오래 걸릴 것이기 때문에 약간 스트레스를 받고 있습니다. 어느 날 주택 담보 대출 회사가 이 사람에게 접근합니다. 회사는 담보 대출을 받아 신용 카드 빚을 갚으라고 제안합니다. 쉬운 해결책처럼 보여, 이 사람은 그 제안을 받아들입니다. 글쎄요, 문제는 대출 기간이 30년이라는 것입니다. 그렇기 때문에 몇 년 동안 열심히 노력했으면 다 갚았을 빚을 30년 동안 갚을 것입니다. 그리고 만약 무슨 일이 생겨 담보 대출을 갚지 못하면, 대출 회사는 집을 가져갈 수 있습니다.

| Sample Response | In his lecture, the professor explains how mortgage refinancing companies prey on people who need money. Mortgage refinancing companies approach people who have a relatively small amount of debt and offer to help them pay off their debt by refinancing their house. The problem is that then the person is stuck paying off a relatively small debt for 30 years because that is the term of the mortgage. Furthermore, if something happens and they miss a mortgage payment, then the refinancing company can take their house. This is an example of a predatory loan practice, because the true objective of the refinancing company is to get the person in a position where they will miss a mortgage payment and then lose their house.

5

| Script | W: Hey, Clark, got a minute? I could really use some advice right now … do you have time? It's about my roommate, Elsa …

M: Sure! Anything for a friend. Why, did you have a fight with Elsa?

W: No… not yet, anyway. Well, she's always using my things without asking my permission first. I mean, basic courtesy, right? I sometimes spend fifteen or twenty minutes looking for something of mine, only to find out later that she has it.

M: Hmm … have you tried talking to her about it?

W: Do I have to? I mean, c'mon. Does it take too much to ask if she can use my stuff? Plus, I don't really want to embarrass her or anything … she's supposed to know such things …

M: Hmm … you may have to be blunt with her. Maybe she thinks it's okay with you, since you are not saying anything about it to her, you know? So talk to her even if it makes you feel uncomfortable … unless you can move in with a new roommate anytime soon.

W: You know, I'm actually thinking of doing that, since Tina's roommate is moving out next week. But I'm afraid I may hurt Elsa's feelings if I leave just like that.

M: Well, if her attitude bothers you so much, do yourself a favor and do something about it, okay? Either you talk to her about it, or leave.

| Script 해석 | W: 안녕, 클락, 시간 좀 있니? 지금 정말 충고가 좀 필요한데, 너 시간 돼? 내 룸메이트 엘자에 관한 것인데.

M: 물론이지! 친구를 위한 건데. 왜? 엘자와 싸우기라도 한거야?

W: 아니, 어쨌든 아직은 아니야. 그니까, 엘자는 늘 물어보지도 않고 내 물건을 사용해. 내 말은, 그건 기본적인 예의잖아? 15분, 20분, 한참 내 물건을 찾다 보면 늘 엘자가 그걸 가지고 있는 거야.

M: 흠, 그 문제에 대해서 얘기해 봤어?

W: 해야 할까? 내 말은, 있잖아. 내 물건을 써도 되는지 물어보는 게 그렇게 어려운 일이야? 게다가 엘자를 당혹시키고 싶지는 않아. 그런 건 당연히 알아야 하는 거 아냐.

M: 네가 솔직한 태도를 보여야 할지도 몰라. 네가 아무 말도 안 하니까 엘자가 그래도 된다고 생각하는 걸지도 모르잖아? 곧 새로운 룸메이트를 찾고 싶은 게 아니라면, 좀 불편하더라도 얘기를 해 봐.

W: 있잖아. 사실 그렇게 할까 생각 중이야. 티나의 룸메이트가 다음 주에 이사 간대. 그런데 내가 그렇게 떠나면 엘자가 상처 받지는 않을까 걱정돼.

M: 흠, 엘자의 태도가 너무 신경 쓰이면 너 자신을 위해서 뭔가 해, 알겠지? 직접 얘기를 하던지 아니면 이사를 가던지.

| Sample Response | The woman is having trouble dealing with her roommate, who doesn't ask permission when taking or using her stuff. She says that she sometimes can't find things because her roommate has taken them. The man suggests she either talk to the roommate about it or move out. I would rather talk to the roommate because the situation might just be a case of miscommunication or poor etiquette on the part of her roommate. If she talks to her roommate, she can probably solve this problem easily. Besides, moving out is too much of a hassle. If she talks things out, she won't spend as much time and effort to try and resolve the situation.

6

| Script | One of the major challenges for companies that wish to introduce a new technology to replace an existing one is overcoming the collective switching cost. The collective switching cost refers to the difficulty of switching from a widely used and available technology to a new technology … uh, even if that new technology is far better. One example of this would be the persistence of the QWERTY keyboard. Uh, that's the keyboard layout that all of us use. This layout was first created in 1868 for typewriters. Its main purpose was to separate the most commonly used letters to avoid mechanical problems in the typewriters. Now, obviously in the age of computers, these mechanical problems are no longer a concern, and keyboard layouts that are more comfortable and allow for faster typing have been created. So why do we still use QWERTY? Because it's everywhere … any computer you buy comes with a QWERTY keyboard, so that's what people are comfortable using … even though there are better keyboards out there. Another example would be the dominance of the Windows® operating system. Unless you buy an Apple computer, any PC you buy is probably going to come with Windows pre-installed on it. The situation is the same as we talked about before. Other operating systems besides Windows exist, and some are arguably better. But Windows is everywhere. Basically, every program you buy is designed to run on Windows, and you can easily transfer files from one computer to another because everyone has the same operating system. So even though some operating systems might offer better performance than Windows, it is very unlikely that they will replace Windows.

| Script 해석 | 기존의 기술을 새로운 것으로 교체하는데 있어서 기업의 가장 큰 도전 과제 중 하나는 집단적 전환 비용을 극복하는 것입니다. 집단적 전환 비용이란 널리 사용되던 기술을 새로운 기술로 바꾸는 어려움을 의미합니다. 신기술이 훨씬 우수하다 해도 말입니다. 한 예로, QWERTY 키보드를 계속해서 사용하는 것입니다. 이것은 우리 모두가 사용하는 키보드 방식이죠. 처음 이 자판은 1868년 타자기용으로 만들어 졌습니다. 이 설계의 주목적은 가장 자주 사용하는 글자들을 떨어뜨려서 타자기의 기계적인 문제를 줄이려고 하는 것이었습니다. 컴퓨터의 시대가 된 지금은 이런 종류의 기계적인 문제가 더 이상 걱정 거리가 아닙니다. 그리고 더 편리하고 빠르게 칠 수 있는 자판 배열도 개발되었습니다. 그런데 왜 여전히 QWERTY를 사용할까요? 그건 어느 곳이나 있기 때문입니다. 구매하는 모든 컴퓨터가 이 자판을 가지고 있습니다. 그래서 사람들이 편리하게 사용하는 겁니다. 비록 더 좋은 자판이 있지만요. 또 다른 예는 윈도우 운영 체제의 우세입니다. 여러분이 애플 컴퓨터를 구입하지 않는 이상, 모든 PC에는 윈도우가 이미 설치가 되어 있습니다. 이 상황은 이미 말씀 드린 것과 같습니다. 윈도우 말고도 다른 운영체계가 이미 존재하고, 논의의 여지는 있지만 더 좋은 것도 있습니다. 그러나 모두들 윈도우를 사용하죠. 여러분이 구입하는 모든 프로그램이 이미 윈도우에서 실행할 수 있도록 고안되어 있습니다. 그리고 모두 같은 운영 시스템을 가지고 있기 때문에 파일을 옮기는 것도 편하죠. 그래서 다른 운영 체계가 실행 면에서 더 나을지 몰라도, 윈도우 시스템을 대체할 것 같지는 않습니다.

| Sample Respone | In her lecture the professor discusses the concept of collective switching costs. The professor gives two examples of this concept. The first is the QWERTY keyboard. The professor says that while better keyboards have been designed since the invention of the QWERTY keyboard, they have not been able to replace it because the QWERTY keyboard is so widely used and it would be too much trouble for people to switch. The professor says the same is true of the Windows operating system. While some operating systems may work better than Windows, they are unable to replace Windows because everyone already has Windows and all the programs we use are written for Windows. These two examples demonstrate the concept of collective switching costs and why it is difficult to replace an existing technology with a new one.

Appendix

Exercise 1 Words with Similar Sounds p232

2	assess	11	ideal	21	ingenious
3	adopt	12	imitate	22	immigrate
4	effect	13	pause	23	persecute
5	aggregated	14	suite	24	censor
6	causal	15	advise	25	biography
7	comprehensible	16	ensure	26	overdue
8	conscience	17	farther	27	personnel
9	cooperation	18	loss	28	principle
10	physical	19	expand	29	stationary
		20	disperse	30	hostile

Exercise 3 Words Stress p234

첫째 음절: mischievous, nuclear, photograph, comfortable, resource, analyze, genuine, feature, compromise, landlord, illustrate

둘째 음절: economy, maintain, analysis, committee, fatigue, photographer, photography, pervade, discuss, mistakenly, statistics, participate

셋째 음절: popularity, engineer, presentation, interfere, educational, economic, disappoint, photographic, recommend, manufacture

Exercise 4 Weakened Sound p235

2	alive	11	around	21	tired
3	prove	12	side	22	sphere
4	assign	13	apart	23	already
5	sure	14	turn	24	cause
6	attain	15	spit	25	irrational
7	accustom	16	forgive	26	abnormal
8	vision	17	logical	27	able
9	enrich	18	irrelevant	28	resolution
10	estate	19	reserve	29	bound
		20	remind	30	immoral

Exercise 5 Sound Comparison p236

A

2	nipple	9	phase	17	Jew
3	cap	10	composer	18	thorn
4	grammar	11	teeth	19	array
5	divine	12	budge	20	rhyme
6	wag	13	edge	21	league
7	prove	14	dare	22	shoot
8	zest	15	seethe	23	though
		16	deadly	24	choke

B
2	lived	9	cede	17	country
3	angel	10	leisure	18	behalf
4	rope	11	blood	19	mother
5	good	12	field	20	these
6	avid	13	coach	21	stalker
7	drought	14	cause	22	pear
8	impossible	15	chess	23	risen
		16	lit	24	latter

Exercise 6 Pronounced or Not? p237

2. The plumber kept (k)nocking on the door, hearing several voices ta(l)king, but got no answer.
3. He fas(t)ened his seat belt and has(t)ened to the hospital immediately.
4. She of(t)en takes a wa(l)k in her nei(gh)borhood, lis(t)ening to music.
5. The mountain was so high that we couldn't get to the top within the day; we clim(b)ed all day, though.
6. He'd bou(gh)t a birthday present for his ei(gh)t-year old dau(gh)ter, and just finished wrapping it up.
7. Matthew took out a (k)nife from the cu(p)board and cut the dou(gh)nut in hal(f) to share with his younger brother.
8. They conducted a signature-collecting campai(gn) opposing nuclear bom(b) tests, and thousands of people si(g)ned their names.
9. I was struck dum(b) by the grand scale of the cas(t)le, but it is un(k)nown who desi(g)ned it.
10. When Jessica sat the baby on her (k)nee, she couldn't feel the wei(gh)t of it.

Exercise 7 Sentence Stress p237

2. That way, you won't have to worry about paying for your tuition.
3. Have you heard about the issue with the sculpture purchases?
4. I think it's really unfair to scrap the teams after what they have done for the school.
5. Telling freshmen that they can't bring a car to school won't help them settle in school.
6. My schedule has been crazy ever since I heard about that stupid policy.
7. Students who want to work aren't limited to finding jobs at the computer labs.
8. The woman is upset because she hasn't gotten into a class that she needs to graduate.
9. Her problems with finances will be more manageable with a full scholarship.
10. The woman says that he could ask his friends to move his things for him.

TOEFL® iBT books from LinguaForum

링구아포럼의 6단계별 토플 교재 eBasic-e-b-m-i-Hooked on

TOEFL® iBT 훅톤 시리즈 | Advanced Level
- New Edition Hooked On TOEFL (훅톤토플)
  Reading / Listening / Speaking / Writing
- 빈출 1순위 TOEFL VOCA / Frequency#1 TOEFL VOCA (영문판) / 빈출 1순위 TOEFL VOCA Workbook
- TOEFL® iBT INSIDER-The Super Guide (영문판) / TOEFL® iBT Test Book 1(영문판)

TOEFL® iBT i,m 시리즈 | High Intermediate ~ Intermediate Level
- New Edition TOEFL® iBT
  i-Reading / i-Listening / i-Speaking / i-Writing
- TOEFL® iBT Core Topic Guide (영문판·총 4권) / INTRO VOCA (한글판·영문판)
- TOEFL® iBT m-Reading / m-Listening / m-Grammar / m-Writing / m-Speaking

TOEFL® iBT b,e 시리즈 | Low Intermediate ~ High Beginner's Level
- TOEFL® iBT b-Reading / b-Listening / b-Grammar / b-Writing
- TOEFL® iBT BASIC VOCA
- TOEFL® iBT e-Reading / e-Listening / e-Grammar

TOEFL® iBT eBasic 시리즈 | Beginner's Level
- TOEFL® iBT eBasic-Reading / eBasic-Listening

"세계가 신뢰하는 **Worldwide on-line iBT Test**"
www.linguaforum.com

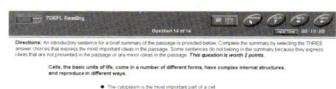

LinguaForum™

우153-792, 서울시 성동구 성수동2가 281-4 푸조비즈타워 5F
교재주문 (02) 3480-6627 대표전화 1577-6167
● www.linguaforum.com 회사 소개·도서 구매·온라인토플테스트·도서 문의 및 상담

🔍 시험 상세 : 시험 화면은 다음과 같이 구성되었습니다.

Reading
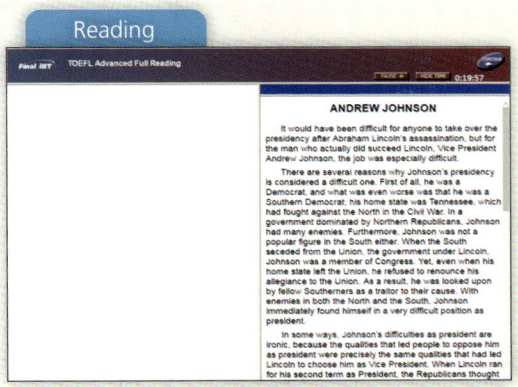
학술적인 내용의 지문을 이해하는 능력을 평가합니다.

Listening
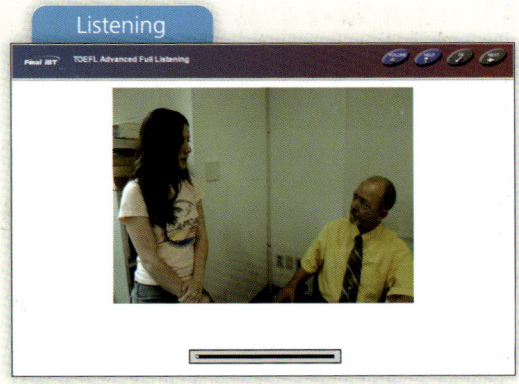
강의, 교실 토론 및 대화를 듣고 이해하는 능력을 평가합니다.

Speaking
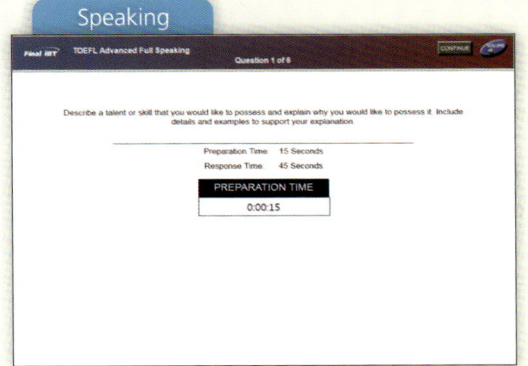
다양한 주제에 대해 말할 수 있는 능력을 평가합니다.

Writing
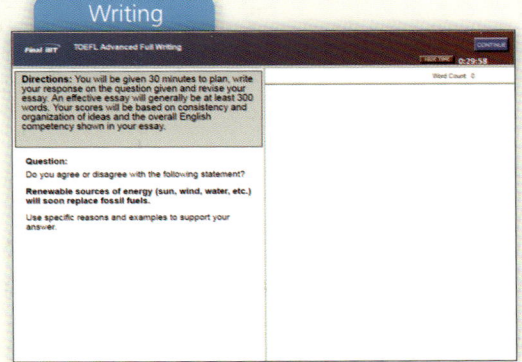
강의내용을 요약하고 자신의 의견을 정리하는 작문능력을 평가합니다.

성적표

각각의 모의 테스트를 마친 후 **예상점수를 확인**할 수 있습니다. SPEAKING과 WRITING 점수는 **채점 전문 인력**에 의해 매겨집니다.

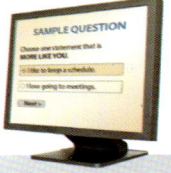

시험 준비 세팅

먼저, 마이크가 있는 헤드셋을 준비해주세요.
그리고 인터넷이 연결된 상태에서 크롬브라우저로 접속하여 시험에 응시하시면 됩니다.

 시험 응시 및 문의 사항 Tel : 02-3483-2786

초급부터 실전까지 토플교재의 바이블
링구아포럼 TOEFL Series

- 아시아 최초로 2003년부터 미국은 물론 전 세계로 영어 교재와 판권 수출
- 온라인 서점 아마존닷컴 토플 판매 1위 (2003년, 2004년)
- 주니어 토플 개념 정의
- 최초 6단계별 토플 시리즈 개발

링구아포럼의 6단계별 토플 교재 eBASIC / e / b / m / i / Hooked on / Insider / Test Book
– eBasic 시리즈를 시작으로 e, b, m, i, Hooked On 순으로 단계가 올라갑니다. 영문 종합서 Insider 와 모의고사집 Test Book이 있습니다.

1단계 — New Edition eBasic Series
중학교 1~2학년 수준으로 토플을 처음 접하는 학습자를 위한 입문 단계로, iBT의 주제와 형식, 문제유형에 입문 수준의 어휘와 문법으로 구성되었습니다.
〈개정판〉

2단계 — New Edition e Series
중학교 2~3학년 수준의 토플 학습자를 위해 개발된 두번째 초급 단계이며, iBT의 주제와 형식, 문제유형에 입문 수준의 어휘와 문법으로 구성되었습니다.
〈개정판〉

3단계 — b Series
중학교 3학년 이상의 영어능력을 가진 학습자를 대상으로 개발. 링구아포럼 eBasic, e 시리즈를 학습한 학습자에서부터, 토플을 처음 접하는 대학생/성인들 모두 토플에 적응하고 중급~고급 단계로 진입할 수 있도록 구성 되었습니다.

   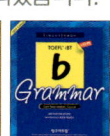

4단계 — m Series
중급 수준(성인 입문)의 토플 학습자를 대상으로 개발. iBT에 등장하는 모든 주제와 문제유형 등을 모두 다루었으며, 실전보다 조금 쉬운 수준으로 연습할 수 있습니다.
〈개정판〉

5단계 — New Edition i Series
실제 토플 시험을 준비하는 학습자를 대상으로 개발. 링구아포럼 토플 시리즈의 중/고급단계로, iBT에 등장하는 모든 주제와 문제유형 등을 모두 다루었으며, 실전과 거의 유사한 수준으로 연습할 수 있습니다.

6단계 — New Edition Hooked On Series
실제 토플 시험을 준비하는 학습자를 대상으로 한 고급단계로, iBT에 등장하는 모든 주제와 문제유형등을 모두 다루어, 실전과 동일한 수준으로 연습할 수 있습니다.